D0848396

READING, PERCEPTION, AND LANGUAGE

Reading, Perception and Language

Papers from the
World Congress on Dyslexia

Sponsored by
The Orton Society
in Cooperation with
the Mayo Clinic

Edited by
Drake D. Duane
Consultant in Neurology
Mayo Clinic
and
Margaret B. Rawson
Language Consultant and
Past President, Orton Society

Published in Cooperation
with the Orton Society

York Press
Baltimore

Library of Congress Cataloging in Publication Data

World Congress on Dyslexia, Mayo Clinic, 1974.
  Reading, perception, and language.

  Bibliography: p.
  Includes index.
  1. Dyslexia—Congresses. I. Duane, Drake D.,
1936-   II. Rawson, Margaret B. III. Orton Society.
IV. Mayo Clinic, Rochester, Minn. V. Title.
RJ496.A5W67 1974   616.8'553   75-23237
ISBN 0-912752-07-6

This book was manufactured in the United States of America.

Library of Congress Cataloging Card Number 75-23237

ISBN 0-912752-07-6

CONTENTS

CONTRIBUTORS

Peter E. Bryant, Ph.D.
Department of Experimental
  Psychology
University of Oxford
Oxford, England   OX1 3PS

Robert C. Calfee, Ph.D.
School of Education,
Stanford University
Stanford, California 94305

Macdonald Critchley, C.B.E., M.D.,
  F.R.C.P., F.A.D. (Hon)
National Hospital
Queen Square
London, England   WC1N BG

Drake D. Duane, M.D.
Department of Neurology
Mayo Clinic
Rochester, Minnesota 55901

Leon Eisenberg, M.D.
Department of Psychiatry,
Harvard Medical School *and*
  Children's Hospital Medical Center
Boston, Massachusetts 02115

Philip B. Gough, Ph.D.
Department of Psychology
University of Texas
Austin, Texas 78712

Robert J. Joynt, M.D. Ph.D.
Department of Neurology
University of Rochester Medical
  Center *and* Strong Memorial
  Hospital
Rochester, New York 14642

Richard L. Masland, M.D.
H. Houston Merritt Professor of
  Neurology
Columbia University,
New York, New York 10032

Margaret Byrd Rawson, M.A.
Reading Consultant *and*
  Former President,
  The Orton Society
Route 12
Frederick, Maryland 21701

Earl D. Schubert, Ph.D.
Hearing and Speech Sciences
Stanford University Medical Center
Stanford, California 94305

Michael Turvey, Ph.D.
University of Connecticut
Storrs, Conneticult 06268
  and Haskins Laboratories,
  New Haven, Connecticut 06510

FOREWORD

Knowledge advances on a ladder of new insights. New insights are merely new ways of looking at old problems. Such flashes of intuition are most likely to occur when human interaction permits one person to see his problem through the eyes of another; thus he becomes aware of aspects of a problem to which he has previously been oblivious.

Fortune favors the prepared mind—success comes to the inquiring scientist whose open mind, constantly scanning the environment, is ready to accept new ideas, and prepared to incorporate them into his established schemata.

It is these concepts which underlie the long standing policy of the Orton Society of bringing together at its Annual Meeting individuals from widely differing backgrounds and disciplines, and of encouraging the broadest possible interpretation of what is relevant to dyslexia.

There are few problems where this is more appropriate, for the ability to speak, read, and write requires a broader scope of psychological and neurological skills than almost any other human endeavor. It is doubtful that we will ever really understand the dyslexias until we have a solid basis of understanding of the diverse underlying mental processes involved in reading, writing, and the use of oral language.

The design of the papers in this series, organized for the Orton Society by a committee of the staff of the Mayo Clinic, and presented at the World Congress on Dyslexia in 1974, is to bring us up to date on new advances in diverse fields of study concerned with these mental processes. Its purpose is to provide for each of us some new appreciation of what it takes to read and write.

Richard L. Masland, M.D.
H. Houston Merritt Professor of Neurology
Columbia University

PREFACE

This volume includes the State of the Arts papers presented as part of the 25th Annual International meeting of the Orton Society, a World Congress on Dyslexia, held in cooperation with the Mayo Clinic in Rochester, Minnesota, November 7–10, 1974.

This meeting commemorated the 25th anniversary of the Orton Society, a non-profit scientific and educational organization for the study and treatment of children with specific language disability (dyslexia). For their silver anniversary session, the Society and designated representatives at the Mayo Clinic attempted to bring together experts in several fields pertinent to an understanding of variations in learning and performance in reading, writing, spelling, and spoken language. Each speaker was to bring to the meeting his or her own contemporary survey of an aspect of perception or language, which it was hoped would facilitate a greater comprehension of the worldwide problem of language learning difficulty in the intellectually intact child and adult.

Each speaker was sponsored by a subvention from the Orton Society. Additionally, the support of the following departments of the Mayo Clinic assisted in bringing these speakers together: the Department of Neurology, the Section of Speech Pathology, the Section of Audiology, the Section of Psychology, the Section of Child and Adolescent Psychiatry, and the Department of Pediatrics.

The Planning Committee in charge of selecting the topics and speakers for this series comprised: F. L. Darley, Ph.D., Head of the Section of Speech Pathology; M. R. Gomez, M.D., Head of the Section of Pediatric Neurology; D. D. Duane, M.D., Department of Neurology; A. R. Lucas, M.D., Head of the Section of Child and Adolescent Psychiatry; and W. M. Swenson, Ph.D., Head of the Section of Psychology—all of the Mayo Clinic.

The efforts of the committee, the speakers, the Local Arrangements Committee headed by Mrs. Paula Rome, Mr. Roger Saunders, President of the Orton Society, and their respective secretaries and associates are gratefully acknowledged by the editors. The editors owe a special debt of gratitude to the staff of the *Bulletin of the Orton Society* particularly to Jan-paul Miller,

associate editor; and to Karen Evjen for her unfailing expertise and cheerful-
ness during the revision of the manuscript.

The papers here presented are issued simultaneously by the Orton Society (paperback) and by the York Press (cloth edition). Other papers from
the same Congress will be found in the *Bulletin of the Orton Society* for
1975, Volume XXV.

The primary interest of the editors and of all of those to whom they are
indebted is, of course, the children and adults whom it is their purpose to
serve.

Drake D. Duane, M.D.
Margaret B. Rawson, M.A.

SUMMARY OF THE WORLD CONGRESS ON DYSLEXIA

Drake D. Duane

One might reasonably inquire why a World Congress on Dyslexia would include discussions in so many potentially diverse disciplines as those within these pages and conclude with a publication entitled, "Reading, Perception and Language." The rationale behind this symposium is that reading is not an isolated behavior; it is by definition part of the language process. Furthermore, language in general and reading in particular are correlated with perception and memory. Understanding of variance in behavior is linked intimately to a comprehension of normative function. Thus, if one is to deal with the "dys" of dyslexia (used in the sense of inadequate management of words), knowledge of the language units that are interwoven within the language, as well as how they are perceived and retained, is implied. Since the role of emotional factors in the causation and consequences of language learning failure has been debated, this topic was felt to merit inclusion. Likewise, as various therapies have been offered in the past, the student of language disability will profit from a review of the rationale behind such therapies and the extent to which objective data support their validity.

Each paper was designed to provide a "state of the art" summary of the present status in that area. Depending upon the background and interests of the reader, some papers may be more pertinent and stimulating than others. However, it should be apparent that comprehending language disability today is a multifaceted, interdisciplinary, and demanding task.

Critchley's historical overview of dyslexia provides the reader with the perspective of how the physician has come to know about and has tried to analyze reading retardation. His classic monograph[4] and comments here should stimulate worldwide epidemiologic investigation into the incidence and possible genetic mechanism underlying developmental dyslexia. It will be important that the countries participating in such studies take into account cultural factors that may skew the results, as well as agree upon what

1

constitutes reading retardation. This is not a simple problem: within the culture of the United States the task of determining incidence based on a generally agreed-upon definition has met with frustration. Those engaged in such research must bear in mind that the target behavior is language-based; epiphenomena such as overactivity, peripheral perceptual deficits, and altered coordination, while recognized, are not of primary concern. Should such cross-cultural studies of reading retardation be accomplished, it would be interesting to note if any cultural or linguistic group has a lower or higher incidence of reading failure. Such an observation would raise the question of what role the native language plays in placing a greater or lesser encumbrance upon mastering the reading process of that language. Such studies must also be controlled in respect to the cultural attitudes toward failure in general and specifically with regard to reading failure. Additionally, prevailing educational methodology of the cultural group must be taken into account. If relatively homogeneous genetic groups have higher or lower frequencies of reading failure, this finding will reinforce the suspicion that, among the causes of specific language disability, constitutional (genetic) factors are important.

However, the implication of Critchley's and Gough's comments is that in all likelihood such cross-cultural studies of reading failure will not detect marked differences that depend on the language system of the culture. This is likely due to the fact that the coding process across western cultures remains similar in that even alphabetic writing systems are not truly a phonetic equivalent of the spoken tongue. Ideographic languages may place some children at a different type of disadvantage, depending upon how those children are able to perceive the sound/symbol relationships of their language graphemes and their symbolic equivalents.

Critchley's concluding remarks on the potential role of brain chemistry are in keeping with current interests in brain research regarding the chemical events within and between brain cells. A disturbance in these events among dyslexics may be uncovered, but the still evolving state of knowledge in this new field of science may not, in the immediate future, permit a definitive statement. At present, our knowledge of the process of myelination and its variations, cellular RNA production, and neurochemical transmitters remains relatively primitive. Furthermore, future studies may suggest the need for closer inspection of the role of those supporting cells of the central nervous system known as the glia. However, whether such research will be bountiful or barren is still to be determined. One must bear in mind that, despite the fact that we use the term "specific" for language disability or dyslexia, within that category there is likely to be relative heterogeneity such that a uniform biochemical alteration may not be documented.

Gough's analogy of coping with one's native tongue in early life as if it were foreign to one's native culture is intriguing. However, in the earliest stages of language evolution, the facility for using language data is developmentally unique; this fact would caution against comparison with the adult attempt to master a second language. Yet it is interesting to note that some bright college-level American students have demonstrated great difficulty in acquiring a second language. These unilingual adults usually have a history of early difficulty with reading English and demonstrate residual impaired English spelling performance.[5]

Despite his protest at the conclusion, Gough's review provides, for those working in the language field, the basis of language structure with which they should be familiar. Witness to that need is the suggestion of Calfee and Rawson that the task of remediation must be directed to the mastery of structured linguistic knowledge. Those involved in the assessment and remediation of persons with specific language disability should follow the work of the linguist in his attempt to elucidate the substrate of language. It is implied from Gough's remarks that when we know more about the nature of language we will know more about how to teach it. The remaining papers provide the corollary of that statement: when we know more about the nature of the student we will know more about how to teach the language to him.

Joynt's historical survey of the anatomic correlates of language is marked by his willingness to accept individual structural differences in what many readers might otherwise have thought to be a static field. The observation of brain asymmetry in structure begs the question of the correlation between brain asymmetry and brain function. Although previous observations have suggested that these morphologic differences are uninfluenced by maturation,[6,7,7,19] a recent report[18] raises the question of developmental changes in structure as well as sex differences. What relationship such morphologic brain asymmetries have to language and reading retardation remains to be determined. However, in addition to traumatic procedures such as cerebral angiography and pneumoencephalography confirming, *in vivo*, such asymmetry,[6,8,11] the newly available computer-assisted transaxial tomogram of the head offers potential for a noninvasive method of studying brain morphology.[2] This work should be done. Moreover, anatomy should be extended to physiology with further clarification of the possible electroencephalographic correlates with delay in language acquisition.[3,14,16]

Calfee's statements have broad application for the researcher and clinician alike. His paper not only provides current findings on the nature of memory but provokes the reader to investigate the developmental aspects of cognition and learning. The suggestions by Calfee regarding future research in

reading acquisition should stimulate those in the field of educational remediation to reassess their methods and results. The observation that memory
mechanisms in the average child of five are as efficient as they will be in
adulthood suggests, as he points out, the need to focus on teaching appropriate to the task at hand. The implication is that the task for individual
students may differ as their development in nonmemorial function differs.
His analogy of the beginning reader as an uninstructed person is one that fits
my own bias. His thesis is one in which Orton Society members will find both
support and challenge. Calfee's paper is especially pertinent to the interests of
educators.

   The papers on auditory and visual perception may find greater appeal
among perceptual psychologists than among those primarily involved in the
remediation of reading disorders. However, those in the educational field will
profit from the study of Schubert's and Turvey's papers. Too frequently the
clinician treats the field of perception cursorily without appreciating the
complexity of the problems facing those who study the basics of perception.
Part of the difficulty in communication between these areas of interest lies in
the need for the perceptual psychologist to be facile with the laws of physics.
The type of rigorous discipline required is one with which those in the clinical
fields seldom feel comfortable. Furthermore, the approach of the perceptual
investigator often involves him in a search for a unitary explanation of
behavioral response to diverse physical events. This suggests a conceptualization of the perceptual process as being uniform throughout the species.
However, it is likely that developmental and individual differences in perception do exist. Unfortunately, our state of knowledge in these fields does not
yet permit sufficiently discriminating attention to those differences that
likely are operative in varying skills in language behavior. Both Schubert and
Turvey have reduced a massive amount of diverse and complex data to
reasonable size while remaining scientifically sound. The next step to be
taken from these surveys is to examine those aspects of auditory and visual
perception that are sensitive to individual difference to such an extent as to
alter acquisition of language function. Additional reading which may supple-
ment one's interest in auditory and visual perception includes the works on
speech perception by the Haskins group[13] and the volume, *Language by Ear
and by Eye: The Relationships Between Speech and Reading,*[9] cited by
several of the authors in this book. Additionally, the area of dichotic listening
tests in assessing language function and dysfunction warrants further investigation.[10,12]

   Turvey's novel and thought-provoking presentation on visual perception should stimulate a reassessment of previous, more traditional attitudes on the subject. His comments on the proprioceptive aspects of visual perception interest the reader as to the manner in which such a view of the visual system may apply to the remediation of reading disorders. His statement that the visual system is not well suited to the task of two-dimensional static analysis of forms such as graphemes seems incongruent with the universal use of such means of communication in developed cultures—or does he subtly suggest one reason why visual symbolic behavior is inefficient for some?

Bryant's review of previous studies attempting to define the role of cross-modal transfer is an interesting exercise in critical analysis. He has shown that the investigator must be especially careful in drawing conclusions about cross-modal influences without intramodal controls. Although those workers who have used tactile-kinesthetic means of enhancing learning have often empirically judged such techniques to be valid, Bryant cautions them to investigate their worth scientifically. However, Calfee has rightly pointed out that the laboratory setting is an artificial environment compared to the real world of the classroom. Yet this should not diminish attempts to clarify so fundamental an issue as whether deficits in cross-modal transfer may impair reading and language acquisition. A little-known but interesting study[1] of good and poor readers among the congenitally deaf suggested that both groups performed equally well on intramodal tactile and visual tasks. The deaf poor readers did poorly on tactile-visual linked tasks. However, the above study and the work of Bryant thus far suggest that intersensory integration and reading ability probably are positively related, but a cause-and-effect relationship remains to be established. Contrariwise, the belief that poor sensory integration leads to poor reading also awaits documentation. While clinicians working on this hypothesis are empirically satisfied with its validity, Bryant has left us with the hope that elucidating this point experimentally is not far beyond our grasp.

Every clinician working with retarded readers, regardless of his primary field, should read and reread Eisenberg's eloquent dissertation on the emotional aspects of reading disability. His paper encompasses the broad scope of the human aspects of reading disorders. The definitions are superb and exhibit the author's breadth and depth of comprehension beyond that sometimes narrowly labeled "psychiatric." He points out (correctly, I believe) the heterogeneity of so-called specific dyslexia. The observation that every disabled reader is predisposed to an emotional problem is one with which on reflection all clinicians must concur. As to the practical question of when psychiatric evaluation is indicated in a given situation, the simplistic answer would appear to be—when its need is suspected. More appropriately, as Eisenberg points out, when the emotional behavior interferes with educational performance or extends disruptively into the student's behavior outside the classroom, psychiatric intervention of perhaps more than one type including therapeutic tutoring may assist in the rehabilitation process. The informed passion of this author reaffirms the appropriateness of the topic for inclusion in this symposium

The ultimate purpose of study and diagnosis is the alleviation of distress and the promotion of positive health. In the development of language competence the treatment of language disability today remains educational. Rawson presents models of language and language learning reflecting an appreciation of variation in the capacities and difficulties of learners. She reviews approaches to the treatment of dyslexia found in language education and re-education during the past half-century in our culture and in others. She reports an accumulation of evidence supporting the effective remediation of dyslexia. Furthermore, she suggests the need to add to the growing body of quantitatively validated long-term studies. Inspection of the remarks of other authorities in education[15] further supports Rawson's observation that there is a paucity of statistical data upon which to report. Eisenberg, earlier in this symposium, pointed out why these data may be difficult to compile. Calfee's suggestions, however, may assist in elaborating this needed information.

A commonality of views exists among many of those who have found educational remediation to be effective, with threads of this fabric running throughout this volume, as well as in Rawson's paper. They include a delicate balance of knowledge of the progression of language acquisition and recognition of the variability in the developmental stage of language acquisition to ensure accurate assessment of the student's strengths within the substrate of language performance. They involve reduction of the task of language instruction to a basic phonemic-graphemic-morphemic level commensurate with the student's capacity to learn these skills; an individualized, hierarchical, sequential program of language skills must be developed, so that the learner relates meanings of combined symbols within the context of the patterns of the language to be mastered in all its forms—reading, writing, spelling, and speaking; and still one must maintain an active respect for the personal emotional needs of the student.

The papers in this volume commemorating the 25th anniversary of the Orton Society vary in content and approach. Their common base of interest results from the proposition already mentioned that the more we know about the nature of the language the more we will know how to teach it. When we know more about the nature of the student, we will know more about teaching the language to him. The more skillfully, flexibly, and therapeutically individualized our remediation the more self-reliant and competent he will become. Perhaps the stimulus of these papers will see the next 25 years of the Society's work brought to a successful conclusion, with difference in language performance treated productively and creatively instead of as a disability.

References

1. Allen DV, Rothman RK: Intersensory integration and reading ability in the deaf. Bull Psychon Soc 1:199–201, 1973
2. Baker HL Jr, Campbell JK, Houser OW, et al: Computer assisted tomography of the head: an early evaluation. Mayo Clin Proc 49:17–27, 1974
3. Conners CK: Cortical visual evoked response in children with learning disorders. Psychophysiology 7:418–428, 1970
4. Critchley M: The Dyslexic Child. Second edition. London, William Heinemann (Medical Books), 1970; (*Also* Springfield, Illinois, C C Thomas, 1970)
5. Dinklage KT: Inability to learn a foreign language. In Emotional Problems of the Student. Second edition. Edited by G Blaine, C McArthur. New York, Appleton-Century-Crofts, 1971, pp 185–206
6. Geschwind N: Cerebral dominance and anatomic asymmetry (editorial). N Engl J Med 287:194–195, 1972; (See also Geschwind N: Anatomical evolution and the human brain. Bull Orton Soc 22:7–13, 1972)
7. Geschwind N, Levitsky W: Human brain: left-right asymmetries in temporal speech region. Science 161:186–187, 1968
8. Hochberg FH, LeMay M: Arteriographic correlates of handedness. Neurology 25:218–222, 1975
9. Kavanagh JF, Mattingly IG: Language by Ear and by Eye: The Relationships Between Speech and Reading. Cambridge, Massachusetts, MIT Press, 1972
10. Kimura D: Cerebral dominance and the perception of verbal stimuli. Can J Psychol 15:166–171, 1961
11. LeMay M, Culebras A: Human brain—morphologic differences in the hemispheres demonstrable by carotid arteriography. N Engl J Med 287:168–170, 1972
12. Leong CK: Dichotic listening with related tasks for dyslexics: differential use of strategies. Bull Orton Soc 25:111–126, 1975
13. Liberman AM, Cooper FS, Shankweiler DP, et al: Perception of the speech code. Psychol Rev 74:431–461, 1967
14. Lombroso CT, Symann-Louett N, Gascon GG, et al: Dyslexia: differences in visual evoked responses to meaningful and nonmeaningful stimuli (abstract). Neurology (Minneap) 24:349, 1974
15. McCarthy JM: The state of the art: where we are in learning disabilities. Read at the meeting of the CANHC-ACLD, Los Angeles, California, Feb 3, 1973
16. Sklar B, Hanley J, Simmons WW: An EEG experiment aimed toward identifying dyslexic children (letter to the editor). Nature 240:414–416, 1972
17. Wada JA: Interhemispheric sharing and shift of cerebral speech function (abstract). Excerpta Medica International Congress Series No 193, 1969, pp 296–297
18. Wada JA, Clarke R, Hamm A: Cerebral hemispheric asymmetry in humans: cortical speech zones in 100 adult and 100 infant brains. Arch Neurol 32:239–246, 1975
19. Witelson SF, Pallie W: Left hemisphere specialization for language in the newborn: neuroanatomical evidence of asymmetry. Brain 96:641–646, 1973

DEVELOPMENTAL DYSLEXIA:
ITS HISTORY, NATURE AND PROSPECTS

Macdonald Critchley

It was kindly suggested to me that I should talk briefly, first of all, on the history of developmental dyslexia—though I fear this may be all too familiar to you; secondly, that I should say something about what is going on today outside the United States; and thirdly, that I might speculate a bit as to the future, indicating possible trends in worldwide research into the problem which interests us all.

The entity we speak of as developmental dyslexia was first described 78 years ago simultaneously, yet independently, by two English doctors. One was a school medical officer in Bradford, Yorkshire, James Kerr.[7] The more explicit account, however, we owe to a general practitioner who lived in Seaford, a small town on the south coast of England. A number of schools were sited there, and Dr. Pringle Morgan[8] was an attending physician to one of these. Stimulated by a paper which dealt with elderly aphasiacs who had lost the ability to read, he submitted a short communication to one of the British medical journals. He said that in one of his schools there was a boy of fourteen who could not master the art of reading, and yet he was of superior intelligence.

The boy's schoolmaster proclaimed that if the teaching had been oral, this boy would have been top of the school. As it was, he was struggling along at the bottom of the class. "Could it be," wrote Dr. Pringle Morgan, "that there exists a condition which one might call 'congenital word-blindness'?"[8] The identity of that boy and his progress are unsolved mysteries which I am still in the process of trying to unravel.

Certain writers have sought to attach priority for the discovery of this syndrome to two Germans, who described cases in 1867 and 1885, respectively, but both of them wrote about children who were dullards and fall outside the group which concerns us. Dr. Rudolph Berlin,[2] who first used the term dyslexia in 1887, was talking of adult aphasiacs.

In Czechoslovakia, the name of Heveroch,[6] a neurologist in Prague, has been put forward as the pioneer writer, but this is so only on the Continent. I tracked down his paper and had it translated, finding that it was written in 1903, seven years after Pringle Morgan's prophetic description. Furthermore, the case discussed was that of a brain-damaged child, whose condition we cannot accept as developmental dyslexia. It was, however, the precursor of the excellent work which has since been done in his country.

After 1896, a steady trickle of case reports appeared in the literature,[*] and congenital word-blindness became well and truly established in the corpus of neurology. Let us here highlight one or two contributions which stand out as landmarks.

In 1906, an American, Dr. Claiborne,[4] advanced the challenging notion that congenital word-blindness was a disorder peculiar to English-speaking peoples, being the product of what seemed to him the wholly illogical spelling of the language. We will discuss this idea more a little later.

The second landmark—and a most important one—was the statement made by the English eye specialist, C. J. Thomas,[10] in 1905, that word-blindness often appears in more than one member of a family. This fact has turned out to be vital to our present conception of the essential nature of this particular learning disability.

The third striking feature which came to light is that among poor readers boys greatly outnumber girls. Who should be given credit for first mentioning this I cannot say, for it seems to have crept inconspicuously into the literature. An early *ad hoc* mention was made by Bachmann[1] in 1927, but although he was perhaps unaware of it, he was anticipated by Orton[9] in 1925.

It is the work of this fourth great man which attracts our attention especially at this current Congress. I refer, of course, to the imaginative, observant and perceptive Samuel T. Orton. Like Pringle Morgan, he was alerted to the condition of this kind of language disability by a boy, the now-familiar 16-year-old "M.P.," whom he saw in an Iowa mental health clinic.[9] Further search led to his finding several, and later many, such children, who were conspicuous by reason of their difficulties in coping with reading and spelling. Need I enumerate the invaluable contributions which Dr. Orton brought to our knowledge of this syndrome? I was far away from Iowa when he was beginning work in this field, but at the very same time I, too, was becoming caught up with the problem, and I naturally appreciated to the full the exciting ideas which Dr. Orton was advancing.

Both he and I came to the problem of backward readers through a study of their handwriting, as well as of their reading and spelling. To me, this problem of penmanship was the most intriguing phenomenon at that time. Many of the children were muddled as to the lateral orientation of the letters they saw and committed to paper. After all, it is a mere convention that the letter "E" should have its prongs pointing to the right and not to the left. Most children soon come to realize empirically the way this asymmetrical letter faces, but the word-blind youngster remains in doubt. Nay more, in putting pen to paper, not only may he rotate individual letters but he may even reverse clusters of letters or whole words. In fact, he may perpetrate mirror writing. It was in 1927 that I published a book on the subject.[5]

Dr. Orton believed that this laterospatial disorientation was so fundamental that he called the syndrome "strephosymbolia," twisted symbols. Many children in his series were left-handed; some were ambidextrous; others were crossed-laterals, preferring one hand but the opposite eye or foot.

Since 1925, interest in this developmental language problem has snowballed, and we have gained experience as to its vagaries. True, we have discarded the terms "word-blindness" and "strephosymbolia." We now speak of dyslexia, and to pinpoint those cases which are idiopathic, constitutional, and genetically determined, we use the term "specific developmental dyslexia." In so doing, we eliminate all those reactionary cases where the dyslexia is secondary to perceptual defect, to intellectual inadequacy, to emotional disturbance, or to brain damage.

Claiborne's hypothesis that dyslexia is due to our troublesome and erratic spelling has not stood up to scrutiny. Obviously he was not correct, for reading difficulties are met with in all raciolinguistic groups. For example Claiborne's predecessor, Dr. Heveroch, unknown to Claiborne, was concerned with children using the phonetically regular Czech language.

However, the linguistic problem is not straightforward. Is dyslexia distributed evenly all over the globe, or are some races and peoples more involved than others? For that matter, just what is the prevalence of developmental dyslexia among *English-speaking* children? I believe we are safe in asserting that at least 10 percent of all school-children are backward readers. Not all of those, of course, are cases of developmental dyslexia, but many are, especially among the boys. Out of this 10 percent, I am sure that at least one-fifth of the boys are dyslexic, the girls constituting perhaps one-twentieth. These figures are probably an underestimate, with many authorities citing a higher incidence.

So we sorely need: first, a statistical study of the incidence in your country and in mine; and, secondly, a comparison of those countries where English is not the mother-tongue.

Early in my eight-year term of office as President of the World Federation of Neurology, I started to explore the problem of contrastive prevalence of developmental dyslexia by setting up a small research group with an international and interdisciplinary membership. The problem proved to be far more complex than we had expected, but some data have emerged. No European country is without its quota of dyslexic children. In Germany, and perhaps also in the Scandinavian countries, the incidence seems to be about the same as in Great Britain. Claims have been made that dyslexia is rare in Italy, but to me the arguments are not convincing. Many fallacies arise, for there is no standardized international procedure for diagnosis. I prefer to think that dyslexia occurs just as often among Italian-speaking children, but that, because of the regularity of the language, it constitutes less of a handicap to them than to learners whose native language is English.

We also know that dyslexics are encountered among the peoples of Asia and Africa, where the structure of the languages is quite different from the subject-predicate, alphabetic-phonetic systems with which we are familiar. Here again there have been certain challenging statements. It has been asserted that dyslexia is rare among the Japanese. I must confess that this surprised me; the evidence so far seems unconvincing. I believe that more work by Japanese neurologists will clear up this point, especially if it it correlated with the situation in China, where, to my knowledge, dyslexia does occur.

There is still a great dearth of information from some other countries, and I hope that during this Congress we shall be hearing something from their representatives. We have really only just started on what will be a very considerable research project, but it is one which must be carried out.

It is true that there have been some recent surveys of what is going on here and there. Some Americans have been peripatetic observers of the European scene. Others have come here to the United States from Great Britain, to familiarize themselves with American remedial techniques. Coordination of this kind is excellent and desirable. However, I envisage research which is far more penetrating. Before we can embark on the task of determining precisely the incidence of dyslexia in the various countries of the Americas, Europe, Asia and Africa, we require statistically valid reading tests, which can be modified so as to apply to the languages concerned, and which can be understood by others.

One promising line of research, barely touched upon yet, is biochemical. The maturation of the brain depends partly upon appropriately timed myelination of the nerve fibers, and partly upon the intimate structure of the nerve cell itself.

A child's pyramidal tract does not myelinate until somewhere between the ages of one and two years. In the case of a foal, however, this function is evolved within a few minutes of birth. The pyramidal tract is a relatively simple structure which transmits volitional movements, so the foal can at once stand and move about. The more complex brain structures naturally myelinate still later in the human child, perhaps as late as six years or even later. Orton gave attention to the significance of this as early as the 1920's.

Myelination is, of course, a pure histochemical transaction and, as such, it could well be delayed by some inherent process which is genetically determined. Equally well, the chemical reaction of myelination might be capable of stimulation by artificial means. Were that ever to come about, we would then be in possession of a method for accelerating the natural learning processes. At one time we thought we had found a pharmacological answer in glutamic acid, but experience eventually proved the drug to be worthless. The same applies to certain so-called "get smart" pills—that is, those pharmaceutical preparations which have been alleged, without justification I believe, to possess powers of stimulating cerebral metabolism in both early age and senescence. Methylphenidate, also, is certainly not the pharmacological answer for developmental dyslexia.

Turning from the chemistry of the myelin sheaths which invest the axon processes of each nerve cell, we can study the neuron itself, with its complicated nuclear structure, as well as the complex means whereby adjacent cells intercommunicate. Again, this is a histochemical process mediated by neurohumoral transmitter substances. Already we know of the existence of at least five of these and the sum-total may eventually prove to be even greater.

This way of thinking might be of enormous promise to us. Recently, we have become familiar with the analogy of the specific loss of one of these neurohumoral transmitters occurring in middle age, with its logical remediation by feeding back the missing material. I am referring to the loss of dopamine in Parkinson's disease and its replacement by L-Dopa. So, if one day it were possible to demonstrate an inborn deficiency of a neurohumoral transmitter in the brain of a dyslexic, then it should be possible to replace it pharmacologically.

The whole human cycle of birth, infancy, childhood, middle age and senescence is a continuous biometabolic process, one which may be temporarily delayed or which may be liable to premature decay. Allow me to quote from a recent paper by Dr. Bromley:

> It is now taken for granted that we start life at conception with a complex genetic make-up, or programme, which guides and limits the development of our biological, behavioural and psychological characteristics within the context of opportunities and constraints provided by the physical and social conditions of our environment. . . . This process of juvenile development is in some ways smooth and continuous and in other ways uneven and abrupt, but the main point is that for normal children, the sequence of development is systematic and progressive, and seems to be under relatively close genetic regulation as regards the ages at which certain stages of development are reached.[3]

Words such as these may hold the key which will unlock the mystery of delayed cerebral maturation. It may well be that at the time of the Golden Anniversary of the Orton Society 25 years hence, the majority of the contributions will be epidemiological, chemical and pharmacological in nature. Today we are fortunate in knowing a considerable amount about remedial techniques for the individual instruction of these unfortumate children. Tomorrow, we may be able to help them in other ways—even by reversing deficiencies in the brain.

References

1. Bachmann F: Über Kongenitale Wortblindheit. Berlin, S Karger, 1927
2. Berlin R: Eine besondere Art von Wortblindheit (Dyslexie) (Monograph). Wiesbaden, Verlag von JF Bergmann, 1887
3. Bromley DB: Mental aspects of aging. Triangle 12 no. 4:171, 1973
4. Claiborne JH: Types of congenital symbol amblyopia. JAMA 47:1813–1816, 1906
5. Critchley M: Mirror Writing. London, Kegan Paul, 1927
6. Heveroch A: About Specific Reading and Spelling Difficulties in a Child With Excellent Memory [in Czech]. Publikováno v Paedagogický Rozhledech, 1904
7. Kerr J: School hygiene, in its mental, moral and physical aspects. J Roy Stat Soc 60:613–680, 1897
8. Morgan WP: A case of congenital wordblindness. Br Med J 2:1378, 1896
9. Orton ST: Word-blindness in school-children. Arch Neurol Psychiat 14:581–615, 1925
10. Thomas CJ: Congenital word-blindness and its treatment. Ophthalmoscope 3:380–385, 1905

THE STRUCTURE OF THE LANGUAGE

Philip B. Gough

I would like to begin by making an extravagant claim about the importance of the structure of language in reading. But I cannot, for no claim about
its importance could truly be considered extravagant. Knowledge of the
language being read is at the heart of the reading process, and without that
knowledge, reading could simply not take place.

When thinking about reading, we are apt to overlook the importance of
language; at least books (e.g., Kavanagh and Mattingly[32]) and journals (e.g.,
Reading Research Quarterly) on the subject seem pre-occupied with the
periphery of the reading process.[54] Perhaps this is because language is so
seldom absent in humans that we are not often led to think about what its
presence means. The loss of language in profound aphasia clearly results in an
inability to read normally, but this loss is so generally devastating that we are
apt to overlook the reading disability and its connection with the linguistic
deficit. Probably more striking is the case of the profoundly deaf child, who,
lacking the knowledge of the language which he confronts when asked to
learn to read, finds that task forbiddingly difficult; many scholars are persuaded that the profoundly deaf child, even one with exceptional intelligence,
never learns to read in anything like the way we take for granted in the
literates around us.

But we need not look to pathology for evidence of the importance of
language to reading; the most persuasive evidence is right behind our eyes.
Here I am, for example, with an intact brain, a sound memory, adequate
visual and auditory perceptual systems; I can recognize letters, organize them
into larger units, make the appropriate saccadic eye-movements and return
sweeps. But I cannot read a word of Polish or Tagalog or Urdu or any other
of the world's several thousand languages, save English. Of course I can learn
to read one of those language, but only, I would submit, by learning the
language.

15

In what follows, I will consider what it is that a man who can read Polish knows that I do not, or more precisely, what it is that I know of English that enables me to read it.

To begin with, a speaker's knowledge of a language (his grammar) can be divided into three parts: he knows the sounds of the language (its phonology); he knows the words of the language (its lexicon), and he knows the sentences of the language (its syntax and semantics). I will try to show that each of these plays an important role in learning to read, and each is crucially involved in the process of reading by the skilled reader. Let me begin in the middle, with the word.

Words

The words of the language are the joints of the grammar, for they connect the forms of the language with its meanings. It is a curious fact that the word has been relatively neglected by linguists. For most of us, the word seems the essence of language. The Bible places it in the beginning. Parents speak proudly of their child's first words. We minimize our knowledge of a foreign language by saying we know only a few words. Yet the linguist has studied the word relatively little; he knows much more about the sounds of which it is constituted and the sentences which it constitutes than he does about the word and its meaning.

There are only two things about the meaning of words which, at this moment, seem incontrovertible: they are in the head, and they are decomposable.

The first point may not seem remarkable. But until fairly recently, there has been a tendency in linguistics and psychology to equate meaning with reference, to identify the meaning of a word with that to which it refers. (Thus the meaning of *chair* would be taken to be the set of all chairs, the meaning of *London* the city of that name.) That this view is mistaken has long been apparent to philosophers,[22] but many linguists and psychologists have failed to recognize their wisdom. Moreover, among psychologists, even when the difference has been recognized, there has been a determined effort to tie meaning closely to reference, to make the meaning of a word simply a residue of one's experience with the thing it refers to. Thus it has been suggested that the meaning of a word is simply a visual image of its referent,[47] or that the meaning of a word is just a conditioned response, a fraction of one's response to that which the word signifies.[46]

There is a grain of truth in both of those views. The meanings of words must somehow reflect the properties of their referents, else they could scarcely represent those things in discourse. And the connection between a word's form and its meaning must be learned ("conditioned"), for the mapping between the forms and meanings of a language is almost totally arbitrary. But there is no more than a grain of truth to these ideas.

For one thing, only a fraction of the words we know can be said to have a referent we can see or hear or feel. (Consider, by way of illustration, the words of the preceding sentence.) Moreover, even in the case of the minority of words which do refer to perceptible objects, it is doubtful that the attributes of their meanings can be equated with, or reduced to, products of a single perceptual system (like a visual image), for the fact that most of the sensible attributes of objects can be apprehended through more than one sense (as, for example, triangularity can be seen or touched or even heard) strongly suggests that those attributes ultimately have a conceptual basis.

What these points suggest is that we have no reason *a priori* to expect that the nature of the meanings of words can be related in any simple or direct way to the nature of the world of the senses. Rather, we should be prepared to find the nature of meanings related only indirectly and in complex ways to the external world.

Arguments like these lead inexorably to the conclusion that meanings must be investigated in their own right, that they lead lives of their own somewhere behind the eyes and between the ears. But this poses a methodological problem for the linguist, for if we locate meanings inside the head, we have no way of investigating them directly. We take them to be neutral events, or states, or structures. But the neurophysiologist is of no help, for he has enough trouble deciding if a man is asleep or not; we can scarcely expect him to tell us the difference between *rutabaga* and *although*. Thus we are forced to treat meanings as abstract, theoretical entities, and to try to discover (or better, invent) the properties which explain a word's behavior (i.e., how it compares with other words, how it fits into sentences, and so forth.)

While we cannot see the meaning of a word directly, we can often see it indirectly: we can often see its reflection in other words, for we can, in many instances, see how that meaning relates to others. We know that the meaning of *boy* is the same as the meaning of *lad,* but that the meaning of *turnip* is not the same as that of *umbrella;* in general, we can say about any two words whether they are synonymous or not. We know that the meaning of *hot* is the opposite of the meaning of *cold,* but that this is not true of (say) *slow* and *wealthy;* in general, we can say about any two words whether they are antonymous or not. We know that the meaning of *adult* is contained in the meaning of *woman,* but that the meaning of *frog* is not part of the meaning of (say) *custard;* in general, we can say about any two words whether they are hyponymous or not.

Moreover, our ability to perceive relations between words is not limited to familiar relationships like synonymy, antonymy, and hyponymy. Even though we have no name for it, we can readily perceive that the relation between the words *attorney* and *client* is the same as the relation between the words *doctor* and *patient.* In general, given any two pairs of words, we have little difficulty deciding whether the members of one pair are related in the same way as the members of the other.

What seems the most natural way to explain these relationships (and, hopefully, to characterize meaning) is to assume that meanings are decomposable, that the meaning of a word is built up out of a set of more basic semantic components. Virtually every modern student of meaning concurs in this assumption. The basic semantic units, the semantic primes, have gone under many names, from "sememes"[8] to "minimal content units"[28] to "dimensions of semantic space";[46] perhaps the most widely used is *semantic features.*[31]

The assumption that the meaning of a word consists of a set of semantic features provides a framework for the explanation of many of the relationships between words. It allows us to explain synonymy; we say that a pair of words are synonyms if and only if they share exactly the same set of features. Thus *boy* and *lad* would be synonymous because they both have the features HUMAN and MALE and YOUNG (etc.), and have no features on which they are different. A pair of words would be antonyms because they share the same set of features except one where they differ; thus *boy* and *girl* would be opposites because they are alike in all respects save the feature representing sex. We could account for hyponymy by positing that word A is a hyponym of word B if and only if the set of features which constitutes the meaning of B is a proper subset of the set of features which define A.

Moreover, the featural framework would enable us to approach another important set of relationships between words, those which concern their combinability. Words cannot be combined freely; truly random strings of words are totally un-interpretible. Most such strings are barred by the syntactic rules of the language; thus we cannot interpret:

(1)   Whenever bicycles Democrat smoked rarity choose.
because we can fit no syntactic structure to it.

But it is easy to find (or at least invent) sentences which could be said to be interpretible, but where the interpretation makes no sense, as in (2–4):

(2)   The truck ran over the perception.

(3)   His billfold died.

(4)   That goldfish is a rock musician.

Though it may be possible to assign metaphorical interpretations to some of these sentences (like interpreting "His billfold died" to mean it wore out), in their literal interpretation each of them is anomalous. Moreover, each of them is anomalous for a different reason. Thus (2) is anomalous because *perception* is not a concrete object, (3) because billfolds aren't animate, and (4) because a goldfish is not a human being.

Linguists try to explain facts like these by asserting that lexical items have selectional restrictions; certain verbs can take only certain kinds of nouns as subjects (or objects), nouns permit only certain kinds of adjectives as modifiers, and so forth. Obviously, the notion of semantic features makes itself very useful here, for one can define selectional restrictions in terms of such features. Thus, for example, *marry* would be defined as a verb which requires subjects and objects with the feature HUMAN, and we could then explain why "John married a dancer" is perfectly acceptable, but "John married a silo" is not.

The notion of semantic features would seem to hold promise for the analysis of word meaning. But that promise has not yet been fulfilled. Only a handful of features have been proposed,[4,5] and these tend to consist of isolated sets of features put forward to account for the relationships between small numbers of words in clearly circumscribed semantic fields, which, like kinship terms,[49] have a transparent structure. It remains to be seen whether a set of features can be developed which will account for the incredibly more complex structure of a speaker's entire vocabulary.

There have been sporadic attempts by psychologists to discover a larger set of semantic features, to discover, as it were, the semantic structure of the lexicon. These attempts[48,44] consistently take the same form. Subjects provide similarity ratings for a substantial sample of words, either directly or indirectly. Then those ratings are subjected to some form of multidimensional scaling, in hopes of revealing the semantic structure which presumably underlies the observed pattern of similarity ratings.

I think it is fair to say that these efforts have proved disappointing. They yield only the obvious (e.g., that *canary* differs from *eagle* on at least two dimensions, like size and domesticity). And I think the reason for this is also obvious: there are inherent limitations in comparing isolated words, for many crucial properties of words reveal themselves only when the words are employed in sentences.

Consider, for example, the words *persuade* and *promise*. Considered in isolation (or in most contexts, for that matter), these words are quite similar. They are both verbs, they both take human subjects, they both take sentential complements, and so forth. But consider their role in sentences (8) and (9):

(8) John promised Harry to go.

(9) John persuaded Harry to go.

Notice that in the first sentence *John* is the subject of the verb *go;* it is John's going that John promised. But in the second sentence *Harry* is the subject of the verb *go;* it is Harry's going that John obtained through persuasion. Yet the only observable difference between the two sentences is that one contains *promised* where the other contains *persuaded;* we must conclude that some difference between those verbs, in conjunction with the syntactic structure of the sentence, alters the grammatical relations between the verb *go* and the nouns of the sentence. I do not know how this difference should be stated, but there can be no doubt that it must be a part of the meanings of these verbs, and it seems very doubtful that it would be noticed in any comparison of the two verbs in isolation.

Or consider the difference between the words *sure* and *sorry* in these two sentences:

(10) John was sure the Dodgers lost the pennant.

(11) John was sorry the Dodgers lost the pennant.

If we hear the second of these, we can conclude that the speaker believes that the Dodgers did, indeed, lose the pennant. But the first of these sentences conveys no such information; it would be perfectly reasonable to say this even if you believed that John was quite mistaken about the Dodgers. The two sentences clearly differ in their presuppositions and that difference must be attributed to the difference between *sure* and *sorry.* How this difference is to be described is not well understood,[33,36] but it seems reasonable to believe again that the difference would not have been detected in a word sorting task.

Observations like these suggest that no standard procedure, no fixed form of analysis, is likely to lead to the discovery of the true set of semantic features, even assuming that they exist. Rather they are apt to be found only as by-products of the analysis of sentences (much as chemical elements have emerged from the study of compounds), and some of them may be detectable only in very unusual, even artificial, circumstances.

This does not mean that the student of semantics must sit idly by, awaiting the millenium. While there has been little progress in the identification of the basic semantic elements, there have been significant advances in our knowledge of what features must be like and how they must be combined. Three seem to me noteworthy.

First, it has been clearly established that not all features are symmetrical, or neutral. Consider pairs of opposites, like *above* and *below, over* and *under, long* and *short.* In the feature framework we assume that the members of each pair have identical sets of features save one, and it would seem immaterial how we would assign that last feature, so long as we gave different assignments to the antonyms. (Thus we might assign + to *above* and − to *below*, or just the opposite.) But it turns out that there are good linguistic reasons for making one of the terms more basic,[4,5] and there is now psychological evidence for the same point.[12] Thus, sentences containing *above* are easier to verify than sentences containing *below*, sentences with *long* are easier to verify than their counterparts containing *short* and so forth. So we are led to suppose that (at least some) features do not have symmetrical values, but instead have a basic unmarked value opposed to a derivative, marked one.

Second, there is persuasive evidence that at least some features must be relational.[6,7] To this point, I have implicitly treated features as if they were nothing but properties, one-place predicates in the language of the logician. But there are many words which must contain at least one feature which, if thought of as a predicate, must be (at least) a two-place predicate. This is clearly the case with transitive verbs like *hit,* or *carry* or *repair;* such verbs clearly make reference to two things, the subject or agent or actor, and an object or victim or recipient of the action. But this is not only true of verbs; it is also true of many nouns, like *father* and *debtor* and *teacher.* And linguistic analysis shows that it is true of many ordinary adjectives as well. Thus an adjective like *small* can easily be shown to be, not an absolute property which can be predicated of an object, but rather a relation, true or false of an object only in relation to some implicit norm. Thus if we say that a certain elephant is small and a certain flea is large, we do not thereby imply that the flea is larger than the elephant. Rather, we mean only that the elephant is small as elephants go, and the flea is large for a flea. This point is surely obvious (and must have long been so), but its implications for our understanding of the nature of word meanings have not been generally appreciated until recently. We can now see that the very meaning of ordinary words like *large, short* and *cold* (indeed, any adjective which seems to refer to a point on some continuum) cannot consist solely of a set of properties.

Instead, it must contain elements which are logically more complex, in the form of relations, two-place predicates where one place is filled by a hypothetical (and variable) norm.

If the complexity of semantic features is increasing, so is that of their arrangement into meanings. To this point, I have treated meanings not only as if they were made up only of properties, but also as if they were nothing but conjunctions of those properties, as if a meaning were nothing but a list of properties and relations. But we now know that meanings must have more complex structure than this. A number of linguistic analyses[2,35] have shown that words like *give* and *lengthen* and *kill* contain relational components whose arguments are not individuals, but rather whole propositions (which themselves may be complex.) Thus it has been argued that *give* should be analyzed as something like *A cause B,* where B itself can be decomposed as *C has D;* and it has been argued that *kill* should be analyzed as *X cause Y,* where Y is the proposition that *Z dies.*

The details of these analyses are controversial,[18] but their general import, that individual word meanings have complex internal structure, is all but universally accepted.

One of the most interesting recent developments is the suggestion that the many components of the meanings of words are not understood all at once, but rather that words are understood, as it were, serially, or piecemeal. For one thing, it may well be that the syntactic properties of a word are revealed to us before the semantic. That this might be so was suggested by the fact that computer programs designed to understand sentences look first for syntactic information in order to parse a sentence. This notion is supported by the fact that we seem to be able to detect syntactic deviance more readily than semantic anomaly. Thus the deviance of (12) seems more obvious to me than that of (13).

(12) Joe Namath faded back and threw a long protect.

(13) Joe Namath is coming to Mayo for his hysterectomy.

Moreover, within the semantic features of a word, it also begins to appear that some are apprehended more quickly than others.[14,42] The evidence here is far from clear,[15,48] but it seems to suggest that one realizes first upon hearing a word features which are specific to or characteristic of that word, and then develops, as if by inference, features which pertain to a word only more remotely. Thus, people have been shown to decide that "canaries are yellow" is true faster than they can decide that "canaries can fly" is, or that 7-Up is bubbly faster than that 7-Up is wet.

All of this is very recent, and although studies of the mental lexicon are burgeoning, our understanding of word meanings is far from clear. But we can say that words are made up of basic and derivative semantic features, at least some of which are inherently relational, arranged into structures of increasing complexity. The closer we look, the more complex they seem. And each of these intricate entities is stored in the head of the reader, available to him in a fraction of a second. This is a most impressive fact, for notice that there is no way to *compute* the meaning of a word on the basis of its form. The connection between forms and meanings is almost totally arbitrary. Thus to understand a word, the reader (or listener) has no choice but to consult his mental lexicon; he must look it up in his semantic dictionary. And this is no small feat, for that dictionary is very large.

It is not easy to estimate the size of a man's lexicon; nor is it impossible. One way to approach it is to draw a random sample of words from a good-sized dictionary, and then to see what proportion of these are known to the subject. If he knows one-tenth of the words we present to him, and if the words we present to him constitute one-fiftieth of the words in the dictionary then we can multiply the number of words he knew in the sample by 500 to get an estimate of the number of words he knows in that dictionary.

Using just this procedure, Oldfield[45] has set the size of the vocabulary of the literate (British) adult at about 75,000 entries. But this has to be an underestimate, for the printed dictionary excludes a goodly number of items which are clearly entered in our mental lexicons. It excludes most place names, the names of streets, and hotels, and athletic stadia. It excludes the names of most people with whom we are familiar, the names of athletes, and musicians, and politicians, to say nothing of our personal friends and acquaintances. It fails to include the titles of familiar novels, and songs, and movies; the names of scientific laws and scientific societies, and brand names. In short, it fails to include a vast number of items which are securely stored in each of our heads. I don't know how to count these items, but I would not be surprised if they numbered in excess of 25,000. And if this is at all accurate, then our vocabularies must approach or exceed 100,000 items.

And the amazing thing is, that confronted with any one of these myriad items, we are able to find exactly the right entry in a fraction of a second. (If I say *register,* or *Mayo,* or *Samuel Orton,* you understand me in what seems to be no time at all.)

The fact that we can accomplish this wondrous feat rests on our knowledge of phonology.

Sounds

If the speaker has as many as 100,000 meanings filed away in his head, the phonological system of the language constitutes the filing system for those materials. Corresponding to each of those meanings is a phonological form; that form serves as an address, a set of instructions as to where the item can be located.

The form of each word is composed of a string of sound segments called phonemes. Each phoneme, in turn, can be decomposed into a set of more basic units, its distinctive features.[29] A given language draws upon a universal set of distinctive features like voicing and nasality to form the pool of phonemes which constitute the auditory alphabet of that language. Each such alphabet is relatively small; English, for example, employs some 46 phonemes. But a small number of phonemes can be combined and permuted to form a staggering number of distinct strings of phonemes to label lexical entries. Given the 46 phonemes of English, for example, we could form 46^4, or nearly half a million, items four characters in length alone.

The great majority of these combinations and permutations do not constitute words in the language; most of them are barred by the language's phonological rules. In English, for example, no word can begin with more than three consonants; indeed, if it contains as many as three, the first must be /s/ and the third must be a liquid (/l/ or /r/). Thus the phonology of a language must contain, in addition to an inventory of phonemes, a set of rules which govern the behavior of those phonemes.

The phonological rules of a language do more than state which combinations of phonemes are permissible. They also specify how those phonemes will interact in combination, for phonemes are not inert objects. Instead, they influence and react to other phonemes in their immediate environment, the nature of the word in which they occur, and even the sentence in which that word is embedded.

There are a variety of such phonological processes. There are processes of assimilation, where a given segment takes on features of a neighboring segment. In English, for example, a vowel which occurs before a nasal consonant like /n/ is often nasalized; thus the /i/ in *see* becomes nasalized in *seen.* The suffix which converts a singular noun into a plural assimilates the voicing of the noun's final consonant; thus the plural of *cat* ends in /s/, but the plural of *dog* ends in /z/. The prefix *in* becomes homorganic to (i.e., takes on the place of articulation of) a following stop consonant; thus *in* prefixed to *balance* or *personal* results in *imbalance* and *impersonal.*

There are processes of addition and deletion, like *epenthesis* and *syncope,* whereby entire phonemes move into or out of syllables having a certain structure. In English, for example, when a suffix beginning with a vowel is added to a noun ending in one, the latter may be deleted; thus *Mexico* or *Arizona* plus *-an* yields *Mexican* and *Arizonan.* A morpheme ending in a consonant-sonorant cluster is subject to *epenthesis,* where a vowel is inserted to break up that cluster; thus the vowel called *schwa* is inserted into the cluster /ntr/ to yield *center* and *winter.*

Finally, there are processes like coalescence and neutralization, where two phonemes merge into one. Thus in English, a final /t/ or /d/, combined with a following /y/, will become /š/ (as in *deletion*) or /ž/ (as in *invasion*), and all unstressed vowels merge to schwa.

Phonemes are also influenced by the nature of the word in which they occur. Whether a phoneme will be stressed is a function of its locus in the category of the word in which it occurs; stress is applied to the same string of phonemes one way in a noun (e.g., *áddress*), another way in a verb (e.g., *addréss*). The application of stress is also influenced by the larger syntactic context; *green hóuse paint* is not the same as *green house páint.*

Finally, phonemes are even influenced by the sentence in which they occur. Whether a phoneme will be stressed is a function of its locus in the syntactic structure of that sentence;[11] how clearly it will be enunciated is a function of the nature of that sentence.[39]

One of the most important and interesting consequences of these phonological processes is that the form of a word *before* it undergoes these processes may differ substantially from the form of that word when it emerges from those processes. Thus when we hear a word, what we hear is not the basic sequence of segments of which that word is constituted, but rather the result of the application of the phonological rules of the language to that basic sequence. We are then led to conclude that there are two sides to the form of every word. Its inner side is an abstract representation, a string of what are called systematic phonemes. Its outer side is a phonetic representation, derived from the abstract form by means of phonological rules.

It follows from this that words which are quite different *phonetically* may result from very similar underlying forms. Thus Chomsky and Halle [11] have shown how word pairs as different as *sign* and *signal, anxious* and *anxiety, divine* and *divinity,* and many more, are derived from common underlying representations, which, combined with different affixes, result in the distinct phonetic representations.

This phonological system, then, yields forms which provide a means of access to the lexicon. Each lexical entry is associated with a form; that form serves as its address in the memory of the speaker.

It is tempting to hypothesize that the mental dictionary is searched in the same way as a printed one, that the words in the mental dictionary are subcategorized from first segment to last. Then as a listener would apprehend the first sound segment, he would (as it were) open the dictionary to the section that corresponds to that segment, apprehend the second segment and turn to that subsection, and proceed in this way until he had found the entry which exactly matched what he had heard. Such a procedure would be very efficient; it would be guaranteed to yield the correct reading for any word in a very short period of time (and surely we must require this of any system which aspires to characterize the way our heads work).

There are a number of problems, though, with this hypothesis. The most crucial one is that the sound segments do not present themselves to the listener in anything like the orderly linear fashion which this mechanism would seem to presuppose.[38] At least we know that the acoustic signals which are the cues for the phonemes do not arrive in serial order, but rather overlap one another in time like shingles, such that it can be shown that it is frequently impossible to identify a given phoneme until you have identified that which follows it. This fact (among others) has led some theorists[52] to argue that we recognize speech by the syllable, or even the word, rather than by the phoneme.

Just how speech recognition works, how the phonological system leads to the lexicon, is a mystery. But for our purposes, this is not important, for however it works, it does provide access. Given a phonological representation, our heads do find the right lexical entry, and in what seems to be nothing flat.

It follows that if one could establish a correspondence between visual symbols and phonological segments, such that a visual representation could be mapped onto a phonological one, and if one could teach this correspondence to someone, then we would have access to that person's lexicon through a new modality.

Now it may occur to you that I have just invented writing and reading. There is a method in my madness (or a point to my inanity); in fact, there are two.

First, I wish to stress the fact that writing systems do not map visual symbols onto *sounds;* they do not embody correspondences between letters or characters and *acoustic signals.* Rather they connect those characters with *phonological representations,* abstract entities in the head of the speaker of a language.

Second, the writing system could tap in at least three different levels of phonological representation.[34]

One could tie in at the phonetic level, the level of the derived representation. Curiously, it appears that no writing system does this (i.e., no natural writing system is truly phonetic). The reason may well be that there would be no point to it, for one would then have to undo the work of the phonological processes to get back to the underlying form.

The more reasonable possibilities are the level of the systematic phoneme, and the level of the syllable. A phonemic system is obviously much more economical; there are less than 50 phonemes in a language, but usually more than a thousand distinct syllables.

The disadvantage of the phonemic system is that you cannot display to the learner the correspondences he must master.[26] You cannot show him this symbol goes with that phoneme, for there is no discrete way of presenting a phoneme. Only a minority of them can be presented in isolation, so all we can do is to present the learner with *strings* of characters, and *strings* of phonemes, and hope that he can break the code. And if the learner is not *aware* of the isolability of the phoneme—if he is not conscious of the fact that *pig* is constituted of three segments—then his problem is well nigh impossible.[51] Still, many do master the system and my concern is with the role of the phonological system in *their* reading.

There is no question that the phonological system plays a role in reading languages like English. It provides the only means by which the reader can (directly) read a word he has never seen written before. As we noted, the reader of an ideographic language who has mastered 2000 characters is helpless in the face of the 2001st; there is nothing which will tell him what word it is. But the reader of a language like English who learns to read two thousand words can read two *hundred* thousand, for he has internalized a set of rules which map the printed symbols into the phonological system, and he clearly must use those rules to read novel or unfamiliar words.

The more interesting (and controversial) question is whether he goes through the phonological system in reading familiar words. I like to entertain the hypothesis that the skilled reader goes through the phonological system all the time. There is evidence which appears to conflict with this hypothesis.[1,21] But there are three facts which are not easy to explain unless we assume the skilled reader automatically transforms print into phonological form.

First, several investigators[16,40] have found that if subjects are asked to proofread material for misspellings, they are much more likely to miss an error whose phonological form (i.e., its sound) is like that of the intended word than a spelling error which leads to a different phonological form. Thus, for example, if *work* were misspelled as *werk,* this mistake will go undetected far more often than would *wark.*

Second, if a reader is presented with strings of letters, and asked to decide if they are words or not, it takes him much longer to decide that a nonsense syllable is a nonsense syllable if it is homophonous with some word.[50] Thus it will take longer to decide that *brane* is nonsense than that *brone* is.

Third, we have found that if someone is asked to name the colors of ink in which each of a series of nonsense syllables is printed, his speed is greatly reduced if the syllables themselves sound like color words. That is, nonsense syllables homophonous with color words produce a Stroop effect[30] almost as large as the color words themselves.

Each of these results is easily explained if we assume that the skilled reader automatically converts printed forms into phonological ones, and hard to explain otherwise. So until better evidence is in, I am prepared to believe that the phonological system provides the reader with access to the lexicon, just as it does the listener.

The whole point of finding word meanings is to understand sentences, for unless he is reading signs on doors or labels on boxes, the reader is confronted with sentences. Let me turn at last to the role of syntax in reading.

Sentences

Someone who knows a language knows the sentences of that language. He can tell you whether something is or is not a sentence of the language. He can tell you whether one of its sentences is meaningful or anomalous, whether it is consistent or contradictory, whether it is ambiguous or unambiguous. He can often paraphrase those sentences, or answer questions about them, or carry out the instructions they convey. But mostly, and most importantly, he can understand them.

Extravagant claims have been made for the influence of sentences and their structure in reading. It has been argued[53] that sentence structure reaches into every corner of the reading process, from the inner recesses of word recognition to the outer movements of the eye across the printed page. For example, it has been argued[37] that the syntactic structure of the line under fixation determines how far the eyes will range ahead of the voice in reading aloud (the so-called *eye-voice span*). It has been claimed that the

syntactic structure of material currently under fixation will specifically determine the next saccadic movement of the eyes.[41] And it has been argued that
the structure of the sentence in which a given word is found will influence the
recognition of that word.[55]

I am skeptical about these hypotheses. Taken in broadest terms, each of
these hypotheses must be true. If the structure of what I am reading is so
complex that I cannot understand it, then eventually I will stop scanning
ahead and make a regressive eye movement; in this sense syntactic structure
surely must influence eye movements in reading. And if I encounter the form
m-i-n-u-t-e in the frame (14), then that structure clearly determines my
recognition of that form as *mínute,* rather than *minúte.* But the claims are

(14) I'll be there in a minute.

more dramatic than this: it is said that the syntactic structure of that part of
the sentence now under fixation determines the nature of the very next eye
movement, that the immediate context of a word influences, not just the
interpretation of what is seen, but the very perception itself. And it is these
dramatic hypotheses which consternate me.

Consider, for example, what would have to happen for the part of the
sentence now under fixation to affect where the eyes move next. First, the
material under fixation must be understood; that is not an instantaneous
process. Next, the material must be used as a basis for calculations of what
might occur next; this, too, must take time. Third, these calculations must be
compared against information arriving from the periphery (i.e., from the
visual pattern to the right of the print falling on the fovea); again, this must
take time. A decision about where the eyes should go must be reached, and a
set of orders for their movement must be drawn up. Finally, those instructions must be issued, and the movement carried out. All of this must take
place during the duration of a single fixation, about 250 milliseconds, or one
quarter of a second. That this sequence of events is implausible obviously
does not mean that it does not take place; the nervous system accomplishes
any number of implausible feats. But it does suggest that we might do well to
subject the apparent demonstrations to careful scrutiny.

They do not stand up to it. The single study which purports to show the
influence of syntactic structure on eye-movements is flawed in design, execu-
tion, and analysis. The research which purports to show the influence of
syntactic structure on eye-voice span is also flawed. In no case, for example,
have the researchers attempted to vary syntactic structure while holding the
confounding variable of lexical content constant. When we have done this in

our laboratory, we have found no effect of syntactic structure on eye-voice span at all. Rather, eye-voice span seems to be primarily determined by the length of the words just ahead of the voice: the shorter the words, the longer the eye-voice span.

The alleged influence of context on word recognition in reading is also open to question. There have been a number of demonstrations that the immediate sentential context of a word influences the recognition of that word. Thus, for example, Tulving and Gold[55] measured the visual duration threshold (the length of exposure necessary for the word to be recognized) for words presented in appropriate and inappropriate contexts, and found a significant difference favoring the former.

This result seems very plausible (and, indeed, it is easily replicable). But the contexts in question were presented to the subjects many seconds before the presentation of the target word, and they remained available throughout the recognition procedure. This is surely very different from the situation which obtains in ordinary reading, where the immediately prior context of a word comes under fixation only a fraction of a second before the word in question. That is, in ordinary reading, one would probably encounter the immediate context of a word no more than one or two fixations before the word itself. Cosky and Gough[17] have found that context does *not* facilitate recognition of a word unless that context is presented at least 500 milliseconds—half a second—before presentation of the word.

All of this is not to say that sentence structure does not influence any or all of these things, but convincing evidence that it does is not yet in hand.

The role of sentence structure in the peripheral components of the reading process is moot. But there is no question of its place at the center of that process. To read a sentence is to grasp the meaning of that sentence, to comprehend it. And the structure of a sentence is crucial to its comprehension.

To fully appreciate this, we must consider what the comprehension of a sentence involves.

First, we must note that the comprehension of sentences is fundamentally different from the comprehension of words. In the case of words, meanings are (so far as we can tell) arbitrarily associated with sounds; hence given one of those sounds, there is no way to arrive at its meaning other than by looking it up in our mental dictionary. But the meaning of very few, if any, sentences can be stored in our memories, because of the simple fact that virtually every sentence we encounter is new to us. I hope this point is obvious, for it is fundamental to an appreciation of the role of sentence structure in reading (or listening, for that matter). If it is not obvious, I think you would be persuaded it is true if you were to randomly select any sentence in today's newpaper or yesterday's magazine, and then to try and find another occurrence of that same sentence anywhere you care to look.

If the meanings of sentences cannot be found in our memories, then they must be arrived at in some other way: they must be *computed* on the basis of the meanings of their constituent words and the syntactic and semantic rules of the language. If this is the case, then we must ask how the meanings of sentences are related to the meanings of their words; we must ask what function must be computed.

We might begin by assuming the simplest of functions: that the meaning of a sentence consists of nothing more than the meanings of it words. But this assumption is obviously false, for the same words in the same order can still correspond to different sentential meanings. Thus, for example, the sentence (15) could mean either that a gentleman should offer his seat to old men and old women, or that he should offer his seat to old men and *all* women. The sentence (16) has one meaning in which *they* refers to children who are starving, another in which *they* refers to some persons who are engaged in the act of starving children.

(15) A gentleman should offer his seat to old men and women.

(16) They are starving children.

The existence of such ambiguities is very important, for they show that a given sentence, with the same words, in the same order, can have more than one meaning. But this means that the meaning of a sentence must consist of more than the meanings of its words plus their order; evidently the meaning of a sentence also depends upon how the reader *groups* its words into larger units. If *old* is grouped with *men* only, as in (17), then sentence (15) means one thing; if *men* and *women* are grouped together as in (18), then it means another. Similarly, in sentence (16), if *are starving* is taken as a unit, then *they* refers to the children, but if *starving children* is taken as a unit, then *they* must refer to the starvers of the children.

(17) (old men) and (women)

(18) (old) (men and women)

We are led, then, to propose that the meaning of a sentence consists, not only of the meanings of its words and their order, but also their grouping. But even this won't work, for the same words, in the same order, grouped in the same way can yield different sentential meanings. Thus (19) can mean either

that visiting relatives sometimes *are* boring, or that visiting relatives sometimes *is* boring.

(19) Visiting relatives can be boring.

Clearly, the meaning of a sentence is determined by more than the
meanings of its words, their order, and their grouping; it depends upon more
than what linguists since Chomsky[9] have called the *surface structure* of the
sentence. Evidently sentences have another, deeper level of structure, a level
at which the crucial grammatical relations (like subject-of, object-of, modi-
fier-of) are defined. This *deep structure,* then, is what must be recovered in
understanding a sentence, and this deep structure must be what the reading
process leads to.

I devoutly wish I could tell you how we do it. But I cannot, for the
brutal fact is that we have no good idea as to how it is accomplished.

The fundamental problem is posed by the fact that the deep structure of
the sentence is seldom directly reflected in the superficial arrangement of its
words. It is related to its superficial structure only by means of a complex
composite of functions called *grammatical transformations.*[9,10]

Grammatical tranformations are inventions of the linguist. The linguist
attempts to describe what a man knows when he knows a language by writing
a grammar of that language. He tries to write a set of rules which will generate
a set of *base* or *deep structures,* structures in which the basic grammatical
relations are simply and explicitly exhibited. (There is a raging controversy in
linguistics over whether these rules are syntactic, semantic, or something in
between the two; for our purposes this controversy is irrelevant.) Given these
base structures, he then writes another set of rules which transforms them
into a form closer to what we hear. These rules are called transformations,
and their function is to permute, delete, add—in short, rearrange—the elements of the base structure into the form we observe. Thus a given configuration in the base structure, with say, doctor as *subject* and patient as *object* of
the verb *heal,* might emerge as sentence (20) or a nominalization like (21) or
a cleft sentence like (22) or any number of other superficial forms.

(20) The doctor healed the patient.

(21) The doctor's healing of the patient.

(22) What the doctor did was heal the patient.

The work of the comprehender could be thought of as the undoing of
these transformations to extract the idea that *the doctor healed the patient.*
Two ideas have been proposed to explain how it is done. But neither is
adequate: one is too simple to be right, the other is too vague to be either
right or wrong.

The first idea was that each of the grammatical transformations posited by the linguist corresponds to a mental operation performed by the comprehender in understanding a sentence.[23],[43]

One difficulty with this idea is that it makes the relation between linguistic complexity and perceptual complexity too pat. The grammar is written, not to predict how hard sentences are to understand (far from it), but rather to provide the simplest and most elegant account of the sentences of the language and their structure. It would have been an amazing coincidence if the number of tranformations required by the linguist in generating the sentence corresponded to the number of operations the comprehender had to perform to understand it. But there appears to be no such coincidence (or at least it isn't consistent). In some cases, perceptual complexity increases with tranformational complexity: passive sentences are harder to understand than actives,[23],[24] nominalizations are harder to understand than their sentential counterparts;[13] and relative clauses whose pronouns have been deleted are harder to understand than those in which they have not been.[27] But in other cases, transformation seems to have no effect (or even to reduce) the perceptual complexity of sentences. Cleft sentences like (23) seem no more complex than their sources, sentences with adjectives are no harder than those without.[19] Thus, while the idea has yet to be conclusively refuted,[25] there seems little reason to believe that this is the way it's done.

(23) It surprised me that the Dodgers lost.

The second idea[3],[20] amounts to little more than a denial of the first. It says that we do not arrive at the deep structure of sentences by means of grammatical transformation, but instead, that we do so by means of perceptual strategies or heuristics—what might be thought of as inductive leaps into the structural abyss. Thus we are supposed to have mastered certain ways of attacking sentences, like assuming that if a noun precedes a verb, it is the subject of that verb, or that an adjective preceding a noun is a modifier of that noun.

The problem with this hypothesis is not that it is refuted by data; the problem is that no data can refute it.[25] If we agree that someone who comprehends a sentence does so by arriving at its deep structure, then the comprehender must do it by some means. And if we call those means perceptual strategies, then the idea that the comprehender employs perceptual strategies is true by definition, and it does not contribute a farthing to our understanding of that process.

Thus we have no good idea about how sentences are understood; we can, in fact, say precious little about it.

One thing we can say is that we seem to understand sentences from left to right, or from start to finish, and usually in a single pass (i.e., once through the sentence). This seems obvious to our introspections, but more trustworthy evidence is provided by what we call garden-path sentences. Garden-path sentences are sentences whose initial words are interpreted in a way which proves incompatible with what follows: one is led blithely down a garden path, only to come up against an uninterpretible wall, and be forced to retrace one's mental steps. For example, consider:

(24) The fat boy weighed 200 grapes.

(25) The freight trains carried weighed more than that shipped by planes.

(26) His face was flushed, but his broad shoulders saved him.

The fact that we are aware of a cognitive derailment while reading these sentences, of the necessity of reinterpreting an earlier part of the sentence, shows that we must have interpreted that part of the sentence before we got to the later.

At the same time, we can safely say that we do not do it in a strictly left-to-right manner, one word at a time. If we did this, we would be constantly garden-pathed, since virtually every sentence offers the opportunity for it. Consider for example, a simple sentence like (27).

(27) The light hurts my eyes.

We obviously interpret *light* as a source of illumination, and we seem to do so as soon as we read the word. But if we did, then a sentence like (28)

(28) A light jacket is heavy enough for spring.

should give us trouble, and it certainly seems not to. Thus it seems that we do withhold our interpretation of words at least momentarily; one is tempted to characterize comprehension as proceeding from left to right by leaps and bounds.

Finally, we can say that the comprehender is aided in his efforts by whatever outcroppings of deep structure appear at the surface. The comprehender understands sentences better when their subjects precede their verbs and their verbs precede their objects than when those elements are rearranged; he understands sentences better with relative pronouns than without;[27] he understands sentences with complementizers better than those without.

So we can say a little about what makes some sentences harder to understand than others. But the simple fact of the matter is that we can understand, quickly and effortlessly, just about any sentence. This is one of the most wondrous feats of the human intellect. And we are essentially ignorant of how it is done.

What this means is that I must leave about where I came in. I would like to conclude with some extravagant claims about the role of language in reading. I need not, for language speaks for itself. Clearly, one can employ language without reading: we speak and understand most of the time without reading or writing, almost all of us speak and understand *before* we ever read or write, and a good many of us (perhaps the majority) *never* read or write. On the other hand, I doubt that true reading is possible—even conceivable— without language. So language is crucial to reading. This being the case, it is sad that I cannot do much more than say so. But that is the state of the art.

References

1. Baron J: Phonemic stage not necessary for reading. Q J Exp Psychol 25:241–246, 1973
2. Bendix EH: Componential Analysis of General Vocabulary. Indiana University Research Center in Anthropology, Folklore, and Linguistics, Publication no. 41. Bloomington, Indiana, 1966
3. Bever TG: The cognitive basis for linguistic structures. *In* Cognition and Language Development. Edited by R Hayes. New York, John Wiley & Sons, 1970, pp 277–360
4. Bierwisch M: Some semantic universals of German adjectivals. Foundations of Language 3:1–36, 1967
5. Bierwisch M: Certain problems of semantic representations. Foundations of Language 5:153–184, 1969
6. Bierwisch M: Semantics. *In* New Horizons in Linguistics. Edited by J Lyons. Baltimore, Penguin Books, 1970, pp 166–184
7. Bierwisch M: On classifying semantic features. *In* Semantics. Edited by DD Steinberg, LA Jakobovits. Cambridge and New York, Cambridge University Press, 1971, pp 410–435
8. Bloomfield L: Language. New York, Holt, Rinehart & Winston, 1933
9. Chomsky N: Syntactic Structures. The Hague, Mouton, 1957
10. Chomsky N: Aspects of the Theory of Syntax. Cambridge, Massachusetts, MIT Press, 1965
11. Chomsky N, Halle M: The Sound Pattern of English. New York, Harper & Row, Publishers, 1968
12. Clark HH: Semantics and comprehension. *In* Current Trends in Linguistics. Vol 12. Edited by TA Sebeok. The Hague, Mouton, 1973
13. Coleman EB: The comprehensibility of several grammatical transformations. J Appl Psychol 48:186–190, 1964
14. Collins AM, Quillian MR: Retrieval time from semantic memory. J Verbal Learning Verbal Behav 8:241–248, 1969
15. Conrad C: Cognitive economy in semantic memory. J Exp Psychol 92:149–154, 1972

16. Corcoran DWJ: Acoustic factors in proof reading. Nature 214:851, 1967
17. Cosky M, Gough PB: The effect of context on word recognition. Read at the convention of the Midwestern Psychological Association, May 1973
18. Fodor JA: Three reasons for not deriving "kill" from "cause to die." Linguistic Inquiry 1:429–438, 1970
19. Fodor JA, Garrett M: Some syntactic determinants of sentential complexity. Perception Psychophysics 2:289–296, 1967
20. Fodor JA, Garrett M, Bever TG: Some syntactic determinants of sentential complexity. II. Verb structure. Perception Psychophysics 3:453–461, 1968
21. Forster KI, Chambers SM: Lexical access and naming time. J Verbal Learning Verbal Behav 12:627–635, 1973
22. Frege G: Über Sinn und Bedeutung. Zeitschrift für Philosophie und Philosophische Kritik. 100:22–50, 1892. Translated in Translations from the Philosophical Writings of Gottlob Frege. Oxford, Blackwell Scientific Publications, 1952
23. Gough PB: Grammatical transformations and speed of understanding. J Verbal Learning Verbal Behav 4:107–111, 1965
24. Gough PB: The verification of sentences: the effects of delay of evidence and sentence length. J Verbal Learning Verbal Behav 5:492–496, 1966
25. Gough PB: Experimental psycholinguistics. In A Survey of Linguistics Science. Edited by JF Kavanagh, IG Mattingly. College Park, Linguistics Program, University of Maryland, 1971
26. Gough PB: One second of reading. In Language by Ear and by Eye. Edited by JF Kavanagh, IG Mattingly. Cambridge, Massachusetts, MIT Press, 1972, pp 331–358
27. Hakes DT, Cairns HS: Sentence comprehension and relative pronouns. Perception Psychophysics 8:5–8, 1970
28. Hjelmslev L: Prolegomena to a Theory of Language. Bloomington, Indiana, Indiana University Press, 1953
29. Jakobson R, Fant G, Halle M: Preliminaries to Speech Analysis. Cambridge, Massachusetts, MIT Press, 1963
30. Jensen AR, Rohwer WD: The Stroop color-word test: a review. Acta Psychol (Amst) 25:36–93, 1966
31. Katz JJ, Fodor JA: The structure of a semantic theory. Language 39:170–210, 1963
32. Kavanagh JF, Mattingly IG: Language by Ear and by Eye: The Relationships Between Speech and Reading. Cambridge, Massachusetts, MIT Press, 1972
33. Kiparsky P, Kiparsky C: Fact. In Recent Advances in Linguistics. Edited by M Bierwisch, KE Heidolph. The Hague, Mouton, 1970
34. Klima ES: How alphabets might reflect language. In Language by Ear and by Eye. Edited by JF Kavanagh, IG Mattingly. Cambridge, Massachusetts, MIT Press, 1972, pp 57–80
35. Lakoff G: On the nature of syntactic irregularity. In Mathematical Linguistics and Automatic Translation, Report No. NSF-16. Cambridge, Massachusetts, Computation Laboratory, Harvard University, 1965
36. Lakoff G: Presupposition and relative well-formedness. In Semantics. Edited by DD Steinberg, LA Jakobovits. Cambridge and New York, Cambridge University Press, 1971, pp 329–340
37. Levin H, Kaplan E: Grammatical structure and reading. In Basic Studies in Reading. Edited by H Levin, JP Williams. New York, Basic Books, 1970
38. Liberman AM, Cooper FS, Shankweiler DP, et al: Perception of the speech code. Psychol Rev 74:431–461, 1967
39. Liberman P: Intonation, Perception, and Language. Cambridge, Massachusetts, MIT Press, 1967
40. MacKay DG: Input testing in the detection of misspellings. Am J Psychol 85:121–127, 1972
41. Mehler J, Bever TG, Carey P: What we look at when we read. Perception Psychophysics 2:213–218, 1967

42. Meyer DE: On the representation and retrieval of stored semantic information. Cognitive Psychol 1:242–300, 1970
43. Miller GA: Some psychological studies of grammar. Am Psychol 17:748–762, 1962
44. Miller GA: English verbs of motion: a case study in semantics and lexical memory. *In* Coding Processes in Human Memory. Edited by AW Melton, E Martin. Washington, DC, Winston/Wiley, 1972, pp 335–372
45. Oldfield RC: Individual vocabulary and semantic currency. Br J Social Clin Psychol 2:122–130, 1963
46. Osgood CE, Suci GJ, Tannenbaum PH: The Measurement of Meaning. Urbana, University of Illinois Press, 1957
47. Paivio A: Imagery and Verbal Processes. New York, Holt, Rinehart & Winston, 1971
48. Rips LJ, Shoben EJ, Smith EE: Semantic distance and the verification of semantic relations. J Verbal Learning Verbal Behav 12:1–20, 1973
49. Romney AK, D'Andrade RG: Cognitive aspects of English kin terms. Am Anthropol 66:146–170, 1964
50. Rubenstein H, Lewis SS, Rubenstein MA: Evidence for phonemic recoding in visual word recognition. J Verbal Learning Verbal Behav 10:645–657, 1971
51. Savin HB: What the child knows about speech when he starts to learn to read. *In* Language by Ear and by Eye. Edited by JF Kavanagh, IG Mattingly. Cambridge, Massachusetts, MIT Press, 1972, pp 319–326
52. Savin HB, Bever TG: The nonperceptual reality of the phoneme. J Verbal Learning Verbal Behav 9:295–302, 1970
53. Smith F: Understanding Reading. New York, Holt, Rinehart & Winston, 1971
54. Smith F: Review of Language by Ear and by Eye (Edited by JF Kavanagh, IG Mattingly). Language 50:762–765, 1974
55. Tulving E, Gold C: Stimulus information and contextual information as determinants of tachistoscopic recognition of words. J Exp Psychol 66:319–327, 1963

NEUROANATOMY UNDERLYING
THE LANGUAGE FUNCTION

Robert J. Joynt

The title, "Neuroanatomy Underlying Language Function," immediately raises several difficulties. By anatomy we imply structure, and this supposes that we know the arrangement or localization of that structure. It will become obvious that localization of function, and especially of the language function, remains one of the ineluctable quests of brain scientists. Language is also in the title, and certainly there is no universal agreement on this. I will not get into the question of whether or not animals have language. Certainly primates have been taught the use of symbols, and how to arrange and how to interpret these symbols when placed in certain sequences. It may have implications for studying the genesis of language, but we need not obscure further a problem which is already obscure.

First, I will trace the historical development of thought in this area. Not only does it give us a perspective regarding brain and language interaction, but it also makes the point which Korzybski made about general semantics in that what is new is not necessarily good, and what is good is not necessarily new. Second, I will look at modern views on localization and lateralization of language. Last, I will attempt to reconcile some of the diverse views.

Historical Development

Language is unique to man. That is likely why it was the first function to arouse serious thought as to its placement within the brain. This may have been a bad choice for the progress of knowledge concerning the brain. Clarke and O'Malley in their excellent history of the knowledge of the nervous system, *The Human Brain and Spinal Cord,* state:

It was perhaps unfortunate that the early clinical investigators chose the complex function of speech as an illustration of cortical localization.

39

This topic is still a much disputed subject, and precise localization of speech 'centers' initiated by Broca retarded rather than facilitated its elucidation. Nevertheless, the interest that was brought to bear on the whole question of functional localization in the cortex was of the greatest significance.[10]

Prior to the nineteenth century the brain was looked upon as a kind of an amorphous gruel without specific functions assigned in different brain areas. Indeed, the ventricular theory of brain function was just dying. This theory placed higher functions such as perception, reasoning, and memory into the different brain ventricles. There was very little experimentation designed to uncover the secrets of the brain. There were exceptions to this holistic view; one was the prescient idea put forth by Prochaska in 1784. He was then professor of physiology at Vienna. He wrote, ". . . and so it is by no means improbable that each part of the intellect has its organ in the brain, with one for perceptions, another for judgment, and perhaps still others for will, imagination, and memory, all of it then working together admirably and arousing one another to action."[38]

The modern era of localization really began with the work of Franz Josef Gall, a Viennese physician and anatomist. He is unfortunately remembered as the founder of phrenology or cranioscopy as he called it. He was an excellent anatomist and his anatomical text on the nervous system was an early classic in the field. He developed his ideas from an early observation that his colleagues with good verbal memories had prominent eyes. He reasoned that the cranial prominence was due to great development of the subjacent frontal lobes of the brain. He stated:

> I regard as the organ of memory of words that part of the brain which rests on the posterior half of the orbital roof (central portion of the posterior third of the orbital surface of the cerebral hemisphere, immediately anterior to the tip of the temporal lobe).[18]

He then equated the presence of various faculties with certain cranial prominences and reasoned that this quality was resident in that underlying area of the brain. He identified 27 qualities and placed these in different areas. His mechanistic views of brain function collided with the academic and clerical community of Vienna. He left and settled in Paris where his ideas were popular, but still raised opposition in high circles. It is said that even Napoleon resisted his advancement in the medical and scientific community. His pupil, Spurzheim, traveled widely and popularized phrenology. He died in 1832 on a lecture tour to the United States.[27] However, phrenology died a hard death, for the British Phrenological Society was just disbanded in 1967, and it is still possible to obtain phrenological consultation along the board-walk at Atlantic City. However absurd we may consider these views now, Gall was the first one who popularized the notion that the brain could be parcellated with certain functions residing in certain areas. That it did not gain more popularity at that time was probably due to the immense influence of Flourens, a French physiologist, who still put forth the idea that intellec-tual powers were diffusely distributed throughout the brain.

There were some advocates of Gall's theories and one of these was Bouillaud, a prominent French physician. He noted the association of frontal lobe lesions with a disturbance in language in 1825 and stated, "The legis-lating organs of speech reside in the anterior lobes of the brain."[4] His ideas were espoused by his dutiful son-in-law, Auburtin. Auburtin had a patient with a cranial defect in the frontal area. He performed one of the first physiological experiments in this field. He observed when he pushed on the frontal lobes with a spatula that the man's speech was interrupted. This he also placed in evidence for the frontal lobe localization of speech function.

It was Auburtin who suggested this brain-speech relationship to Paul Pierre Broca. Broca was a French surgeon with an interest in anthropology. During a meeting of the Society of Anthropology in 1861 Broca was discus-sing brain size and its correlation with intelligence, Auburtin suggested it was not brain size, but the size of certain areas which corresponded to certain faculties. Broca had a chance to test this out in his clinical practice with a brain-damaged patient who was able to express only a single syllable. This was the nonsense syllable, "tan," which the patient repeated over and over again.[25] The patient soon died of a cellulitis and at autopsy, there was found a lesion in the frontal lobe as predicted by Auburtin. Broca presented his findings. He continued to collect cases, and, by 1863, he reported on eight.[7] At that time he stated, ". . . and, a most remarkable thing, in all of the patients the lesion existed on the left side. I do not dare to draw a conclusion and I await new facts." Two years later, Broca was sure enough of his findings to put out his dictum, "We speak with the left hemisphere."[8] This pro-nouncement led to great controversy, both of priority and of validity.

The question of the priority of Broca's findings has come up again and again. Dax, a French physician, noted that his father, Marc, had made this observation in 1836, and stated it publicly in a medical congress.[28] Research has revealed, however, that Dax probably did not present this finding at a medical congress but had written a small paper on it and distributed it to some of his colleagues. Thus, it was somewhat in the form of a sealed communication. If we follow the Oslerian admonition that the man gets credit who brings it to the attention of the public, we must give full credit to Broca. The arguments concerning the validity of Broca's discovery came from many areas. Even theologians got into the discussion as it seemed to be a continuation of the views of Gall.[26] Language, they reasoned, reflected the higher mental processes which were guided by non-corporeal soul, and the discrete localization of language to certain areas of the brain seemed to be too materialistic. Biologists were greatly disturbed as Broca's thesis was a direct refutation of the old biological law, "functional unity with organic duality." That is, two symmetrical organs should have the same function. Certainly nothing seemed to be more symmetrical than the two cerebral hemispheres.

Broca's discovery set off an intense search for various "centers" within the brain. The last half of the nineteenth century was flooded with ever more elaborate diagrams explaining brain function. Various disruptions of these patterns were proposed to explain different language disturbances. Along with this was the early work on stimulation of the cortex by Fritsch and Hitzig in Germany, and Ferrier in Britain which confirmed motor areas and extended the concept of "centers." Anatomists such as Meynert and Flechsig were involved in describing myelination patterns, association tracts, and various cellular patterns. These anatomical and physiological observations buttressed theories supplied by the clinicians.

There were reactions to this "diagram making," as Henry Head derisively called it. Hughlings Jackson, for instance, while accepting localization, viewed language not as discrete units but as a hierarchical organization whose dissolution followed certain predictable patterns.[24] Freud, in his 1891 monograph on aphasia, also warned against strict localization.[17]

Even now, the issue is far from settled. All accept the view that language is lateralized; the degree of this lateralization and the organization within the hemispheres continues to be an issue argued as much today as it was 100 years ago in the time of Broca. It is pertinent to review the concept of localization as viewed by the holistic and "localization" proponents.

Localization and the Holistic View

Lenneberg puts the question right at the anatomists: "It would be satisfying if we could explain the mechanism of human language by certain unique structures of the human brain. Unfortunately, this is not possible. The difficulty is largely because of a general discrepancy between our knowledge of neuroanatomy and our knowledge of behavior."[30] Scientists would be less than truthful if they did not admit to this discrepancy.

The major problem is that we know a great deal more about what disturbs language than about what constitutes the neural basis for language. To explain function from observing dysfunction is always dangerous. This admonition was first put forward by Hughlings Jackson, who pointed out the error of localizing a cerebral function on the basis that a focal lesion was followed by the loss of that function.[24] Jackson, throughout his clinical career, became more and more skeptical of localizing function within the brain. He emphasized the effects of "momentum" of a lesion which further complicated the problem of localization. By this he meant that a rapidly developing lesion was often more disruptive than one which developed more slowly but occupied the same anatomical area. Freud was influenced by Jackson, and was also against strict localization. He envisioned the speech area as a broad zone surrounding the Sylvian fissure on the left side. He states:

> The apparatus of speech therefore presented itself to us as a continuous cortical area in the left hemisphere extending between the terminations of the acoustic and optic nerves and the origins of the motor tracts for the muscles serving articulation and arm movement. The necessarily ill-defined parts of the speech region which border on these receptive and motor cortical fields, have acquired the significance of speech centres from the point of view of morbid anatomy but not in respect of normal function; their lesions cut off one of the elements of speech association from its connexions with the others.[17]

Goldstein, in an even more holistic view of brain function, defined localization as follows:

> A particular locality in the brain matter is characterized by the influence which the structure of this locality exercises on the total process. . . . To different localizations of lesions correspond different symptom complexes because the different performance fields are affected in a different way by the process of dedifferentiation.[22]

The strict localizationists denigrate the contributions of the holistic school of brain function. It must be pointed out in fairness that in spite of the holists' unwillingness to tie an area of the brain closely to a language function, they recognize that certain disturbances in language function could be predicted on the basis of the location of lesions.

Localization and the Localizationists

Strict views on localization were triggered off by the demonstration of a speech area in the left posterior frontal region by Broca. As noted earlier, there was a spate of publications identifying various centers of the brain with many interconnections which were invoked to explain brain function. Disturbances in these centers or connections were invoked to explain different language problems. For a time it was believed that most examples of aphasia were due to lesions in Broca's area. However, Wernicke, in 1874, described a different type of aphasia,[42] and, although his anatomical confirmations were scanty, it was recognized that this type of aphasia was associated with lesions in the superior temporal area. Wernicke also put forth a notion that the posterior and anterior areas constituted two separate centers for language but suggested that there was a connection between the two running through the area of the insula. He conjectured that certain lesions could disconnect these two areas and account for some of the varieties of aphasia. It is likely that the connection is not in the insula but by the way of the arcuate fasciculus. This is a white matter band which streams out of the temporal lobe beneath the parietal region and through the suprasylvian opercular areas to the frontal speech area (Figure 1). Wernicke termed this disconnection as a conduction aphasia. One of the striking clinical characteristics of this type of aphasia is the inability to repeat verbal patterns, presumably because of severing the immediate input in the sensory areas from the motor speech area.

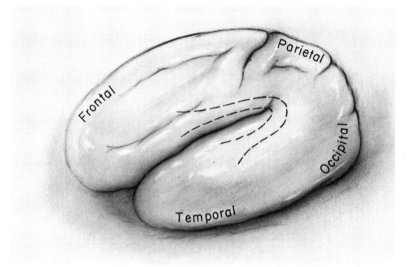

Figure 1. Lateral view of a left hemisphere, demonstrating the relationship of the arcuate fasciculus to the temporal, parietal, and frontal lobes.

Recently, there has been a resurgence of interest in looking at language disturbances and other behavioral disturbances from a point of view of disconnection of various areas in the brain.[20] This connectionistic view of brain function depends upon several anatomical facts. Flechsig[16] in 1901 pointed out that primary sensory areas had long subcortical connections, but these primary sensory areas had only short intracortical connections to adjacent parasensory zones. Also, these parasensory zones had long intracortical connections with other zones. These parasensory zones are the association cortex. They are part of what is called the "uncommitted cortex," so named by Penfield.[36] They are not concerned with the primary sensory and motor functions of the cortex. It is in man that these association or uncommitted areas are most highly developed. It is a view of the connectionists that learning, including language, takes place because these long association pathways are capable of intermodal connections. Thus, the human brain, because of its anatomy, is prepared for the acquisition of language. During the usual course of language learning, intermodal connections (i.e., auditory-speech) are accomplished. It is a view of those espousing this idea that various language disturbances can be predicted from the interruption of these connections. For example, it has already been pointed out that interruption of the posterior from the anterior speech areas results in a characteristic type of language disturbance, conduction aphasia. Other disconnection syndromes have been described. These connections may be of three basic types: intrahemispheric, interhemispheric, or a combination of both. Dejerine[14] in 1892 described alexia without agraphia. This is one of the prime examples of a disconnection syndrome. There was a lesion involving the left occipital cortex producing a right homonymous hemianopsia, thus only the left visual field was intact. However, the visual impression could not cross to the other side for interpretation because of an infarction in the posterior corpus callosum. Other disconnection syndromes were described by Liepmann who predicted the correct lesion for auditory word deafness in 1898,[31] and for "sympathetic dyspraxia" of the left hand in cases of right hemiplegia in 1907.[32] The lesion in this latter instance was in the area disconnecting the praxis area in the left hemisphere from that controlling motor movements in the right hemisphere. Various types of interhemispheric deficits have now been described in studies of the split-brain man. While early studies of Akelaitis[1,2] failed to confirm any behavioral change of consequence following callosal section, tests involving interhemispheric transmission of information do demonstrate a defect. Indeed, when an original patient of Akelaitis was tested 30 years later, she did demonstrate problems with interhemispheric transfer of information.[23]

There is widening evidence that various deficits can be explained in this simplistic way. However, there are detractors to this scheme of brain function. For instance, Bender and Feldman[3] have pointed out that visual agnosia is not a disconnection syndrome as claimed by Geschwind.[20] They find that their patients with this disorder have a combination of total mental impairment and impairment in visual perception to varying degrees.

Anatomical-Clinical Correlates of Language

While proponents of a more holistic or of a more strict localization view continue to argue regarding theory, clinicians have been involved in anatomic-clinical correlations. But here there are also problems difficult to resolve. Much of the material which has been used for anatomic-clinical correlations is a result of vascular accidents. Unfortunately for the anatomist, it is rare that patients do not have rather widespread vascular disease prior to the time that they succumb to their fatal infarct or hemorrhage. Examination of these brains often shows multiple areas of involvement which complicates the interpretation of the anatomic findings. Likewise, patients with neoplasms often have marked distortion of brain structures so that assigning the location of the lesion to only that of the neoplastic involvement ignores many of the associated structural changes. Many of the studies of localization have been on material collected during wartime by the unfortunate occurrence of missile wounds. While this material does not have some of the complications of vascular and neoplastic material, often the localization is made on the basis of roentgenographic findings which neglect the damage occasioned by passage of the missile through the brain and also the consequent pressure changes at the time of entry. Localization by cortical stimulation and after cortical excision provide a different type of material. Here the localization can be rather strictly controlled so that estimates of the area of brain involvement are more accurate. But almost all of this material is provided by surgery on patients with epilepsy who are having epileptogenic areas removed. In many instances, these patients may have suffered early brain damage so there may not have been normal brain development. Comparison of these findings to normal behavior may be misleading. Newer types of diagnostic procedures such as computer-assisted tomography can define discrete areas of brain involvement during life and will add to our knowledge of localization.

While it is easy to carp at the problems put before us by nature, it is necessary to proceed in spite of these, and to attempt correlations which will give us a greater insight into brain function. Indeed, most of the studies on various types of material are in general agreement on those areas producing aphasia. Two of the best studies on missile wounds are those of Conrad[11] and Russell and Espir.[40] These studies show that lesions around the Sylvian area in the left hemisphere do produce aphasia, and lesions outside these areas are generally without effect on language function. Corroborating this is the work of Penfield and Roberts.[37] They demonstrated that cortical stimulation in the areas bordering the Sylvian fissure anteriorly and posteriorly would cause speech arrest. What is more significant is that they were able to correlate the effect of cortical excisions on patients with either left or right hemispheric dominance for speech. The dominance was established by intracarotid amytal injection. Cortical excisions could be carried out in extensive areas of the dominant left hemisphere without disturbing speech if these zones around the Sylvian fissure were left intact. Also, patients with extensive damage to the left hemispheric speech areas had developed right hemispheric dominance for language.

Therefore, irrespective of a broad or restricted view of language localization, most clinical studies do agree on a relatively restricted zone around the Sylvian fissure which, when destroyed, leads to language dysfunction. Again, we must recall Jackson's warning against ascribing a functional capacity to an area if destruction of that area disrupts function.

Thalamic Contributions to Language

Discussion about the theoretical and anatomical substrate for language function has been confined to the cortex and the immediate subcortical structures, but there is evidence that deeper structures may play a role. Specifically, the thalamus has been suggested for a number of reasons to be an integral part of the speech mechanism. There have been numerous clinical examples of thalamic hemorrhages and tumors causing aphasia. Thalamotomy has occasionally resulted in aphasia. More recently, stimulation of thalamic nuclei has elicited anomia and speech perseveration.[35] There also appears to be lateralization of the effects of stimulation to the left thalamus in the righthanded patient. Within the thalamus, it was in the ventral lateral region from which these alterations in language were obtained. This area included the pulvinar and fibers related to the centrum medianum and the dorsal medial nuclei. As pointed out by Ojemann and Ward,[35] this is very similar to the model for the thalamic role in speech proposed by Penfield and Roberts.[37] The latter authors suggested that the centrum medianum and the dorsal medial nuclei connections were related to the frontal cortical speech area and the pulvinar to the parietal temporal speech area. Penfield and Roberts viewed the thalamic areas as providing an interrelationship between the frontal and posterior speech areas. Ojemann and Van Buren[34] had noted earlier that stimulation in this area would inhibit respiration and produce prolonged expiration. The left thalamus had a significantly lower threshold than the right in producing this response. It was suggested that this might represent the respiratory substratum necessary for proper vocalization.

Cerebral Dominance

Broca's views on lateralization of speech function soon gained ascendancy, as already discussed. Jackson,[24] who was not predisposed to exact localization, stated, "The two hemispheres cannot be duplicates if damage to one alone can make a man speechless." Jackson proposed that the left hemisphere was the "leading hemisphere" in speech, although he did believe that more automatic speech might be represented in both hemispheres. The concept of dominance was extended by Liepmann and Maas,[32] who showed that this was not confined to language function only but included lateralization of manual dexterity. Jackson also reported some instances of left hemiplegia with aphasia, but pointed out that not every case was aphasic. Bramwell[5] in 1899 reported a case of "crossed aphasia" in a lefthanded man who had disease of the left hemisphere. Chesher[9] suggested that the relationship between speech and handedness was not a simple one. He described ambidexterous patients with the lesion causing aphasia on the left side. Numerous studies have since confirmed that in righthanders, the left hemisphere is almost always dominant. The few exceptions are when there is early brain damage to the left hemisphere and when there is a history of lefthandedness in the family.

The problem with lefthanders is much more complicated. It is difficult to arrive at a definite figure of laterality, as many of the studies have been done with different types of case material or using different techniques. However, it appears that well over half of the lefthanded patients still have left hemisphere dominance for speech. Not all of the remainder have right hemisphere dominance because there is occasional bilateral dominance, as demonstrated by the intracarotid injection of amytal.[6] There are two extensive series reported by Conrad[26] and Penfield and Roberts.[37] Conrad reported on 203 aphasics, 17 of whom were lefthanded; 10 had left hemisphere and 7 had right hemisphere lesions. In the operative series of Penfield and Roberts, aphasia was reported in only two of 22 lefthanded patients after right hemisphere operation as compared with 19 of 67 lefthanders following operations on the left hemisphere. There have also been observations that the aphasia occurring in lefthanders is often mild and transitory.[45] It is also noted that the character of the aphasia may vary so that marked defects in oral comprehension are seldom observed in lefthanded patients with aphasia. Thus, it appears that not only is the absolute degree of dominance less in lefthanded patients, but also the character of the aphasia might be different.

There are frequent observations that damage to the so-called dominant hemisphere in children does not preclude normal language development. For example, hemispherectomy in patients with infantile hemiparesis does not produce lasting aphasia, even if the left hemisphere is removed.

Role of the Right Hemisphere in Speech

The right hemisphere is the dominant one in some lefthanders, and it is often responsible for speech in patients with early damage to the left hemisphere. What part, if any, does the right hemisphere play in speech in a normal situation?

One hundred years ago, Jackson[24] suggested that automatic and emotional speech might be a function of the right hemisphere. This was based on his clinical observation that emotional speech often remained after more abstract speech had disappeared in cases of right hemiplegia. Critchley,[12] on the basis of clinical observations, noted that some of his patients with right hemisphere lesions had word finding disturbances, difficulty in learning verbal material, and some loss of literary creativity. Eisenson, testing a series of patients with right hemisphere lesions, noted they did more poorly than normals on tests of vocabulary recognition and sentence construction. He put forth the idea that the right hemisphere may

> be involved with super or extraordinary language function, particularly as this function calls upon the need of the individual to deal with relatively abstractly established language formulations, to which he must adjust. The modifications are not such as to be picked up in casual conversation, in which precision of language is not expected.[15]

Smith[41] reported a patient in whom the left cerebral hemisphere was almost totally removed for treatment of a glioblastoma. The patient was severely aphasic. However, there was some recovery of speech. The patient could use simple sentences and sing familiar songs. More notably, he was able to identify many objects when given the name. Thus, he did have some language function in the right hemisphere, mostly of the receptive type. In experiments on split-brain man in which the stimulus and response are limited to the right hemisphere, it was found that some fairly complex words and phrases are understood by the right hemisphere.[19] In addition, simple spelling tasks can be performed by the right hemisphere. So it appears that there are some language mechanisms operative in that hemisphere, mainly in the receptive field. There are two pertinent studies recently reported. Kinsbourne[29] performed intracarotid injections of amytal in three patients with right hemiplegia and dysphasic speech. Injection of sodium amytal into the left carotid artery did not alter the dysphasic speech. However, injection of amytal into the right carotid artery in two patients rendered the patients mute. A more extensive study was done by Czopf,[13] who confirmed this finding on a larger series. Therefore, the vestiges of speech remaining in aphasic patients appear to be mediated by the right hemisphere as predicted by Jackson.

Interrelationship of the Two Hemispheres

It is obvious that the two hemispheres are not symmetrical in function. Also, it has been sufficiently demonstrated in recent years that there are functions peculiar to the right hemisphere, particularly in the area of visual and spatial capacities. It has also become obvious that there are peculiar interrelationships between the two hemispheres so that certain tasks may require the participation of both, but often not to the same degree. Even in the language areas as has already been pointed out, the right hemisphere does have some speech function. This asymmetric distribution of brain function appears to be unique to man. However, there is the unusual report by Nottebohm[33] in 1970 who noted that in songbirds, destruction of the nerve to the organ of song on the left was much more effective in disrupting song patterns than destruction of the similar nerve on the right.

There are two fundamental questions which relate to the asymmetry of language function that seem evident: first, how does this asymmetry arise and do the commissures play any part in this, and secondly, when does this asymmetry arise? While disrupting the major commissures between the two hemispheres has a marked, although variable, effect on behavior in many spheres, there is little evidence that it disturbs normal language. Formal language testing without resorting to specific tests for interhemispheric cooperation shows no defects. In one of our split-brain patients, detailed analysis of linguistic patterns revealed no obvious disturbance.[39] That much useful information for normal communication is transferred is evident as, for example, in the patient previously alluded to, with alexia without agraphia, described by Dejerine.[14] Although their disruption does not alter normal speech, there are many possible roles that commissures may play in language development. Two possibilities seem most likely. First, as language develops with various intermodal connections, the commissures act as conduits gradually transferring information to speech centers in the dominant hemisphere. This assumes equipotentiality of the two hemispheres prior to the acquisition of language. That it is the left hemisphere which becomes dominant may have something to do with handedness as it would be advantageous to integrate communication with motor patterns of the more facile hand. The second possibility is that one hemisphere is predestined to language development, and that the commissures are used for inhibition of a similar function in the opposite hemisphere.

The latter possibility has some anatomical and clinical evidence in its favor. Overt anatomical differences between the two hemispheres have been a subject of discussion since the time of Broca. Recently, Geschwind and Levitsky[21] noted in 100 brains that the planum temporale was larger on the left side in 65 percent and on the right side in only 11 percent. This is the area posterior to Heschl's gyrus on the posterior surface of the temporal lobe in the region which, when it is destroyed, disrupts language reception. Perhaps of more significance is the finding by Witelson and Pallie,[43] who observed that this area on the left side was statistically significantly larger in 14 neonatal brains. This strongly suggests a biological preprogramming of the language function. There is also clinical evidence suggesting hemispheric specialization at birth. Woods and Teuber[44] studied children with congenital or early postnatal hemipareses. A group with left hemisphere involvement had language retardation and marked defects on visual spatial tasks when tested years later. Those with right hemispheric lesions had massive losses on visual constructive tests, but only slight difficulty with linguistic development. Therefore, it appears that the functions of the right hemisphere may be more vulnerable and that speech function may be more resilient or is established earlier. However, this pre-eminence of language is at the expense of functions not related to language. It appears that these aptitudes may compete in the developing brain for space, and that there is a definite crowding when one hemisphere is called upon to do more than it would normally do.

Conclusions

It is difficult to amalgamate these diverse views on the anatomy of language. Neurologists, philosophers, linguists, and educators have blunted their lances on this problem for centuries. However, there are some points which emerge which do suggest an acceptable theory of brain-language relations.

It does seem that there is biologic preprogramming for language and that hemispheric specialization is part of our heritage. It also appears that with damage to the brain, there are adaptive mechanisms but these are not perfect. It is likely that the brain puts language high on its priority list, but as it assigns a favored spot to language, other functions may suffer in the process. It also seems obvious that many of our problems with localization stem from the fact that we are not working with the same brain in all cases. For example, it is clear that some left-handers do have different language organizations. It is also clear that each of us has a different genetic makeup, so we are all unique. Therefore, it is likely that we "normal people" are not all supplying the same map to the clinician for his localization exercise.

The great unanswered question is: why does man have this asymmetry of function? On hasty reflection, it may even seem to be a detriment as damage to the left hemisphere, for instance, produces irrevocable language disabilities and we have little reserve in the other hemisphere. However, further examination of this asymmetrical function has great appeal to one with an economical turn of mind. It is easy to see the sense of the system when one sees what happens in his own work. We are deluged with great amounts of information, and more often than not it is in duplicate or triplicate. Our file cabinets are stuffed not only with useless information, but with copies of useless information. Now the great purpose behind our cerebral organization makes sense. We receive information, classify it, quickly sort it either to the one or the other side so that we do not have two warehouses full of the same product. This theory might be called the Sherlock Holmes concept of cerebral organization. For it was the great master himself who introduced it many years ago in his first adventure, "A Study in Scarlet." The prophetic insight of this great detective is revealed in the following pertinent passage:

> (Dr. Watson) I found incidentally that he was ignorant of the Copernican theory and of the composition of the solar system. That any civilized human being in this nineteenth century should not be aware that the earth travelled round the sun appeared to me to be such an extraordinary fact that I could hardly realize it.
>
> "You appear to be astonished," he said, smiling at my expression of surprise. "Now that I do know it I shall do my best to forget it."
>
> "To forget it!"
>
> "You see," he explained, "I consider that a man's brain originally is like a little empty attic, and you have to stock it with such furniture as

you choose. A fool takes in all the lumber of every sort that he comes across, so that the knowledge which might be useful to him gets crowded out, or at best is jumbled up with a lot of other things, so that he has a difficulty in laying his hands upon it. Now the skillful workman is very careful indeed as to what he takes into his brain-attic. He will have nothing but the tools which may help him in doing his work, but of these he has a large assortment, and all in the most perfect order. It is a mistake to think that little room has elastic walls and can distend to any extent. Depend on it there comes a time when for every addition of knowledge you forget something that you knew before. It is of the highest importance, therefore, not to have useless facts elbowing out the useful ones."

"But the Solar System!" I protested.

"What the deuce is it to me?" he interrupted impatiently: "You say that we go round the sun. If we went round the moon it would not make a pennyworth of difference to me or to my work."

References

1. Akelaitis AJ: Studies on the corpus callosum. VII. Study of language functions (tactile and visual lexia and graphia) unilaterally following section of the corpus callosum. J Neuropathol Exp Neurol 2:226–262, 1943
2. Akelaitis AJ: A study of gnosis, praxis, and language following section of the corpus callosum and anterior commissure. J Neurosurg 1:94–102, 1944
3. Bender M, Feldman M: The so-called "visual agnosias." Brain 95:173–186, 1972
4. Bouillaud JB: Recherches cliniques propres à démontrer que la perte de la parole correspond à la lésion des lobules antérieurs du cerveau, et à confirmer l'opinion de M. Gall, sur le siège de l'organe du langage articulé. Arch Gen Med 8:25–45, 1825
5. Bramwell B: On "crossed aphasia" and the factors which go to determine whether the "leading" or "driving" speech centers shall be located in the left or in the right hemisphere of the brain. Lancet 1:1473–1490, 1899
6. Branch C, Milner B, Rasmussen T: Intracarotid amytal for the lateralization of cerebral speech dominance. J Neurosurg 21:399–405, 1964
7. Broca P: Localisation des fonctions cérébrales: Siège du langage articulé. Bull Soc Anthropol (Paris) 4:200–203, 1863
8. Broca P: Sur la siège du faculté de langage articulé. Bull Soc Anthropol (Paris) 6:377–393, 1865
9. Chesher ED: Some observations concerning the relation of handedness to the language mechanism. Bull Neurol Inst NY 4:556–562, 1936
10. Clarke E, O'Malley CD: The Human Brain and Spinal Cord. Berkeley, University of California Press, 1968
11. Conrad K: New problems of aphasia. Brain 77:491–509, 1954
12. Critchley M: Speech and speech-loss in relation to duality of the brain. In Interhemispheric Relations and Cerebral Dominance. Edited by V Mountcastle. Baltimore, Johns Hopkins University Press, 1962
13. Czopf J: Über die Rolle der nicht dominanten Hemisphäre in der Restitution der Sprache der Aphasischen. Arch Psychiatr Nervenkr 216:162–171, 1972
14. Dejerine J: Contribution à l'étude d'anatomie-pathologique et clinque des différentes variétiés de cécité verbale. Mem Soc Biol (Paris) 44:61–90, 1892

15. Eisenson J: Language and intellectual modification associated with right cerebral damage. Lang Speech 5:49–53, 1962
16. Flechsig P: Anatomie des menschlichen Gehirns und Rückenmarks auf myelogenetischer Grundlage. Leipzig, Thieme, 1920
17. Freud S: Zur Auffassung der Aphasien, eine Kritische Studie. Leipzig, Deuticke, 1891. Translated by E Stengel, London, Imago, 1953
18. Gall FJ, Spurzheim JC: Anatomie et Physiologie du Système Neoveux en Général, et du Cerveau en Particuler. Paris, Schoell, 1810–1819
19. Gazzaniga MS: The Bisected Brain. New York, Appleton-Century-Crofts, 1970
20. Geschwind N: Disconnexion syndromes in animals and man. Brain 88:237–294; 585–644, 1965
21. Geschwind N, Levitsky W: Human brain: left-right asymmetries in temporal speech region. Science 161:186–187, 1968
22. Goldstein K: Language and Language Disturbances. New York, Grune & Stratton, 1948
23. Goldstein M, Joynt RJ: Long-term follow-up of a callosal-sectioned patient. Arch Neurol 20:96–102, 1969
24. Jackson JH: Selected Writings. New York, Basic Books, 1958
25. Joynt RJ: Centenary of patient Tan; his contribution to the history of aphasia. Arch Intern Med 108:197–200, 1961
26. Joynt RJ: Paul Pierre Broca: his contribution to the knowledge of aphasia. Cortex 1:206–213, 1964
27. Joynt RJ: Phrenology in New York State. NY Med J 73:2382–2384, 1973
28. Joynt RJ, Benton AL: The memoir of Marc Dax on aphasia. Neurology (Minneap) 14:851–854, 1964
29. Kinsbourne M: The minor cerebral hemisphere as a source of aphasic speech. Arch Neurol 25:302–306, 1971
30. Lenneberg EH: Basic correlates of language. In The Neurosciences. New York, Rockefeller University Press, 1970
31. Liepmann H: Ein Fall von reiner Sprachtaubheit. Breslau, Schletter, 1898
32. Liepmann H, Maas O: Fall von linksseitiger Agraphie und Apraxie bei rechtsseitiger Lähmung. J Psychol Neurol 10:214–227, 1907
33. Nottebohm F: Ontogeny of bird song: different strategies in vocal development are reflected in learning stages, critical periods, and neural lateralization. Science 167:950–956, 1970
34. Ojemann G, Van Buren JM: Respiratory, heart rate, and GSR responses from human diencephalon. Arch Neurol 16:74–88, 1967
35. Ojemann G, Ward A: Speech representation in ventro-lateral thalamus. Brain 94:669–680, 1971
36. Penfield W: Engrams in the human brain. Proc R Soc Med 61:831–840, 1968
37. Penfield W, Roberts L: Speech and Brain Mechanisms. Princeton, New Jersey, Princeton University Press, 1959
38. Prochaska J: Adnotationum Academicarum. Prague, 1784. Translation. In The Human Brain and Spinal Cord, Berkeley, University of California Press, 1968
39. Reiff D, Joynt RJ: Linguistic analysis of speech in callosal-sectioned patient. Read at the Academy of Aphasia, 1969
40. Russell R, Espir MLE: Traumatic aphasia. Oxford, Oxford University Press, 1961
41. Smith A: Speech and other functions after left (dominant) hemispherectomy. J Neurol Neurosurg Psychiatry 29:467–471, 1966
42. Wernicke C: Der Aphasische Symptomenkomplex. Breslau, Cohn and Weigert, 1874
43. Witelson SF, Pallie W: Left hemisphere specialization for language in the newborn. Brain 96:641–646, 1973
44. Woods BT, Teuber HL: Early onset of complementary specialization of cerebral hemispheres in man. Trans Am Neurol Assoc 98:113–117, 1973
45. Zangwill OL: The current status of cerebral dominance. Res Publ Assoc Res Nerv Ment Dis 42:103–113, 1964

MEMORY AND COGNITIVE SKILLS
IN READING ACQUISITION

Robert C. Calfee

Memory processes and their development have been a topic of continuing interest to educational psychologists such as myself. The area has seen some outstanding research in the past decade. Research on how children learn to read is more scarce, a fact which needs to be emphasized in public forums. Finally, trying to piece together the abstractions of basic research with the puzzlements of applied needs is an opportunity and a challenge.

As I have worked on this paper, several matters have proven perplexing and troublesome. One is, whom am I addressing? How many are practitioners (teachers, reading specialists, and so on), how many researchers or evaluators, how many administrators or program developers? Then there is the question of how to relate what is known about this topic to the particular concerns of those who work with dyslexics. Another problem is the generally piecemeal character of behavioral research, and the lack of comprehensive, longitudinal studies bearing on how a child learns to read, and what happens in his head during that experience. I have dealt with this as best I know how by proposing criteria for such research.

The Interrelatedness of Memory and Other Cognitive Processes

The last problem confronting me has been how best to sort out memory from other ongoing information-processing activities in the mind. But if recent work in cognitive psychology has pointed in any single direction, it is toward the interrelatedness of mental processes.

DiVesta described the assumptions of contemporary cognitive psychol-

Portions of the research described herein were supported by a grant from the Carnegie Corporation.

ogy with exceptional clarity when he spoke of ". . . the *prepared mind,* or the knowledge the person brings to the learning situation; the *attending mind,* or how the person responds to informational inputs; and the *processing mind,* or the way the knowledge structure interacts with learning strategies to influence subsequent behavior."[18] The prepared mind, the attending mind, the processing mind—all are a single entity, and memory processes thread their way through each of these aspects of mind.

Memory and "Visual Perceptual Skills"

My point can be illustrated fairly easily. I want you to take a reading readiness test much like the kind that many beginning readers have to deal with under the label, "visual perceptual skills." Your performance on this test may well determine how serious an effort will be made to teach you to read. In Figure 1 is a list of four-letter words. Look at the top word (T); then scan and check each of the other words to see if it is the same as the original target word. Choice 4 was correct, as you can now see if you study the entire item rather carefully. Where is memory required in this test? In the storage of the target string while your eyes move from one test "word" to another. As I have pointed out elsewhere,[14] if the target word is coded as a purely abstract visual image, then by the time your eye has come to rest on the second test word in the series (i.e. after a delay of a quarter of a second or more), you are matching that word with a ragged image, in which detail and order of the symbols are faint at best. Of course, you could go back to the target and refresh your memory, but that implies that you have the time, and that you realize that this is a reasonable thing to do.

What is wrong with the second test word? Check it. All four symbols are there—not in quite the same order as the target word, to be sure, but does that matter? Of course it does, and you know that, because this is writing. But you might have forgotten the order while examining the previous word, or, if you happen to be five years old and don't know anything about written language so that "same" is ambiguous,[24] you might think that order was not important.

Coding and "Visual Perceptual Skills"

The important word is "forgotten." An uncodable visual image begins to fade from memory within less than a second, and even in this simple task, the way the information is processed and stored is a critical determinant of subsequent performance. To demonstrate this point, would you study in Figure 2, the correspondences between synthetic letters like those shown earlier and selected Roman letters?

Figure 1. Example of visual discrimination test for measuring reading readiness.

Now look at a new target word at the top in Figure 3, read it if you can and then mark the test words in the list that are the same.

The ability to recode these symbols into a pronounceable "chunk" for short-term storage over a few seconds greatly facilitates performance on this "visual perceptual" readiness task. The primary reason for this facilitation is that you can *remember* the target word while you are scanning the list of test words.

Definitions

Before proceeding further, let me define three key terms: *reading, learning to read,* and *memory.* You need not necessarily accept these definitions as your own, only allow this usage for the moment.

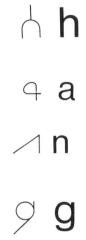

Figure 2. Correspondences between synthetic letters and Roman alphabet; an aid to performing on the visual discrimination test.

Reading

Following the lead of the National Institute of Education Task Force on Linguistic Communication[44] with a few extensions, I here define the major elements in reading. Each of these "definitions" of reading serves a useful purpose in some context, and each is included within the rubric of reading in this paper.

1. *Decoding*—The skill of translating an alphabetic code into some phonological rendering of the spoken language. The reader may not fully understand everything he has decoded.

2. *Comprehension*—The reader is able to extract from the printed page a reasonable idea of what the writer meant. There is no need for the reader to be able to pronounce the written material; the focus of this component is gaining an understanding. I can imagine a situation in which a few words are mixed with pictorial and diagrammatic information, so that a person with a minimal reading vocabulary is able to understand the gist of what is being communicated.[69,70] If he can show evidence of such understanding, then he can read in the sense of comprehending.

3. *Functional literacy*—This "definition" actually refers to a level of reading competence. If an individual can read well enough to carry out the tasks required by his work and daily life, then he is functionally literate. This may require various combinations of decoding and comprehension abilities. Research on this problem might focus on

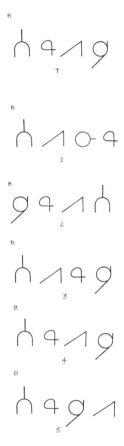

Figure 3. Second example of visual discrinimation test of reading readiness.

simplifying what is to be read as well as on improving the skills of the reader.

4. *Rapid reading*—At this end of the continuum is the individual who can read rapidly, can decide what he needs to read, and can focus attention, perhaps only on a summary or table of contents. For him reading is so well developed that it is natural and fluent. These are characteristics of rapid reading.

5. *"Creative" reading*—I am not sure that there is a need for a separate category here, but it may prove useful to distinguish between rapid reading and situations in which a reader is actively thinking and working through problems as he reads, without regard to speed.

These categories are more like an "in-basket" file than a model of reading, which may distress you. I think that such a categorical listing may serve better for our present purposes than any of the multitudinous "models" scattered throughout the literature. These categories seem to make sense as broad instructional goals, and that is our need here.

Learning to Read

I take it that the aim of reading instruction is competence in one or more of the areas mentioned earlier. But competence and the acquisition of competence are often two different matters. Driving an automobile provides a good analogy. A reasonably competent driver can make his way along a crowded freeway at 55 while carrying on a conversation with a passenger. But this does not mean that in order to train someone to be a competent driver, we should begin by putting him behind the wheel under such conditions. It is not likely that this training method will produce many successful drivers; even though anyone who makes it through is likely to be very good, a lot of people may be killed.

A Task Analysis of Learning to Decode. The acquisition of decoding skills is one of the primary goals of beginning reading instruction. It very likely poses a great challenge to many young children and constitutes one of the major sources of reading failure. This is a controversial point of view in some quarters, to be sure, and by no means a position with which all reading experts will agree.[25,57] Whatever the truth of this proposition, it will serve as a useful context for examining the role of memory in acquisition of a reading competency; the exercise may serve us as a model that could be applied to other aspects of learning to read.

The diagram in Figure 4 represents some of the processes that might be used by a young child to say a word to himself during the early stages of learning to decode.

Using this model as a basis:

1. He has to learn to attend to words and letters as critical sources of information; he must be able to match and identify letters; he may be asked to learn the names of letters.

2. He has to learn certain basic symbol/sound correspondences from the set that form the alphabetic foundation of English writing. This may entail learning of individual letter-sound correspondences by rote association—B → /b/, SH → /s/. It may entail learning "rules" like "final-e/long-vowel," or of patterns based on larger units like rhyming sequences. The child may be taught these correspondences as isolated units, through presentation of related patterns, or by exposure to random collections of words that appear to follow no discernible pattern. The child may or may not be able to verbalize the correspondences or rules he has learned.

Some children can "read" even though they have no knowledge of the English letter-sound correspondence system—for them, reading is a matter of hieroglyphics—but there is a direct and strong relation in the general population between reading achievement level and ability to apply knowledge of the letter-sound correspondence system to vowels or rare words.[67] I am saying nothing here about how best to teach this system, nor how best to describe it—only that the successful beginning reader behaves as if he were acquiring this knowledge.

3. He has to learn to integrate. He does this by visual-phonetic analysis and synthesis, so that his knowledge of letter-sound correspondences allows him to generate an integrated (though possibly tentative) pronunciation of a printed word. In many instances, the training that leads to acquisition of letter-sound correspondence incorporates training in analysis-synthesis, but these two sets of knowledge are separable. One does not necessarily include the other. One instructional approach in this area is exemplified by the Pittsburgh LRDC program[5] in which a student is taught explicit letter-sound correspondences by rote study and then is taught a "synthesis" or blending algorithm based on movement of the finger from left to right. The kinesthetic continuity of the finger movement appears to serve quite well to help the child in linking the individual sounds—/b/, /b-ă / → /bă /, /bă -t/ → /bă t/.

The Bloomfield-Barnhart[8] technique, in which the child always studies complete words—never isolated "sounds"—represents a different approach, in which it is more difficult to observe the processes of analysis and synthesis. Presumably, the child is reconstituting initial consonants and vowel-consonant segments, and pronouncing these as a unit, which seems relatively easy to do.[21]

4. In addition to these foundation skills, the student must acquire and apply a variety of integrating skills. The feedback or TOTE loop[45] in Figure 4 is an instance of such skills. It is assumed that the child has some kind of working vocabulary. For some children, vocabulary may be inadequate or inappropriate to meet the demands of the text being presented. In any event, the child must learn to use the initial decoding as a stepping stone for reaching a reasonable approximation to what pronunciation makes most sense in a given context. More broadly, control skills include learning to be sensitive to when one needs help, knowing where to find help, and adjusting one's tempo to the demands of a given text and situation.

The point of this too-brief task analysis of learning to decode is this— every one of these tasks requires the student to *select, translate, store, organize,* and *retrieve* information from the environment; every one of these tasks makes major demands on one or more *memory processes.*

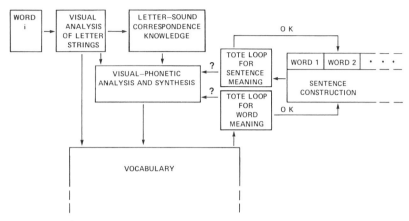

Figure 4. Information-processing model to describe stages in reading acquisition.

Memory

As used in this paper, memory comprises an interrelated set of psychological processes for encoding, storing and retrieving information. At one end, memory becomes indistinguishable from perception, at the other it merges with skilled performance. During the past decade or two, experimental psychologists have given much attention—theoretical and empirical—to the study of memory processes, as evidenced by an out-pouring of books on the topic.[1,46]

There are a few theoretical models of memory that spring from current research. A personal favorite distinguished by its elegance and simplicity was developed by Landauer[35] at Bell Laboratories. Here human memory is a circular chunk of graph paper, forming a collection of boxes—a lot of them. Hovering over this graph paper is a randomly moving finger. Whenever something happens that is to be stored away, the finger writes it in the nearest empty box. Whenever something is to be retrieved, the finger looks in the nearest box with something in it; if it doesn't find what it was looking for, it continues to search in an everwidening spiral until it gets tired. This may strike you as an absurd model, but it works quite well as a description of numerous research findings.

Another popular explanation of memory phenomena builds upon concepts of the modern digital computer. The match-up is a natural one, because computers do have memories. Some computer models (Figure 5) tend to be, on the surface at least, as complicated as the phenomena they are designed to

```
00100  ; CY15F; CRYPTARITHMETIC PRODUCTION SYSTEM
00200  ;         FOR S2, TRY 15 (BOOK VERSION) ON CROSS+ROADS=DANGER
00300  ;         REQUIRES PSGF, U1F, DICTF, UTILF
00400  ;
00500  DEFINE.SYMBOLS!
00600  ;
00700  CY.CONTEXT SET.CONTEXT!
00800  ;
00900  ; MAKE NAMES AVAILABLE FOR USE IN CY.CONTEXT
01000  TD* TD CHANGE.NAMES!
01100  ;
01200  DEFINE.PROCESSES!
01300  ;
01400  ; NOTICING OPERATORS;
01500  ;   SET VALUES OF VARIABLES AND (POSSIBLY) PRODUCE <NTC-EXP>
01600  ;
01700  FC: (OPR CALL)  ; FIND COLUMN CONTAINING LETTER <L> (=> <COL>)
01750
01800  FNC: (OPR CALL) ; FIND NEXT UNPROCESSED COLUMN (=> <COL>)
01900  FLA· (OPR CALL) ; FIND LETTER ABOVE LINE IN COLUMN <COL>(=> <L>)
02000  ;
02100  ; STM OPERATORS;
02200  ;   PRODUCE NEW ELEMENTS OR MODIFY EXISTING ELEMENTS IN STM
02300  ;
02400  PC: (OPR CALL) ; PROCESS COLUMN <COL> (=> <EXP>, <GOAL>)
02500  AV: (OPR CALL) ; ASSIGN VARIABLE <VAR> (=> <EXP>, <GOAL>)
02600  TD: (OPR CALL) ; TEST DIGIT <D> FOR LETTER <L> (=> <EXP>,<GOAL>)
02700  RA: (OPR CALL) ; RECALL ANTECEDENT OF <EXP> (=> <EXP>,<COL>)
02800  RV: (OPR CALL) ; RECALL VARIABLE <VAR> (=> <D>)
02900  ;
03000  DEFINE.SYMBOLS!
03100  ; DEFINE CLASSES FOR USE IN PRODUCTION CONDITIONS
03200  ;
03300  ; CLASSES FOR CRYPTARITHMETIC KNOWLEDGE
03400  ;
03500  <D>:    (CLASS 0 1 2 3 4 5 6 7 8 9)
03600  <L>:    (CLASS A C D E G N O R S)
03700  <C>:    (CLASS C1 C2 C3 C4 C5 C6)
03800  <COL>:  (CLASS COL.1 COL.2 COL.3 COL.4 COL.5 COL.6)
03900  <VAR>:  (CLASS <L> <C>)
04000  <OBJ>:  (CLASS <L> <D>)
04100  <EQ>:   (CLASS = <-->)
04200  <IEQ>:  (CLASS > < >= <= )
04300  <REL>:  (CLASS <EQ> <IEQ>)
04400  <TAG>:  (CLASS NEW OLD NOT)
04500  <EXP>:  (CLASS (<VAR> <REL> <OBJ>) (<TAG> <VAR> <REL> <OBJ>))
04600  ;
04700  ; CLASSES FOR GOAL EXPRESSIONS
04800  ;
04900  <G>:    (CLASS GOAL OLDG)
05000  <SIG>:  (CLASS * % + -)
05100  <END>:  (CLASS + -)
05200  <COND>: (CLASS -COND +COND)
05300  <SIG-EXP>: (<SIG> <COND>)
05400  <COND-EXP>: (COND <COND> <END>)
05500  <GOAL-TYPE>: (CLASS USE GET CHECK RECALL SOLVE <OPR>)
05600  <GOAL-SPEC>: (CLASS <COL> <VAR> <OBJ>
05700                        (<VAR> <COL>) (<COL> <VAR>) (<VAR> <OBJ>))
05800  <GOAL>: (CLASS (<G> && <SIG-EXP> <GOAL-TYPE>)
05900                 (<G> && <SIG-EXP> <GOAL-TYPE> && <GOAL-SPEC>))
06000  ;
06100  <OPR>:  (CLASS PC AV TD RA RV)
06200  <NTC>:  (CLASS FNC FC FLA)
06300  <NTC-COND>: (CLASS MORE END)
06400  <NTC-EXP>: (CLASS (<NTC-COND> <NTC>) (OLD <NTC-COND> <NTC>))
```

Figure 5. Example of program listing for computer-simulation model of human memory. (After Newell 1972.)

model.[47] Computer-based semantic-associative networks[50] are also popular at present.

Other models have relied on the computer as a source of analogy, as a way of representing independent elements in the human memory system and their functional properties. The model in Figure 6 of Shiffrin and Atkinson [58]

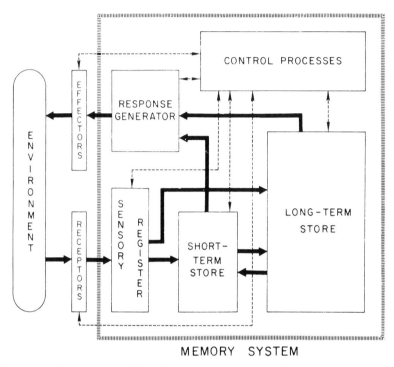

MEMORY SYSTEM

Figure 6. Three-stage model of memory, based on theory of Shiffrin and Atkinson. (This version after Atkinson, Herrmann, and Wescourt 1974.)

is one of the best-known examples of this approach. There are numerous variations on this theme; in Figure 7 is a version that currently appeals to me.

The major components of this system are *perceptual memory* (sizable capacity for uncoded information but extremely rapid loss of information, unique storage system for each sensory mode); *long-term memory* (unlimited capacity, little if any loss of information except by overwriting, but retrieval of information is highly dependent on the organization of sets of information, much like a library, ERIC file, or the papers in my office); *short-term verbal memory* (limited capacity of about 5 to 9 chunks of information, rate of loss is dependent on the individual's ability to concentrate on rehearsing the list of chunks); and, *control processes* (link the system components with one another and other cognitive processes, determine attentional priorities, and decide on coding and storage strategies).

I will not try to characterize the research literature on human memory in any further detail at this point. It must suffice to say that there is a large and

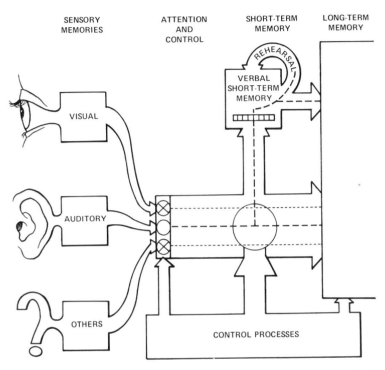

Figure 7. Another version of three-stage model of memory, emphasizing points of contact with control processes.

energetic enterprise underway built upon the activities of college sophomores (who are, for the most part, reasonably skilled readers), a research effort that is noteworthy for its breadth (ranging from simple rote and serial recall tasks to an accounting of the reconstruction in memory of prose passages), rigor of experimental control, and elegance and richness of theoretical development. It may also be criticized for its disregard of individual differences, and for what verges at times on contempt for practical applicability.

Information-Processing and Memory

In this paper memory is being examined from what has come to be known as an information-processing point of view. A few words about this approach are in order.

Hagen, Jongeward and Kail, in a review of memory development, make some lucid observations on the sundering of what had previously been considered a monolithic intellectual structure:

. . . [During the early years of the mental-test movement] memory was treated more or less as a unitary construct and was not analyzed further by . . . differential psychologists. Experimental psychology did recognize that memory performance was, to a large extent, a function of the technique of measurement; but not until the advent of information-processing models [has] memory [been] pursued vigorously as a construct in its own right.

. . . The information-processing model suggests critical points in the memorial process where developmental changes occur—initial encoding, acquisition, storage, and retrieval—and where this process may be linked to other important aspects of cognition.[30]

An information-processing analysis attempts to specify the cognitive mechanisms and operations required to perform a task.[27,37] With regard to memory, one can inquire—what are the functional requirements for *selecting, coding, translating, storing,* and *retrieving* information? To toss some or all of these operations into an undifferentiated grabbag called *memory* sheds little light on how a child actually handles the task, and provides little guidance about what to do if the child encounters difficulty along the way.

Nor is the situation helped by nonfunctional descriptions of memory processes. For instance, here are two tasks that were both described as visual memory. In the first,[54] a nonsense figure is shown, which has to be selected from a highly similar set of alternatives. In the second,[56] the student looks at a series of three numerals while simultaneously hearing three other numerals, and subsequently has to recall all six numerals. Both papers refer to these tasks as "visual memory," but an information-processing analysis of task requirements suggests little if any overlap in cognitive processes. To the degree that performance on the two tasks is correlated, one would expect the commonalities to reflect general factors (control-process variation, if you will) rather than specific factors. This seems an unprofitable way to describe the workings of the mind.

Criteria for Research
on the Acquisition of Reading

In an ideal world, what would I want to see when I looked at a research paper on how children learn to read? This is a dangerous question for someone to pose if they happen to be in the business of producing such papers.

If we think, in the most general terms, about the classes of variables that might affect a child's success in learning to read, there are three primary areas with which we must concern ourselves—the child and his internal workings; the school situation, including the teacher and the curriculum, and the home and social environment from which the child comes. Some of these variables are much easier to control (experimentally or correlationally) than others. Any systematic research on reading acquisition that completely ignores any of these classes of variables will prove less than adequate when we attempt generalization of the results.

Let me propose that research on this topic should be as experimental as possible. Many variables cannot be brought under experimental control in the best of circumstances. Confounded studies, in which a number of factors covary naturally in intricate ways, are likely to provide little new knowledge. We need to try to isolate and orthogonally vary those factors over which such control can be exerted, if we are to determine the independent contribution of potentially important factors, and if we are to discover significant inter-actions.

The next set of criteria I would suggest is substantive in nature. I would propose that research on reading acquisition must take into account three classes of psychological processes—cognition, learning, and development.

By cognition I mean simply how the child thinks. Reading is a thinking process of a most interesting sort. Recent methodological advancements in cognitive psychology have added greatly to our ability to explore thought processes. It is refreshing that psychologists have rediscovered the mind after a long period in which it was forbidden territory. It is necessary and possible to do more than draw flow charts describing complex interrelations among thought processes. Work by a number of theoreticians and experimentalists has provided some powerful methodological tools for testing models of the mind. The work on independent cognitive processes[12,63] strikes me as especially fruitful. Work on computer simulation is still a mixed blessing, in my opinion.

The next major area is the learning process. Reading entails learning. With the advent of mathematical models for learning in the 1950's, a powerful technology evolved for the precise study of learning. Developments have continued in this area over the past two decades, but, to the best of my knowledge, there is not one study of reading acquisition that takes advantage of the tools for the analysis of learning protocols now available. The bulk of the work on learning to read (and there is a paucity of such studies) uses rather gross characterizations, such as the mean learning curve.

Finally, children in the learning-to-read age range are still developing, in the truest sense of the word. I am not referring to the plethora of data showing that the older the child becomes, the faster and more accurately he can perform various tasks. Rather, I mean that these children are changing in the way that they think. We do not know the degree to which such changes are developmental in the "flowering" sense of the word, as opposed to environmentally induced. Much of the research is flawed, given the criteria for the investigation of developmental processes proposed by Kessen[33] some years back. A number of fruitful ideas about Piagetian methodology can be found in Green, Ford and Flamer.[26]

Mental Models for Beginning Readers

Before leaving this topic of general developmental change, I would like to pose a question: How can we best describe the mind of a beginning reader—a child with average abilities and attitudes, between the ages of four and nine?

I would like to propose a few simple models in answer to this question.

1. One possibility is that the child is well described as progressing through a number of different *stages of development,* à la Piaget.[2] The level of development of an individual child at a given time will determine strongly what he can learn and how he can best be instructed. Environmental influences, including teaching, may promote and facilitate this development, but cannot substantially hasten it in other than a superficial way.

2. The *reading readiness* model promulgated in past years is a kind of stage development model, but linked to reading and with little theoretical elaboration. According to this model, one determines whether a child is ready to learn to read by various testing procedures. If the child is not ready, then the best thing to do is wait for awhile until he gets ready.

3. We might consider a child to be a *miniature adult,* possessed of the same potentialities, the same basic processes of perception, cognition, and language as an adult. The main difference is that everything takes a bit longer to operate, because skills are not so highly practiced; and the associative and linguistic base for organizing, coding and chunking information is not so elaborated. According to this model, research on college students is directly applicable to many beginning readers, at least to those in the normal and above-average range of intelligence.

4. The *uninstructed person*—we might imagine that a beginning reader is similar in many respects to an adult, but that skills and knowledge of a particular sort remain to be learned. According to this model, the functioning of the beginning reader differs from that of a skilled reader in a number of important respects, but the appropriate

action to take is not to wait, but to find out what the child does know, and using that as a starting point teach him what he needs to know next on his way to some terminal goal. This model is more or less congenial with the notions of Gagné.[23]

It is not my goal here to argue the merit of one or the other of these ideas. In the period during which reading instruction takes place, developmental change may take a variety of forms, which carry with them quite different implications for education. As part of the American functionalist movement, my biases are much more toward the last-mentioned model—the beginning reader as an uninstructed person—than toward stage-development models. The truth may be best represented by some combination of these ideas. To do more than guess, however, requires substantially better evidence than is now available.

White's 1970 Review of Cognitive Development

A comprehensive review of cognitive changes in the age range of interest here—five to seven years—was reported by White in the Orton Society Bulletin a few years ago.[68] He covered a broader range of topics than I will attempt here. The physiological, affective and motivational changes between the ages of five and seven are substantial. White's language was not that of information-processing, but the parallel between his analysis and what I will present is remarkable at points. Some of his major conclusions provide a broad framework for considering the role of memory processes in learning to read.

White notes the interplay of maturational, experiential, and educational changes at this age level. He points out the futility of ascribing behavioral variations to any single factor. Children's bodies (and brains) are undergoing major development during this period. The opportunity for new experiences in the world are increasing markedly with the child's growing independence, competence and sensitivity (you can take a seven-year-old out to dinner at a good restaurant; for most three- and four-year-olds, McDonald's or Jack-in-the-Box are safer bets). And at five or six the child enters school, where he is expected to acquire knowledge and skills of a character and in a manner quite unlike that of previous years. For all of these reasons, behavioral change between five and seven (one might equally well say four to nine) is rich and varied.

One of the more notable developments is described by White as ". . . a sharply enhanced ability to form a system of behavior in accord with a proposition offered to the child, and then, an ability to maintain the proposition over an extended period of time." What this means is that little kids don't understand what you want them to do, and when they do get it, they quickly forget about it.

White is referring here to what I have labeled control processes—a child's sensitivity to and understanding of the task demands in a situation, and the ready availability of tactics and strategies for handling a problem. Along with published references to investigations bearing on this point, White gives the reader a peek backstage at some of the important boundary conditions for obtaining reasonable data from young children in psychological experiments:

1. You must make sure that the child is comfortable and interested in the situation.

2. You must minimize distractions, and arrange for the relevant stimuli to be as salient as possible.

3. You should use simple, clear instructions; a demonstration or a little practice with feedback helps.

4. You should encourage the child where possible, especially when he is first getting started.

For older children, these "precautions" are less vital; a seven- or eight-year-old is likely to catch on quickly to what he is to do, and to do it as well as he can.

These caveats may strike a familiar chord; they bear an amazing resemblance to principles followed almost automatically by an experienced kindergarten or first-grade teacher, whether or not the subject matter is reading. The fact that developmental psychologists must observe such measures in dealing with young children is not surprising—the fact that there has been little effort until recently to investigate systematically the character of this class of variables does cause a practical person to ponder on the behavior of researchers.

White also remarks, ". . . even with such precautions, a significant proportion of preschoolers will 'fail' the (experimental) task."

For those of you who teach, it should be reassuring to hear a developmental psychologist admit to difficulty in getting a child to do something. The matter has not been investigated, to the best of my knowledge, but I suspect that some researchers are more successful than others in reducing the "failure rate" among the younger subjects in psychological experiments. A whole new area of research might open up here! To be sure, a researcher does have an out—if he doesn't succeed with a child, then the youngster is simply "excluded from the sample for failure to follow instructions."

To quote a few more lines from White, because they fit so closely the line of argument to be made in this paper:

> The youngest [subjects] lapse into . . . positive habits or other stereotypies. . . . They will show . . . a 'failure set.' This presumes discouragement, but discouragement is only occasionally evident and most often is not. [It appears] ,. . . that the child has simply lost sight of his target, his end-state, and remains content to exercise his motor routine, accepting those rewards that chance will bring. . . . [As he grows older] . . . the child improves in ability to hold the plan which is to guide his behavior. . . . In the younger child, the sheer passage of time and concurrent distraction is apt to dissipate the plan.

One cannot speak reasonably about the acquisition of reading and the accompanying development of memory skills without reference to the control mechanisms that mediate and direct behavior. Indeed, the message of my paper is that, given proper attention to control mechanisms, memory functions from age four or five are more than adequate to meet the needs of a child who is learning to read.

Criteria for Research—A Reprise

I have suggested a number of criteria that impose strong constraints for acceptable research on reading acquisition. Such research needs to consider the child, the school environment in which the child is located, and the home environment from which the child comes. The research should explore in a reasonably integrated fashion the cognitive and developmental learning dimensions of reading. The model for the study of reading that many researchers now follow is based on the implicit assumption that parts of the larger problem can be carved out for study in the laboratory or other isolated environments, and that somehow all of the pieces can then be fitted together. I am not a believer in strong and complex interactions, but investigators should provide guideposts to larger problems.

One might also raise questions about whether or not large-scale, well-controlled research designs required for such investigations are feasible. In my opinion they are.[13] It is also my strong conviction that we need to utilize efficient, multivariate research designs and instrumentation systems if we are to move reading (and education more generally) out of the morass in which it is currently mired. In each of the areas described above, we have strong methodological tools, and individuals who are well trained to use them precisely. The problem would seem to call for collaborative research in which investigators who pool their talents are encouraged and rewarded for such collaboration. Consortia of researchers and schools spanning more than a single geographic location may have to be established. It may also be necessary to provide for some continuity of funding, so that efforts of this sort will be worth the large initial investment. All of this may be quite fanciful. Still, I see it as the only alternative to independent investigators' finding their own results, developing their own programs, with little solid evidence as to how everything fits together for the general improvement of instruction in the acquisition of reading.

The Research Literature on the Acquisition of Reading

The character of substantive investigations of reading acquisition is particularly depressing. There is certainly an enormous research literature labeled "reading." But, it tells us little about how a child learns to read, as Gibson and Levin noted:

> Despite all the current emphasis on literacy, the wealth of 'programs' commercially available, the 'learning specialists' who have set up in shopping centers and the arguments over phonics or whole-word methods, it is the beginning phase of learning to read that we seem to know least about. All the talk is of what the teacher does or should do and not of what happens or should happen in the child. This is a very peculiar situation. There is presumably a learning process going on, but it is a rare psychologist who studies it.[71]

The number of studies, good or bad, bearing directly on this topic is unbelievably small. There is, to be sure, a very large number of predictive/correlational studies, but these have led to little in the way of trustworthy conclusions about the nature of reading acquisition or the reading process. There is also a number of large-scale demonstration field studies, efforts to show that one method or another of teaching reading has some special merit. The Cooperative First Grade Reading Study[9] is the best known of these. The problems with such studies—inadequate control over the programs being compared, confoundings due to multiple differences between programs, questionable control over between-subject and between-class variability and inadequacy of the assessment instruments—all of these problems are well known and need not be described in detail here.

There are a few studies built around a miniature reading curriculum paradigm.[7,21,31,53,61,64] These are studies in which children are taught a small number of simple letter-sound correspondences (3 to 6) and then acquire a small vocabulary (usually 4 to 10 words). Further work in this direction should be worthwhile. Although this paradigm would seem well suited to a careful examination of learning processes during decoding acquisition, most of these studies have reported gross measures like mean trials to criterion, or total errors on a post-test. Computer-assisted instruction systems provide another potential source of data about the acquisition of reading, but thus far this potential is largely unrealized.

The case-study approach represents another way of examining how a child learns to read. We are currently engaged in a rather extensive effort along these lines, which we call a Reading Diary. A carefully selected sample of first-graders, whose kindergarten profiles indicate probable success in first-grade reading, is being observed and tested at weekly intervals during the year. Similar studies[22] have been quite limited in time, range of students, character of testing (analysis of oral reading miscues has been quite popular), and observation of the instructional program (in most investigations the classroom has been totally disregarded).

In general, there is little to be learned from the enormous literature on "reading" about the character of cognitive processes that are operative during reading acquisition. By its very nature, this question requires concerted study over a period of months of individual children who are learning to read in a classroom. There has been little payoff from such research up until now.

Current Research on the Development of Memory Processes

When we turn to recent research on the development of memory processes in the age range of 5 to 9 years, the situation is quite promising. To be sure, these studies have their limitations for our purpose. Children's performance is examined under restricted, laboratory conditions, with unusual materials and artificial constraints on instruction and expectation. Individual differences other than age are largely ignored. We have black and white snapshots where we would like color movies with sound. But the research is well controlled, extensive, often imaginative and provocative.

The psychological/developmental literature on memory has been intelligently and comprehensively reviewed by several scholars.[6,16,20,28−30,41]

This literature suggests the following conclusions:

1. Memory function and structure for children in this age-range are identical in virtually all respects to that of adults. The Atkinson-Shiffrin multi-stage model presented earlier serves as well to describe memory for the beginning reader as it does for the college student.

2. There is a dramatic change between 4 and 9 in the operation of control processes—children undergo major developmental changes in how they use their memory resources, how they respond to task and situational demands requiring memory, and in the degree of "planfulness" in their strategies for processing information. In a related vein, though there is less support for the proposition, it appears that individual differences within an age level also reflect variation in control processes more than variation in memory structure per se.

3. Memory control processes in young children are extraordinarily labile; they are subject to large and immediate change as a result of instruction and training. However, the effects of such training are short-lived unless the training is extensive and broad in coverage. A young child is quite capable of adopting mnemonic tactics that substantially improve memory performance in a particular context, but these tactics may be ignored ten minutes later in a different context.

Memory Structure and Function—Constancy from Age 4 Onward

Let me turn now to the first proposition, the invariance of memory processes from age four onward. The gist of work on this point is (a) that if we can ensure comparable attention, selection, encoding, and organization for storage and retrieval, there are negligible developmental trends in memory performance after age four, and (b) within remarkably broad limits, it is feasible to establish such comparability through instructions or organization of the materials. For instance, storage, organization, and retrieval processes can be neutralized by a recognition task, and numerous studies show that recognition is little if at all dependent on age level. When such differences do show up, they probably indicate either that the child was not attending to what was presented, or that he had no way of encoding it.

These remarks apply to short-term and perceptual memory tasks, but also to tasks requiring semantic integration and other high-level cognitive and linguistic skills. To quote again from Hagen, *et al.*:

Initial encoding, not surprisingly, involves language even in preschool-age children. . . . Semantic information is coded for storage in a wide variety of experimental tasks across a wide age range. Other features may be used depending on the circumstances. Further, children as young as five years can deal effectively with semantically integrated information, such as series of short sentences. They can encode and use the semantic information in ways that are independent of the original formal structure. The lack of age differences, across a rather wide range (preschool to adolescence), points to the early (and seemingly automatic) abilities children have in encoding and using considerable amounts of information.[30]

Typical of studies finding negligible developmental change between kindergarten and fifth grade in comprehension and semantic integration are those of Barclay and Reid,[4] Paris and Mahoney,[49] and Paris and Carter.[48]

Obstacles to Achieving Comparability. There is no question but that older children have a richer and more efficiently organized experiential and language base, which makes it possible for them to handle a wider range of information from the environment. That is not the issue here. Young students do have a well-developed knowledge base—they know a lot of things, even if many don't yet know that whales aren't fish, or can't define (or spell) *onomatopoeia.* They will learn such things as the need and opportunity arises. The important point is that, in most significant aspects, young students' memories are structured and can be used much like an adult's. Whether through a *lack of understanding of conventions* (if somebody asks you to listen to something, they expect you to make some effort to attend to it and remember it), or *lower motivation* (why exert cognitive energy in remembering something that may seem irrelevant), or whatever the reason, younger students are less likely spontaneously to study and memorize materials put before them. When the tester or the testing situation clarifies task requirements, then age-related differences become negligible—given, of course, that the materials fall within the child's grasp.

Reasonable materials, clear instructions, efforts to equate experience with a task format—all sensible steps to minimize extraneous variability in measurement—may be for naught if a child's answers are too hasty, or represent too little thought and effort. The implications for test construction, administration and interpretation seem substantial—if poor performance is likely to reflect either lack of knowledge *or* lack of interest, then the information from the test is of uncertain meaning and value. The younger the student, the more likely that such concern is warranted. Group-administered "reading readiness" tests seem particularly vulnerable to this criticism, but many of the so-called "criterion-referenced" tests used in classrooms today seem to me to raise similar questions.

There are two steps to remedying this situation. Put yourself in the child's place and ask, "What do I have to be able to know and do to perform adequately and with confidence in this situation?" Then ask, as the instructor-tester, "What could be done to alter the situation so that the task demands are directly related to the skill or knowledge under investigation, and so that the student understands and accepts the task presented to him?" I have described such tests elsewhere as "clean" tests.[14]

For instance, it might be suggested that a recognition-test format yields a clean measure of encoding and storage processes. But even in a "simple" two-choice task we cannot be certain that response demands are inconsequential. In a study by Siegel, Kirasic, and Kilburg,[60] preschoolers were first shown a series of pictures to remember. Then they were shown a series of test cards, each with two pictures, one of which had been in the original study list. The other picture was either quite unlike any of those that had been studied, was more or less similar, or was virtually identical to the "correct" picture. The child's task was to point to the picture that he had seen earlier.

Half the children were judged impulsive (rapid, inaccurate responses) and half reflective (slower, more accurate responses), based on a test developed by Kagan.[32] Impulsive children made more recognition-memory errors under all conditions, the more so as the two test pictures on a card were more similar. This might be taken as evidence that an impulsive child is less likely to attend to and/or store away a picture presented to him for memorization. A reasonable conclusion, perhaps, but a passing remark in the paper merits attention:

"Five subjects (3 reflectives and 2 impulsives) [4 boys and 1 girl, these from an original sample of only 21 preschoolers and hence 25% of the sample] showed such marked position biases on the test of recognition memory (on the last 40 cards the children chose either the left or the right figure on all 40 trials) that their data were excluded from further consideration."

Position biases generally reflect a breakdown in cognitive processing—if a situation seems hopeless, if you can't think of anything sensible to do, or if the circumstances seem to call for a slapdash response, then why not arbitrarily pick an alternative and perseverate on it. No data were reported on the degree of position bias by those children who were included in the final analysis, and so we cannot tell whether this might account for differences between impulsive and reflective children's recognition memory. The observation I want to make is this: Even in a simple, two-choice pointing task with sensible materials, a student's response style may critically affect observable performance. How fast he selects an answer, whether he checks the alternatives carefully, whether he checks his memory at all, all these reflect processes that intervene between any knowledge available in memory and actual test performance. We cannot safely assume that any test measures an individual's underlying knowledge in a direct way.

Improvements in Memory Through Clear Instructions and Demonstrations
Dramatic examples of the significance of control processes on memory performance have been achieved by the introduction of clarifying instructions, demonstrations, modeling, or short-term training with feedback. To illustrate the matter, Figure 8 shows a page from a teacher's manual of a well-known reading curriculum. Would you look at this material for a moment, and then I'd like to ask a few questions. Don't look back at the figure.

What is the stated purpose of the activities on this page?

What is the gist of the directions; how does a student do the kind of exercise presented on this page?

If you are like most people who have tried this task, you may find it a little hard to answer these questions, because you didn't read the fine print at the bottom of the page. The point here may seem a trivial one—you can't remember what you didn't process. But in many real-life classroom situations, a child is presented with a task in which relevant information (i.e., information he needs for present or later purposes) is obscured by more salient cues.

There are two ways to remedy this situation. One is to give the student a clear idea of what is important in the task—what he should look at or listen to, what criteria are important in evaluating each cue, what can be disregarded. The other approach is up to the teacher, tester or program developer—clean up the test. Simplify the task requirements as much as possible; make sure that relevant cues are salient; choose the substance of the task to match as nearly as possible the student's past experiences and knowledge.

Pictures, Meaningfulness, and Learning to Read
An effective way of improving a young child's "memory" performance is to assure that he has selected cues that carry the critical information. Contrariwise, one of the best ways to decrease performance is to present competing, salient, irrelevant information. The use of pictures to accompany printed text in beginning reading is one of the most distressing examples I know of this latter practice. If the goal in a particular lesson is to teach a child something about the correspondence between letters and sounds, a surefire way of distracting the student from the printed stimulus is to flash an attractive, four-color picture. Samuels[51,52] has reviewed this literature, and

78   ROBERT C. CALFEE

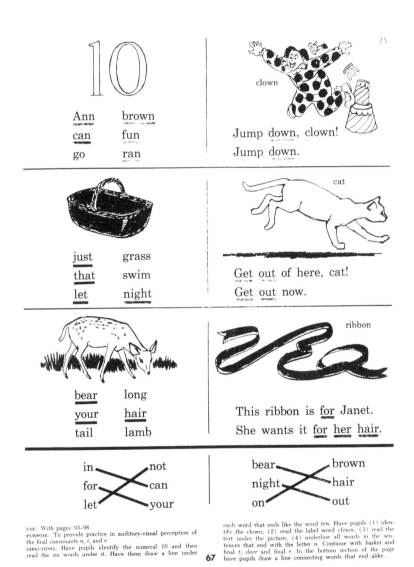

Figure 8. Sample page from teacher's manual of a reading curriculum. (From Workbook for Around the Corner, Teacher's Edition, by Phyllis Wilson. Copyright © 1966, by Harper & Row, Publishers, Incorporated. Used with permission.)

the evidence for this conclusion is very convincing. In a recently published study, Samuels, Spiroff and Singer [55] replicated earlier findings, and showed that presenting words in "meaningful sentential context" also slowed down acquisition of decoding knowledge. If the intention of a lesson is to teach a student to pronounce a set of target words, the best approach is to eliminate all extraneous cues—present the words plain, in isolation.

The use of familiar, high-frequency words in beginning reading series is another instance where the situational cues probably are counter to acquisition of the desired generalizations. It is well known that spelling-sound irregularities are more typical in high-frequency words—*of, was, said* and *don't* are samples. Many such words are easily accessible in memory. They come easily to mind given minimal information. Byers put it well: "[High-frequency words] may facilitate reading acquisition, but only at the cost of the child's early texting response being controlled by single-letter cues. He may even learn a rather generalized set that attention to the whole word (i.e., all the letters) is *not* important for word recognition." [10] The salient meaningfulness of familiar words may in itself sidetrack attention (and consequent analysis and storage) from cues vital in the acquisition of decoding knowledge. The alphabetic principle may be the best-kept secret about reading for many beginning readers. McNeil and Stone's data [40] suggest that semantic associations should be minimized when the goal is to instruct a student about decoding.

In Figure 9 is an example from a workbook in current use in California schools. I visited a first-grade classroom recently in which the students were cheerfully filling in the blanks with letters. I asked one child if he could read any of the words—he said, "No," as did his partner. A boy on the other side of the table then said, brightly, "I can read the words." And he proceeded to do so, including some that he had not printed; in one instance his response had no relation to the graphemic clues, though it matched the picture. The other children caught on quickly, and suddenly all the students at the table became "readers"—that is, they could name the pictures.

I am not categorically opposed to pictures. Concrete representations are often the best way of communicating with someone, particularly with the young and those unused to handling abstractions. But curriculum developers, testers and teachers need to consider more carefully the effects of the cues presented to children during reading instruction. A principle of "least effort" makes sense to most learners—select and use those cues that are most salient, familiar and distinctive in a situation. They will be the easiest to remember. But eventually the piper must be paid: reading is not just picture-naming, and

Figure 9. Sample page from reading workbook, illustrating distracting effect of pictures when teaching decoding skills. (From Skills Handbook for a Duck Is a Duck and Helicopters and Gingerbread, *by Theodore Clymer and Billie Parr, of the READING 360 series,* © *Copyright, 1969, by Ginn and Company [Xerox Corporation]. Used with permission.)*

at some point the student must learn something about translating from graphic cues to a spoken form.

Knowing What You Have to Do

    Intention can be as significant in memorization as *attention.* Young students vary in the way they tackle a memory task, but generally speaking they tend to focus more on details, less on the "big" picture. This represents a decision on their part, rather than an innate developmental necessity. The critical factor here is the match between the student's intentions and plans for handling a task, and the expected criterion—what do you have to be able to do when you are tested.

    For instance, here is a demonstration you can easily perform with a small group of willing subjects, friends or students. The subject's task is to read a prose passage or, better yet, a list of unrelated items like these "anti-rules for reading teachers" taken from a recent book by Smith:[62]

1. Aim for early mastery of the rules of reading.
2. Ensure that phonic skills are learned and used.
3. Teach letters or words one at a time, making sure each new letter or word is learned before moving on.
4. Make word-perfect reading the prime objective.

Before starting to read, half the subjects are given "detail" instructions like, "Count the number of *e*'s" or "Memorize each statement verbatim." The other subjects are asked to "Remember the gist of each statement" or "Try to remember the statements in an organized manner." Next they are given a brief time to read the material. Then, after a little chatter on your part, you ask them to write down the gist of what they just read. The subjects in the detail groups generally can recall little if anything, because of the mismatch between what they were studying and what the test required. The subjects asked to remember the meaning do quite well.

Informal demonstrations as well as more formal investigations have generally shown that intention, the variable being manipulated here, has large and practically significant effects; statistics are not needed to make the point. And the role of this factor in beginning reading is all the more important because it is generally disregarded in instruction and testing. It is simply assumed that when a class of first-graders listens to a teacher, looks at a text, or works on an exam, that they bring a common set, a uniform expectation, of what it is that they are to do with the information and how they are to spend their time.

Individual Differences in Reaction to Instructions

With regard to the benefits of clear instruction, demonstration, modeling, and short- or long-term training on a task, it is important to keep in mind the needs and resources of students. The situation is complex, as shown in a recent review of the aptitude-treatment-interaction literature (Cronbach and Snow, in preparation).

If a child already knows what to do and how to do it, then supplementary instruction is a waste of time. We have found, in testing visual-discrimination skills in preschoolers and kindergartners, that those children rated "high" in general ability by the teacher are not helped by instructions clarifying the criteria for making a same-different judgment, whereas those students with a "low" rating do noticeably better with such clarification than without.[14]

On the other hand, if a situation is unclear for all students in a sample, then a relatively brief amount of training or instruction is likely to benefit the more able students but do little for less able ones. Schultz, Charness and Berman[59] report results of this sort in a free-recall task with first and fourth graders from middle and lower-class backgrounds. Children were given a list of pictures to remember. In one condition, each picture was accompanied by a category label: "Truck. Something to ride in." In another condition, the picture was simply labeled: "Truck." This was the extent of the "instructional" procedure. It is known that categorical organization greatly facilitates recall. The data showed that the middle-class children used the categories during recall, and increased their recall by 50% from the no-label to the label condition. The lower-class sample gained only about 20% from one condition to the other. Thus, in this experiment, with minimal instruction, individual differences were actually amplified; a hint about how to memorize the picture list sufficed for the middle-class children, but was largely ignored by the lower-class students. This does not mean at all that the latter could not profitably employ such a mnemonic strategy. To the contrary, there are a number of studies showing that, with adequate and appropriate instructional intervention, class differences can be eliminated. Incidentally, results similar to those of Shultz, et al.,[59] were found in a study comparing normal and retarded subjects on a recognition memory task.[12] Preschoolers in a normal to bright range of I.Q. saw the categorical organization in a list of pictures and used it to improve performance—without any comment by the tester. Retarded subjects appeared altogether oblivious to the potential for organization, although they were quite proficient at sorting the pictures into categories when so instructed.

To recapitulate, the effects on memory of instruction, training and the like will depend on the student's needs and competencies, and on the appropriateness of the instruction. The effect may be to increase or to decrease individual differences. This doesn't mean that the situation is hopelessly complicated or chaotic. You simply have to consider for a given situation what the students need to know and what instructional resources can be developed.

Mnemonics and Memory Development

The research literature on mnemonics and memory development is scanty, but the dominant themes important in adult memory seem to hold for younger students as well. The critical process in productive memory (i.e., *not* recognition memory) is retrieval—how do you get back to information once it has been stored in memory. Enormous improvement in memory performance can be realized if to-be-remembered information is studied in a framework that facilitates later retrieval (in a free recall task, put all the vegetables together, all the animals together, and so on). It also may be important to point out to the younger or less able student the nature of such organization, and to encourage him to use it in memorizing. Providing retrieval cues during recall is as helpful to young children as to older students. In all these areas, the parallels between child and adult performance are quite close, except that adults are more likely to spontaneously adopt strategies that make efficient use of categorical or other structural information. It is natural to ask, what can be done to increase the likelihood that a young student takes appropriate and effective steps toward studying and memorization—how can full use of mnemonic resources become natural and automatic?

Practice and Automaticity

The younger child's approach to memory tasks seems quite labile. He will readily adopt new strategies on request, but the effects of instruction or short-term training are short-lived. Numerous studies have found that the child who today greatly improved his performance by using a mnemonic strategy (perhaps nothing more complicated than rehearsing the materials aloud, or making a more definite effort to remember something by some other means), this same child is unlikely to try the same strategy tomorrow when given the same task, or even today in a different task context. Changes in time and context erase the influence of otherwise successful interventions.

A number of investigators have conjectured that the degree of automaticity of mnemonic techniques may be critical. The student who does a good job of remembering doesn't have to stop and think about it. Like any other well-practiced skill, the appropriate techniques come into play naturally when they are needed. And what is required for a skill to become automatic? The universal answer seems to be, *practice,* with feedback and encouragement, in a variety of situations like those in which the skill is likely to be needed later. I do not know of studies along this line that bear directly on the acquisition of memory skills, much less memory skills related to reading acquisition. But here is a study by Egeland[19] that provides an example and interesting results in a related area.

Egeland was curious about the effects of slowing down impulsive children, and showing them what to do with the additional time they thereby provided themselves. Impulsive children generally make lots of errors—on reading, discrimination, almost anything they do. Several studies have shown that it is possible to get such children to work more slowly, but this seems to do little to decrease their error rate. Moreover, the effects of instructions to work more slowly do not seem to last very long, nor to transfer to very many situations other than the one in which the instructions were given.

Egeland trained impulsive inner-city children over a four-week period, in eight 30-minute training sessions. A variety of materials and exercises was employed in the training. A "delay-training" group of children was told that it was important to try not to make mistakes, and that one way of doing this was to "think about your answers and take your time." This suggestion was enforced by having the trainer tell a child when a 10—15 second interval had elapsed, after which the child could make a response. A "strategy-training" group was given similar instructions, but was also provided a variety of rules and strategies to try out during the delay interval.

I think that this training procedure incorporates several important components. Training is extensive and extended in time; it includes variation in contexts and materials; and it provides children with positive ideas about how to improve their performance.

The question is—is it worth it? The answer is encouraging. On Kagan's Matching Familiar Figures Test, the strategy-training group reduced their error rate by one half, compared to the pretest level, and this improvement persisted over a two-month interval. The delay-training group showed similar improvement when first tested, but showed a substantial increase in errors on the two-month test.

Even more impressive was the effect of the training on a totally unrelated task, the Gates-MacGinitie Reading Test. The strategy-training group showed a substantially greater gain from pretest to posttest than the delay-training group, which did not differ from a no-treatment control. There was no differential effect of training on the Stanford Achievement Test, a group-administered multiple-choice test.

Here are Egeland's conclusions: ". . . for the impulsive child to become efficient at processing information he must be able to use the reflective approach without having to concentrate on ways of making the acquired reflective approach more automatic." Egeland's study focused on children in real classrooms, training under conditions that in extent, intensity, and comprehensiveness approximated real-life conditions, and measured payoff on tasks of importance in the student's academic career. It seems a good model to follow, and a hopeful one.[42]

The Mnemonic Power of Rules, Principles and Algorithms

Reading provides opportunities for training in general-purpose memory techniques. Take the alphabetic principle. Whatever your particular feelings about the regularity of English letter-sound correspondences, you probably accept with Gough (this volume) the advantages of learning a relatively modest number of correspondences as a way of gaining pronunciation control over a virtually infinite number of written words. Most of you can come fairly close to pronouncing "correctly" every word in Webster's unabridged, even though many of them are meaningless to you, and you have not seen them in print. Here are some words which I am fairly certain you have never seen, yet I warrant you would be in substantial agreement on how they should be pronounced:

GIDDER

PARKLE

GOMPLETE

MIGENT

PLIMBLE

DRATION

A tremendous feat of memory? *No!* This knowledge is not the result of rote association between letter patterns and speech patterns. One way or another, you have acquired a knowledge of letter-sound generalizations or algorithms. You may pick out letter patterns similar to those in other familiar words; you may "compute" the pronunciation from a mental register resembling Venezky's[66] correspondences or the SWRL list.[17] In any event, you use previously acquired information to attack a new problem. I am not arguing here that skilled readers always translate to sound and thence to meaning. That's a separate issue. All I am saying here is that you can with relative ease "attack" novel words and pronounce them in good agreement with other skilled readers.

All this seems so easy, so natural. Why should anyone have trouble? Well, let me take you back to first grade and show you how it feels. Here are a series of six symbol-sound pairs (Figure 10). The symbols—hieroglyphs— were recently discovered on Mars, together with sound tracks. There is every evidence that Martians were a highly analytic and rational folk who would never permit the evolution of a language so erratic and idiosyncratic as spoken or written English. Study these six pairs and then turn to Figure 11 and test yourself against the symbols in the top panel. There are only six pairs, so you should not have any trouble, but I'll bet many of you find it rather difficult. Now for the kicker: there are three other symbols in the list, in the bottom panel of Figure 11, similar to the ones you have already seen. If you are smart, you will have figured out the system

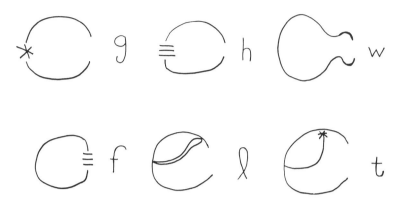

Figure 10. Symbol-sound pairs recently discovered on Mars. Study these and you will be tested on them later.

for this alphabet—it is direct, simple, and rational. Can you name the three bottom symbols?

Now I'm going to demonstrate the probable existence of individual differences among people. You may have recognized that there is a system to this set of symbol-sound correspondences—if not, you may detect it when you see the system organized in matrix form (Figure 12), where the rows and

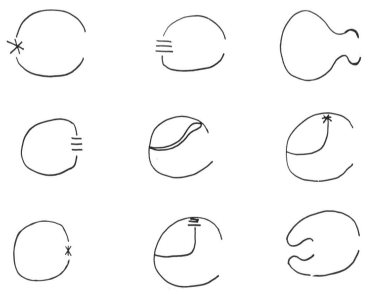

Figure 11. Test list for measuring your recall of Martian symbol-sound pairs. The list includes some new items you should be able to figure out.

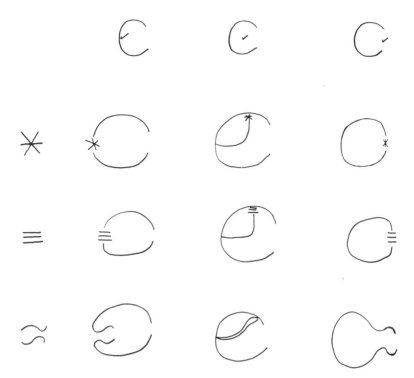

Figure 12. Matrix of Martian symbol-sound pairs, which shows structure of critical features.

columns denote critical features. If you have now seen the rule, performance should be error-free; indeed, I could readily expand the system. For virtually everyone in this category, the names Chomsky, Halle, and Fant are likely to have special meaning. If my conjecture is right, I could even design a simple readiness test to determine whether an individual would be likely to learn the system quickly or not.

The system is based on phonological features, rather than being pho-neme-based. One feature denotes the *manner* of articulation of a consonant (* is stop; ≡ is fricative, ∿ is semivowel), the other feature is the place of *articulation* (front, middle and back). If you are a phonologist, linguist, or speech clinician, these are meaningful terms, and the writing system should now be readily comprehensible to you. It may not be perfect, but it is reasonably easy to construct and store an algorithm or rule-oriented entry in your memory—easy to construct and easy to use because it is built upon pre-existing knowledge. On the other hand, you may not yet know what I'm talking about, and then you will have to rely on rote memory, which takes time and has limited generality.

Am I arguing by analogy that beginning readers must be taught "phonics rules"? No, I am not saying anything about what must be taught. The illustration is meant to make two points: (a) Rule-based knowledge may represent quite a saving in memorial and learning effort, and (b) rule-based knowledge requires a concrete foundation if it is to be readily acquired. The best way of applying these principles in reading acquisition remains a mystery; although it seems likely that lots of good practices now exist, research to date has been inadequate to identify them in any convincing way.

I might mention that the use of articulatory features (such as manner and place of production) to help beginning readers grasp the alphabetic principle might be a promising idea. It is well known that nonreaders experience great difficulty in handling phonemes, and training nonreaders in this area is not easy. But at least one program—the Lindamood's Auditory Discrimination in Depth (A.D.D.) system[36] attempts to help nonreaders over this difficulty by linking phonemes to method of production.

Separability of Curriculum Components

One of the implications of an information-processing approach to memory and cognition is that instructional techniques should match the cognitive requirements of an educational goal. The simple generalizations that grace the paths of "how to teach reading" manuals are then seen to have limited generality. In their place can be proposed a more rational principle: organize educational goals into separable domains where the cognitive requirements within a domain are reasonably coherent, and between-domain differences are large. Teach together those topics that go together in the child's thinking; do not force him to keep shifting cognitive gears.

Word Familiarity and Comprehension

For instance, acquisition of basic decoding skills comprises a markedly different domain than improvement of comprehension skills. The conditions that facilitate learning to decode English writing stand in the way of comprehension and vice-versa. Earlier it was argued that for several reasons high-frequency, familiar words were poor materials to use in teaching decoding. If comprehension is the instructional goal, then choice of familiar words becomes a critical requirement. If a student is to grasp the meaning of a passage with ease, then it is important that the vocabulary make sense to him, that it consist of words represented in the "subjective lexicon," to use Miller's term.[43] "People remember concrete things much better than abstractions. Human memory is quite unlike a computer memory in this respect; not logical simplicity but concreteness counts."[34] Studies bearing on this issue are legion.

Comprehension of a passage requires that the reader create a structural model of the passage content in his mind. The form that such a model might take has been described by a number of theorists.[15,37,65] In these models the reader constructs linkages among words from the passage. It seems likely that highly skilled reading also depends on preexisting structures. It is relatively easy for me to understand a technical article on short-term memory, because I have a rich associative vocabulary relevant to that topic, as well as a number of existing memory structures which provide a ready framework for organizing new knowledge. Little work has been done on the latter topic. The bulk of the work on the former topic is correlational, showing that there is a relation between the degree of unfamiliarity of the vocabulary in a passage and the ease of comprehending it. There is one nice experimental study by Marks, Doctorow, and Wittrock.[38] They modified a number of Science Research Associates passages, either replacing low-frequency vocabulary with high-frequency synonyms, or vice versa. Only 15% of the words were so altered. The effect of this modification was to increase or decrease comprehension performance by amounts ranging from 20% to 40%, a change that is practically as well as statistically significant.

The moral for instruction in comprehension in beginning reading seems clear. Changing the character and quality of a child's semantic memory is a slow and demanding task. If a student is to understand and remember something he has read, it must be meaningful to him. While changing a child's vocabulary may be difficult, virtually every child comes to the classroom with a rich and varied vocabulary of some sort. Combining a strong decoding program with a language-experience approach to comprehension and vocabulary expansion may be an odd combination. I do not personally know of any existing curricula of this sort (although one was described to me recently by Venezky), nor am I suggesting that the research shows that this approach would work better than any other—but it strikes me as an interesting way of dealing with what appear to be two quite separable cognitive skill areas.

Memory, Comprehension and Decoding Speed

Another reason for separating instruction aimed toward decoding skills from that aimed toward comprehension also relates to characteristics of human memory. There is reason to believe that short-term verbal memory is vital to the understanding of a sentence, if not of higher-level units. As words and phrases are decoded, they are stored in short-term memory until enough information is accumulated to allow reorganization. In normal conversation, words come in at a rate of less than five per second; five to ten independent chunks can be stored for up to 15 seconds; if the speech message makes any sense, there is a continuous process of reorganizing and creating a structure in long-term memory for storage of the information. Young children possess this cognitive-linguistic competence by age three or four.

But the process depends on the fluid, rapid flow of words into short-term verbal memory. If . . . I . . . present . . . to . . . you . . . a . . . complex . . . proposition . . . at . . . . . . a . . . slow . . . disconnected . . . pace . . . then . . . chances . . . are . . . that . . .   by . . . the . . . time . . . I . . . get . . . to . . . the . . . end . . . you . . . will . . . have . . . forgotten . . . the . . . beginning. McNeill has discussed this problem in connection with spoken language:

> The computation of sentence structure evidently must take place within a certain limited period. If a sentence is uttered too slowly—say one word every five seconds—its structure collapses . . . sentences, to be understood, must be experienced within a certain span of time. Beyond this span, there is a string of words; within it, a sentence. Forgetting may in part be responsible for this effect, but it does not seem to be the entire story.[39]

The analysis seems even more relevant in reading. If a student is asked to read prose that makes substantial demands on his existing decoding skills, so that his production of words is slow, error-prone and faltering, it seems unreasonable to expect that he will understand very much of what he has read. Short-term memory capacity will not allow it nor is there any need to place a child in such a position.

You may have forgotten what it feels like to read for meaning under conditions in which decoding is not fluent and automatic. Try reading the passage in Figure 13 aloud, or ask a friend to do so. Most people can decode every word correctly. Occasionally a letter reversal raises a problem; but unless or until you have had some amount of practice in reading mirror printing, your oral (and silent) reading will be slow, halting, and painful. Comprehension will be poor unless the material is familiar and redundant.

Many experts have suggested that a beginning reader must find meaning in what he reads, or he will lose interest. This is taken to mean that primer prose should be meaningful, that the child should read only meaningful materials, and should be directed from the earliest experience in reading to seek to understand what he reads. My analysis of the situation as a researcher

One of the oldest drinks known to man is milk, and the oldest milk taken from animals may be horse's milk.

Greek travelers around 450 B.C. wrote about the use of a form of mare's milk, called kumiss. Kumiss was made by letting the milk sour in a large leather bag for several days. The drinks had a pleasantly refreshing taste and the tang of two or three percent alcohol. Kumiss was particularly popular among the Tartars. Even the children frequently drank kumiss as well as nonalcoholic mare's milk.

Figure 13. Mirror-image reversed prose, illustrating difficulty of comprehending a passage when automaticity of decoding process is interrupted.

and my experience with young children suggests that this is bad advice. Young children are quite willing to work at developing skill in a specific and limited task on the promise that it will pay off in a larger context—"meaningfulness" inheres in the very performance of the act. Working on phonics is an acceptable task to most children, if they understand what is to be done and have a reasonable chance of success when they attempt it.

Comprehension skills can be developed without doing any reading at all. Being read to, being asked to explain something you have seen or heard, being asked to create a story, are all reasonable activities for young children that will enhance their skill at organizing prose of a "schoolish" character. As skill at translating letters to sounds begins to develop, then it makes sense to ask the child to read connected prose for meaning—to combine the two skills.

Summary

Let me try to tie together some of the threads spun here. I have not given simple answers to what might seem a simple question—what is the role of memory in the acquisition of reading? I hope you will at least give thought to the absurdity of talking about *memory* as a monolithic process. Teachers, testers and curriculum developers could profitably direct more attention to an analysis of the functional and structural requirements of the tasks that make up beginning reading; they could profitably work toward assuring that a student can make efficient use of those cognitive resources uniquely available to him in handling a task. Comparability in control processes—in how a student understands and approaches a task requiring encoding, storage and retrieval of information—is critical. Some concrete suggestions along this line take an exceptionally simple form. The California First-Grade Entry Level Test (1973), for instance, provides each teacher with a practice test, to be given to each student prior to the "real" test as many times as necessary to insure the child knows what is required of him. This does not insure that individual teachers will have the time and energy to carry out this pretraining. Chances are that in those first-grade classes where the need is greatest, the practice test will not be administered. But the principle is a sensible one. Opportunities for practice must be rich, varied and extensive if they are to have any trust value.

The information-processing approach to memory and cognition makes it natural to probe continuously and in varied ways to find out how a child thinks. In many respects, this approach could lead to a rapprochement of analytic-behaviorist and clinical techniques. Many teachers see their major function as the discovery of how a particular student's head works; information-processing models could contribute theoretically and empirically to this activity.

This approach also permits a new look at general vs. specific skills.[13] It makes it feasible to think more clearly of diagnosis for specific deficits. Similarly, it suggests the creation of instructional programs aimed at specific skill areas—neither nit-picking small, nor so general as to be irrelevant, but reasonable in terms of the tasks confronting the child and the mental structure he brings to bear on the task. I have suggested elsewhere some empirical and theoretical methods that might be useful in this connection.[12,13]

These remarks imply that it is possible to transfer the works of information-processing theorists from the isolated laboratory to the raucous real world—real children, real teachers, real classrooms. This is perhaps a pessimistic moment in education and social science research to propose such possibilities, but for some of us hope springs eternal. I spend a fair amount of time in classrooms with children. Whether it is the knowledge that I bring to the situation as a cognitive psychologist, or the clarity and reasonableness of thought in the children I meet, I feel I have reason to be optimistic about the outcome of such an endeavor.

References

1. Anderson JR, Bower GH: Recognition and retrieval processes in free recall. Psychol Rev 79:97–123, 1972
2. Athey IJ, Rubadeau DO: Educational Implications of Piaget's Theory. Waltham, Massachusetts, Ginn/Blaisdell, 1970
3. Atkinson RC, Herrmann DJ, Wescourt KT: Search processes in recognition memory. Read at the Loyola Symposium on Cognitive Psychology, Chicago, 1973. *In* Theories in Cognitive Psychology. Edited by RL Solso. Potomac, Maryland, Lawrence Erlbaum Associates, 1974
4. Barclay JR, Reid M: Semantic integration in children's recall of discourse. Dev Psychol 10:277–281, 1974
5. Beck IL, Mitroff DD: The Rationale and Design of a Primary Grades Reading System for an Individualized Classroom. Pittsburgh, University of Pittsburgh Press, Learning Research and Development Center, 1972
6. Belmont JM, Butterfield EC: The relations of short-term memory to development and intelligence. *In* Advances in Child Development and Behavior. Vol 4. Edited by LP Lipsitt, HW Reese. New York, Academic Press, 1969
7. Bishop CH: Transfer effects of word and letter training in reading. J Verbal Learning Verbal Behav 3:215–221, 1964
8. Bloomfield L, Barnhart CL: Let's Read: A Linguistic Approach. Detroit, Wayne State University Press, 1961
9. Bond GL, Dykstra R: The cooperative research program in first-grade reading instruction. Reading Res Q 2:5–126, 1967
10. Byers JL: Verbal and concept learning. Rev Educ Res 37:494–513, 1967
11. Calfee RC: Short-term recognition memory in children. Child Dev 1:145–161, 1970
12. Calfee RC: Sources of dependency in cognitive processes. To appear in Cognition and Instruction: Tenth Annual Carnegie-Mellon Symposium on Cognition, 1974
13. Calfee RC: The design of experiments and the design of curriculum. Occasional paper for Stanford Evaluation Consortium, 1974
14. Calfee RC: Assessment of independent reading skills: basic research and practical applications. *In* Contributions to Symposium on Reading. Edited by AS Reber, D Scarborough. Sponsored by the Center for Research in Cognition and Affect of the City University of New York and the Eastern Verbal Investigators League (in press)
15. Carroll JB, Freedle RO: Language Comprehension and the Acquisition of Knowledge. Washington, DC, VH Winston & Sons, 1972
16. Corsini DA: Memory: interaction of stimulus and organismic factors. Hum Dev 14:227–235, 1971
17. Desberg P, Cronnell B: An Instructional Sequence for Spelling-to-Sound Correspondences for the One- and Two-Syllable Words in Vocabularies of 6–9 Year-Olds (Technical Report no. 16). Inglewood, California, Southwest Regional Laboratory for Educational Research and Development, July 3, 1969
18. Divesta FJ: Cognitive structures and symbolic processes. Teachers College Rec 75:357–370, 1974.
19. Egeland B: Training impulsive children in the use of more efficient scanning techniques. Child Dev 45:165–171, 1974
20. Flavell JH: Developmental studies of mediated memory. *In* Advances in Child

Development and Behavior. Edited by HW Reese, LP Lipsitt. New York, Academic Press, 1970

21. Fletcher JD: Transfer From Alternative Presentations of Spelling Patterns in Initial Reading (Technical Report no. 216). Stanford, California, Institute for Mathematical Studies in the Social Sciences, 1973

22. Foorman B: A Look at Reading Diary Studies: the Art and Implications From Cognitive Developmental Theory (unpublished). Berkeley, University of California Press, 1974

23. Gagné RM: The Conditions of Learning. New York, Holt, Rinehart & Winston, 1970

24. Goodnow JJ: Rules and repertoires, rituals and tricks of the trade: social and informational aspects of cognitive and representational development. In Information Processing in Children. Edited by S Farnham-Diggory. New York, Academic Press, 1972

25. Gough PB: One second of reading. In Language by Ear and by Eye. Edited by JF Kavanagh, IG Mattingly. Cambridge, Massachusetts, MIT Press, 1972

26. Green DR, Ford MP, Flamer GB: Measurement and Piaget. New York, McGraw-Hill Book Company, 1971

27. Haber RN, Hershenson M: The Psychology of Visual Perception. New York, Holt, Rinehart & Winston, 1973

28. Hagen JW: Some thoughts on how children learn to remember. Hum Dev 14:262–271, 1971

29. Hagen JW: Strategies for remembering. In Information Processing in Children. Edited by S Farnham-Diggory. New York, Academic Press, 1972

30. Hagen JW, Jongeward RH Jr, Kail RV Jr: Cognitive perspectives on the development of memory. In Advances in Child Development and Behavior. Vol 10. Edited by H Reese. New York, Academic Press, 1975

31. Jenkins JR, Bausell RB, Jenkins LM: Comparisons of letter name and letter sound training as transfer variables. Am Educ Res J 9:75–86, 1972

32. Kagan J: Reflection-impulsivity and reading ability in primary grade children. Child Dev 36:609–628, 1965

33. Kessen W: Research design in the study of developmental problems. In Handbook of Research Methods in Child Development. New York, John Wiley & Sons, 1960

34. Kintsch W: Learning, Memory, and Conceptual Processes. New York, John Wiley & Sons, 1970

35. Landauer TK: Memory without organization: explorations of a model with random storage and undirected retrieval. Read at the Psychonomic Society, St. Louis, 1973

36. Lindamood CH, Lindamood PC: The ADD Program, Auditory Discrimination in Depth. Boston, Teaching Resources Corporation, 1969

37. Lindsay PH, Norman DA: Human Information Processing: An Introduction to Psychology. New York, Academic Press, 1972

38. Marks CB, Doctorow MJ, Wittrock MC: Word frequency and reading comprehension. J Educ Res 67:259–262, 1974

39. McNeill D: Production and perception: the view from language. Ontario J Educ Res 10:181–185, 1968

40. McNeill JD, Stone J: Note on teaching children to hear separate sounds in spoken words. J Educ Psychol 56:13–15, 1965

41. Meacham JA: The development of memory abilities in the individual and society. Hum Dev 15:205–228, 1972

42. Meichenbaum DH, Goodman J: Training impulsive children to talk to themselves: a means of developing self-control. J Abnorm Psychol 77:115–126, 1971

43. Miller GA: A psychological method to investigate verbal concepts. J Mathematical Psychol 6:169–191, 1969

44. Miller GA: Linguistic Communication: Perspectives for Research. Newark, International Reading Association, 1974

45. Miller GA, Galanter E, Pribram KH: Plans and the Structure of Behavior. New York, Holt, Rinehart & Winston, 1960

46. Murdock BB Jr: Human memory: Theory and Data. Potomac, Maryland, Lawrence Erlbaum Associates, 1974
47. Newell A: A theoretical exploration of mechanisms for coding the stimulus. In Coding Processes in Human Memory. Edited by AW Melton, E Martin. Washington, DC, VH Winston & Sons, 1972
48. Paris SG, Carter AY: Semantic and constructive aspects of sentence memory in children. Dev Psychol 1:109–113, 1973
49. Paris SG, Mahoney GJ: Cognitive integration in children's memory for sentences and pictures. Child Dev 45:633–642, 1974
50. Rumelhart DE, Lindsay PH, Norman DA: A process model for long-term memory. In Organization of Memory. Edited by E Tulving, W Donaldson. New York, Academic Press, 1972
51. Samuels SJ: Attentional processes in reading: the effects of pictures in the acquisition of reading responses. J Educ Psychol 58:337–342, 1967
52. Samuels SJ: Effects of pictures in learning to read, comprehension and attitudes. Rev Educ Res 40:397–407, 1970
53. Samuels SJ: The effect of letter-name knowledge in learning to read. Am Educ Res J 9:65–74, 1972
54. Samuels SJ, Anderson RH: Visual recognition memory, paired-associate learning, and reading achievement. J Educ Psychol 65:160–167, 1973
55. Samuels SJ, Spiroff J, Singer H: Effects of pictures and contextual conditions on learning to read. Occasional paper no. 25. Minneapolis, Minnesota, Research, Development and Demonstration Center in Education of Handicapped Children, 1974
56. Senf CM, Freundl PC: Memory and attention factors in specific learning disabilities. J Learning Disabilities 4:94–106, 1971
57. Shankweiler D, Liberman IY: Misreading: a search for causes. In Language by Ear and by Eye. Edited by JF Kavanagh, IG Mattingly, Cambridge, Massachusetts, MIT Press, 1972
58. Shiffrin RM, Atkinson RC: Storage and retrieval processes in long-term memory. Psychol Rev 76:179–193, 1969
59. Shultz TR, Charness M, Berman S: Effects of age, social class, and suggestion to cluster on free recall. Dev Psychol 8:57–61, 1973
60. Siegel, AW, Kirasic KC, Kilburg RR: Recognition memory in reflective and impulsive preschool children. Child Dev 44:651–656, 1973
61. Silberman HF: Experimental analysis of a beginning reading skill. In The Psychology of Language, Thought, and Instruction. Edited by JP DeCecco. New York, Holt, Rinehart & Winston, 1967. (Also in Programmed Instruction 3:4–8, 1964)
62. Smith F: Psycholinguistics and Reading. New York, Holt, Rinehart & Winston, 1973
63. Sternberg S: The discovery of processing stages: extensions of Donder's method. In Attention and Performance II. Edited by WG Koster. Amsterdam, North-Holland Publishing Company, 1969
64. Sullivan HJ, Okada M, Niedermeyer FC: Learning and transfer under two methods of work-attack instruction. Am Educ Res J 8:227–239, 1971
65. Tulving E, Donaldson W: Organization of Memory. New York, Academic Press, 1972
66. Venezky RL: The Structure of English Orthography. The Hague, Mouton, 1970
67. Venezky RL, Johnson D: Development of two letter-sound patterns in grades one through three. J Educ Psychol 64:109–115, 1973
68. White SH: Some general outlines of the matrix of developmental changes between five and seven years. Bull Orton Soc 20:41–57, 1970
69. Wright P: Writing to be understood. Why use sentences? Appl Ergnomics 2:207–209, 1971
70. Wright P, Reid F: Written information: some alternatives to prose for expressing the outcomes of complex contingencies. J Appl Psychol 57:160–166, 1973
71 (Addendum). Gibson, E. J. and H. Levin. The Psychology of Reading. Cambridge, Massachusetts; MIT Press, 1975.

THE ROLE OF AUDITORY PERCEPTION
IN LANGUAGE PROCESSING

Earl D. Schubert

Most audible signals are useful to the human listener; only in rare instances is sound a noxious kind of stimulus. Recently, it does seem in both the musical and industrial spheres of activity we have allowed things to get out of control on the sound dimension, hence the recently popularized concept of noise pollution; but basically man makes use of sound not only in verbal communication with his fellows but in numerous other ways. Occasionally one of my students decides our double-walled sound room seems a good place to study when it is not scheduled for subjects, only to discover that he doesn't really like that much isolation from environmental sounds. For many of us sound at appropriate levels is a welcome accompaniment of our daily activities, partly because it can also be a useful one. I have a good, and otherwise tractable, secretary who will not change to the Selectric typewriter because it doesn't sound like her old one. Many familiar tasks with mechanical devices become more difficult when auditory monitoring is impossible. Yet, as you will see, we have only the beginnings of a theory about auditory perception, and auditory processing of meaningful sounds.

A Perceptual System

The most general purpose of the auditory system is to serve as a perceptual system, i.e., as a device for contributing to the usefulness of acoustic information from the environment. Viewed only superficially, the system does its task so well that it is difficult for us to be aware of the intricacy of that chore. On the other hand, faced with the task of explaining how the system processes its input data, it is impossible not to be impressed with the sophistication of the analyzing system. If we tend to view it as essentially a simple sort of system it is enlightening to consider the history of attempts to devise a proposed partial substitute—the automatic typewriter—a gadget that would accept the spoken word and furnish the corresponding string of phonetic symbols. This desirable device was the focus of many hours of sophisticated search and many, many dollars of research funds. It still pops up full blown occasionally in science fiction but is not even close to complete operation elsewhere to my knowledge. However, one principle that was brought into sharp focus by the struggle to fabricate a phonetic typewriter is the lack of sound-for-symbol correspondence in our attempts to transcribe spoken language. We will attempt a more analytic look at this problem in talking about the perception of speech, but for now our inability to simulate speech perception, even with modern technology, serves to emphasize the complexity of auditory processing.

By now, of course, we are aware that the auditory system alone also cannot transform the acoustic speech input into a discrete string of phonemes that can be read by an independent receiving system. The auditory analyzer appears instead to operate in something like a complex interactive feedback loop involving other sensory inputs and the brain, drawing heavily on the stored results of past experience when processing complex sound sequences. But the fact that much of the auditory input is comparatively useless in the absence of interaction with other systems has certainly not simplified the study of auditory perception. Part of the problem is that even while it is cooperating in the difficult task of speech processing, it can report the identity of the speaker, something about the environment he is speaking in and a great deal about concomitantly-occurring acoustic events. Then, in addition to the considerable variety of outputs contributed to by the auditory system, our difficulty of reaching an understanding of its operation is increased by the nature of the input signal. The rapidly changing pressures that constitute sound waves present a challenge to an inherently slow recording system. Individual peripheral auditory nerves seldom fire at rates higher than 100 per second, yet frequently the detail necessary to differentiate one auditory event from another may be contained in an interval much smaller than 1/100 of a second. In fact, as we shall see, the system resolves time intervals considerably smaller than those encountered by other sensory or motor systems—intervals at least as small as a few thousandths of a second. Immediately some such operation as time multiplexing or rotation is called for; at least some comparatively elaborate scheme is required for capturing these rapidly changing patterns for subsequent perceptual analysis.

One regrettable result of this situation is that the auditory system is such an intriguing gadget simply from the engineering point of view that many of us who should be working with auditory perception have become so entangled in the solution of the engineering problem, that is, the problem of explaining how the auditory system converts the elusive and rapid changes in sound pressure into a usable perceptual code, that we have spent too little of our time attacking the problem of the auditory system as a sensory input—or better still, as part of a larger sensory system.

With the possible exception of pitch and loudness, strong systematic, perceptually-identifiable variables are singularly lacking in auditory perception. Gibson pointed out in 1966 how *long* the study of auditory sensation and perception has been fettered by reluctance to go beyond pitch, loudness and duration in systematizing responses to sound. But though Gibson furnishes an excellent discussion of auditory perception, he doesn't really advance us very far toward finding more suitable systematic variables in sound patterns that might be relevant to perception; though he clearly makes a start in the right direction. Gibson says in *The Senses Considered as Perceptual Systems:*

> Meaningful sounds vary in much more elaborate ways than merely in pitch, loudness and duration. Instead of simple duration, they vary in abruptness of beginning and ending, in repetitiveness, in rate, in regularity of rate, or rhythm, and in other subtleties of sequence. Instead of simple pitch, they vary in timbre or tone quality, in combinations of tone quality, in vowel quality, in approximation to noise, in noise quality, and in changes of all these in time. Instead of simple loudness, they vary in direction of change of loudness, the rate of change in loudness and the rate of change of change. In meaningful sounds, these variables can be combined to yield higher-order variables of staggering complexity.[28]

Many of us who find ourselves working in auditory engineering rather than in auditory perception share this disenchantment with such preoccupation with pitch, loudness and duration. It is certainly true that too much of older psychoacoustics was concerned with the implication of the basic ability of the ear (or auditory system) to distinguish under laboratory conditions the smallest possible difference in the intensity of two auditory signals that could reliably be detected as a loudness change and the smallest change in frequency that could be distinguished as a change in pitch. When viewed more closely, studies of loudness and pitch have not contributed much to a body of knowledge about auditory perception. Particularly, judgments of actual loudness figure only weakly in auditory perception, in fact most of us are aware that one of the necessary tasks of the auditory system is to learn to recognize auditory signals irrespective of large changes in loudness. Loudness changes *are* specifically involved in prosodic accents in speech, but even here they are not necessary to the understanding of speech and not absolutely vital for its naturalness; duration changes serve at least part of that function. This statement about the trivial contribution of loudness, *per se,* should not be interpreted as diminishing the importance in audition of rapid changes in intensity, too rapid to permit perceptual judgments of loudness change. In the auditory literature considerable confusion between these two concepts exists. We are becoming increasingly aware that rapidly changing intensity patterns may be the most important information-bearing elements in audition.

In like manner, tonal pitch, which is central to the perception of music, is at best a secondary factor in the perception of speech and the identification of environmental sound sources; but frequency sequences not responded to as pitch patterns may be quite significant.

There are, of course, a few other terms that serve as descriptors in our attempts to communicate about sound and sound perception. Sound quality has become a multidimensional omnibus term that we will deal with briefly later on. Tonal *vs* atonal is a considerably more functional distinction; consonance/dissonance lends itself to some experimental systematization; but these are essentially weak variables in dynamic auditory perception. If one runs laboratory experiments on complex sounds these terms seldom appear spontaneously; in fact, one finds it difficult to elicit universally acceptable descriptions from subjects, even though the differences being explored may be consistently heard by all subjects.

In addition, though there is a highly sophisticated and very useful body of literature on how the auditory system detects a signal in the presence of noise, and a wealth of material on the interference of simultaneous signals, that aspect of the literature is much more pertinent to understanding the intrinsic operation of the system—what I have called the engineering of the auditory system—than it is to generating principles widely applicable in auditory perception.

Gibson's larger point in his discussion of auditory perception is that the perceiving system extracts from the waveform information about specific relevant events in the environment. This view does run parallel to the kinds of response most frequently elicited from listeners in laboratory experiments. They usually offer some sort of similarity identification. Something has a clarinet quality, a flute-like character, a snap or a pop, a click or a thud, a sound like whining, it is reminiscent of wind in the trees, etc. In everyday listening, the listener doesn't appear to apply generic descriptive labels to organize his rather large repertoire of familiar sounds: hence such labels aren't available to him when he is asked to characterize a new auditory item. Helmholtz[35] may have started the trend when he used the term "nasality" to describe the quality of the clarinet. If there is a distinctive-features pattern or a minimum-dimensions model suitable for nonverbal auditory perception, it does not materialize in the descriptive language of the listener.

Source Identification

Gibson points out that "the sounds of rubbing, scraping, rolling and brushing, for example, are distinctive acoustically and are distinguished phenomenally." He might well have added that such sound sources as dogs, birds, doors and drums are quickly identified. The point is that, for a perceptual system, it is the identification of objects and events that is its proper function. Whatever data reduction scheme the system employs, it must contribute to that function. Identification of qualities and attributes may well be part of its data reduction scheme, but so far, for the auditory system, the dimensions we impose seem to be a source of comfort to us as students of the system rather than something inherently useful to the system itself.

This situation harks back to the seemingly strong statement of Bruner[10] in 1957 that perception *is* categorization. Why do I apply this especially to the auditory system? My concern is that in studying the system we have tended to give too little weight to the maxim stating that for the auditory system the primary assignment is to inform the organism about sound in its environment; that, in turn, the most important datum is the identification of a sound source and the recognition of the behavior of the identified source.

Over twenty years ago, Huggins[39] attempted to systematize this view by suggesting that when the sound wave from a source reaches the auditory system, the minimum information stored for identification is the characteristic resonant frequencies and damping rates of the sound source. Huggins called this principle the System Function Theory of sound perception. The reason for that particular title was that Huggins wanted to employ a specific mathematical model to demonstrate that the peripheral auditory system was capable of extracting the appropriate information. That aspect need not concern us here. For the student of perception the principle is more directly suggested by calling it the Source Identification Theory of auditory perception; with the understanding that we include recognition of source behavior also. Even on an intuitive basis it is roughly apparent that the vibratory behavior of a natural sound source will correlate with some invariant identifying physical properties: size, construction, etc.

Suppose you explore this just superficially with your own auditory imagery by imagining that you experience, or perceive, the following sound-oriented events:

> the kicking of a tin can
> the dropping of a dish
> laughter
> a door closing
> hammering
> footsteps

In each of these familiar instances what happened is identified unmistakably, but what physical clue one responds to primarily is difficult to describe in any abstract generic terms that tend to organize auditory perception. Obviously the signals received do contain information about the details of the source of the occurrence: Was the can large or small; of heavy or light construction; was it in contact with a hard surface like concrete, or an absorbent one like earth or grass? Did the dish shatter or bounce? Each of these properties or conditions has a predictable effect on the specific acoustic output of—and therefore the auditory input from—such natural sources.

You might be persuaded of the efficacy of this principle of data reduction by the fact that you can auditorize each of these events in the absence of the physical stimulus, but if so, you did not do so in the abstract. A different specific image is needed for each property that changes. Huggins' principle states that we store the characteristic resonant frequencies and damping ratios of the source in order to identify that source, but this is really not complete. We also create, or have created, larger general categories. We need to note, however, that the inductions involved in creating larger categories are not possible, or at least in practice they are not accomplished, without the cooperation of other senses, notably the visual system. How do I learn initially that the sound of a large dish shattering is similar but also differs in certain ways which one can generalize from the same happening with a smaller dish? For most of its utility as a source of information about environmental sounds, the ear depends heavily on concomitant information through the eye. Faced with a previously unheard sound, the auditory system alone is not at all skillful in deducing the properties and behavior of the source. Though certain congenitally blind listeners provide striking evidence that such auditory skills can be developed, normally-sighted listeners routinely take the easy way—they explore the properties of the source with the rest of the perceptual system—visual, tactile, etc. Perhaps we should expect, then, since the auditory system seldom works alone, that there are no intrinsic organizing principles of auditory perception. Mostly cross-modal perceptions occur and become functional through experience.

We have been emphasizing environmental sounds. Two other classes of sounds ought to be mentioned at this point: The sounds of speech and the sounds of music. They differ from the kind of environmental sounds just considered in that, indirectly at least, they have been gradually tailored to the capabilities of the auditory system. They are similar, however, in the fact that with some exceptions the ear associates each of them with a particular source. This has some useful implications for our perception of speech.

Artificial Sources

There is, in addition, a class of sounds produced mostly in auditory laboratories, with which the listener does not readily associate a familiar source. Moreover, the differences we ask the subject to distinguish in these sounds are more nearly abstract than they are source-related. This class—laboratory sounds—has had a distinct influence on my willingness to subscribe to the Source Identification principle as the most firmly established unifying principle of auditory perception; specifically, it is the difficulty of handling these non-source sounds perceptually. To take an extreme case, one of our tasks in the laboratory for a couple of years has been to explore the "learning" of a list of abstract sounds. One can think of the process as much like the memorizing of a list of nonsense syllables, except that these syllables are short bursts of random noise, not recognizable speech units. They can be differentiated from one another on an A/B comparison but they resist extrinsic association with any familiar sources. They are distinctly laboratory sounds. They also resist memorization, as we have discovered after hundreds of training and testing trials. I take this as additional proof that the auditory system does not work well alone. The job is not impossible—it is just much more difficult than with extrinsically identifiable sounds. Almost perversely, if subjects are exposed to such sounds repeatedly for other purposes, recognition of specific sounds begins to have its influence. Pfafflin and Matthews [63] encountered this latter problem: so they investigated the identification of noise bursts by encouraging subjects to attach numerical labels to twelve different 100-millisecond (msec) bursts. Some of the noises were reliably identified after 96 to 168 trials per stimulus; some of the others remained almost at the guessing-performance level.

Now learning twelve environmental, source-associated sounds to perfection should take far fewer trials than that. The authors report that the task was a difficult one. They also report that even after applying Shepard's multidimensional scaling program, the error matrix yielded no straightforward interpretation, which I interpret to mean the errors were not explainable on any set of identifiable acoustic or auditory dimensions. Using a greater variety of signals, Webster, Woodhead and Carpenter[82] asked subjects to assign the appropriate numerical label to each of nine line spectrum sounds which they called meaningless buzzes. After four forty-minute sessions subjects were able to identify the nine sounds with about 33 percent accuracy. Their better subjects noted on their cue cards that three of the sounds were like fog horns, two were like car horns; so although perhaps these were meaningless sounds a certain amount of source categorization was apparently being used as an aid. And, of course, it is of interest to me, in promoting the Source Identification principle, that it was the more successful subjects who reported using this mnemonic device.

Related to this notion of identification of sound sources is the concept of a continuum of sounds ranging from actual speech through speech-like to definitely non-speech sounds. House et al.,[37] in their experiment on the learning of speech-like sounds, found no experimental evidence for a corresponding response continuum. They found rather that categorization was the typical operation for identification of speech sounds; ordering along the classical dimensions of loudness, pitch and duration was the rule for their non-linguistic sounds; and generally poor performance held for their speech-like—but non-speech—sounds. My prediction is that the outcome would be the same if they had dealt with source and non-source classes of about equal physical complexity rather than linguistic and non-linguistic classes. In any event, this kind of evidence tends to emphasize the rule that sounds characterized by temporal and spectral complexity but no intrinsic source association are usually learned only with great difficulty; and that, possibly even more than any other sensory input, the auditory system functions mostly as part of a larger perceptual system comprising also the visual, haptic and proprioceptive inputs.

Recognition of Natural Sources

Actually, endorsing the principle of Source Identification as the organizing rule of non-linguistic auditory perception does not mean forsaking any search for other organizing rules. It means only that whatever principles we do invoke must not be at variance with the primary purpose of the perceptual system. For instance, frequency is one physical dimension we know the ear is admirably suited to exploit. The peripheral ear accomplishes at least a rough spectral or frequency analysis of complex signals. This is the recently-emphasized critical-band concept stemming from mounting evidence that one pervading function of the auditory analyzer is to act as a bank of filters about one-third octave in width. If we apply the filter model, it soon becomes apparent that these are much more versatile filters than we have available in the laboratory; but at least for steady-state complex tones—tones like sustained vowel sounds or typical musical tones—the nature of the ear's spectral analysis is well documented. On the surface, this makes it appear that spectral envelope, in this case the pattern of the relative outputs of these omnipresent filters, would be a most likely auditory clue. Classically, in fact, spectral envelope—the relative strengths of the harmonic partials of a complex tone— has been assumed to be the physical correlate of sound quality or timbre. Is spectral envelope a clue that remains perceptually invariant with changes in fundamental frequency? Naively one might suppose this is the identifying characteristic of a musical instrument, i.e., that, since the sound of the trumpet remains the sound of the trumpet as it moves up and down the scale, the relative strengths of the harmonics remain the same over a range of pitches. This is not true of the trumpet, nor of musical instruments in general; instead the formant or fixed resonance region type of characteristic seems to be the rule.[14,15] However, if the source wave remains relatively constant, then both formant influence and constant spectrum characteristics are present in the series of tones, and a sophisticated analyzer like the auditory system could register both and make perceptual use of them. To decide whether constant spectral envelope is one of the unifying perceptual characteristics; i.e., whether the system can recognize invariant spectrum shape, we fed the listener a pair of complex tones with the second one higher than the first by some musical step.[68] Sometimes the waveform was the same for the second tone; sometimes it changed. The subject's chore was to say whether for the second tone—differing in pitch—the quality was the same or different. The result was that when the fundamental frequency was changed by more than three semitones, listeners could not tell whether the waveform had also changed. At least for unfamiliar waveforms, that kind of constant spectral envelope does not furnish a perceptual clue that stays constant with any change greater than a musical major third in fundamental frequency. (That change co-incidentally is about the ratio corresponding to the width of a critical band.) Of course, these are tones without a stable formant region. The question of constancy of tone quality with fixed formants appears to be answered empirically—at least for familiar tones—by the spectra of musical instruments.[76]

However, it is an oversimplification to assert that either the constancy of spectral envelope or the presence of one or more constant formant regions is sufficient to identify a large number of familiar sounds.

One other thing we know about these sounds with no clue but spectral envelope or fixed formant regions (a fact which applies to such familiar steady-state complex sounds as sustained vowels and familiar musical tones) is that they are no longer reliably identifiable when starting and ending characteristics are removed. This has been demonstrated in a number of formal experiments,[3,48,49,66] and I am certain it has been shown in any number of classroom demonstrations. Now the useful meaning of this is not that those steady-state sounds are no longer auditorily differentiable, because they are. What is demonstrated is that the *label* that has been applied to those sounds in previous experience has been reliable, not because of their steady-state spectrum, or steady-state sound quality alone, but rather because of some characteristic rapid temporal variation during their onset and offset. That such rapid transient variations are present, particularly during the build-up of sounds produced by everyday sources, is quite apparent when we view them with the appropriate analyzer. The question, then, is the degree to which the ear is capable of registering these transients and what kind of perceptual differentiations are dependent on their sensory preservation.

The ability of the auditory system to make differentiations on the basis of rapid timing patterns has been the focus of auditory research during the past decade and we now know it is central to the processing of speech sounds, environmental sounds and even the seemingly slower sounds of music. Our primary interest is to understand the role of auditory perception in the processing of speech sounds. A closer look at that problem will bring us back to the topic of the temporal resolution of the auditory system.

Processing of Speech Sounds

The sounds of speech stand in somewhat different relation to the auditory system, of course, than do other environmental sounds as a class. Whether the organism can successfully classify and respond appropriately to sounds in the environment has had some bearing on the probability of the organism's survival, but there is a much closer relation between the sounds of speech and the capabilities of the auditory system. Sound changes not differentiable by the auditory system supposedly would not be functional in the spoken language; sound contrasts once functional in the language but consistently masked by environmental sound would presumably not persist. In this sense speech sounds are more nearly the peculiar province of the auditory system than is the case for environmental sounds. One salient difference is that, instead of performing a role distinctly subservient to the visual system, in the case of speech sounds the auditory system becomes the prime processor. In spite of this situation, there is not a large overlap in the literature of audition and that of speech perception. Auditory workers have been occupied with signals much simpler than speech sounds, and it has been only recently with the ready availability of synthetic speech sounds that systematic probing of the auditory processing of speech signals has begun. In the current body of knowledge on speech perception, three descriptive models of different but intersecting aspects of speech processing make good vehicles for ascertaining how the auditory system contributes to the perception of speech. They are, first of all, speech analysis by feature detection; secondly, the so-called motor theory of speech perception, and last, the analysis-by-synthesis model.

Recognition by Feature Pattern

As we have already noted, the complexity of speech perception became dramatically apparent with the attempt at automatic speech recognition. One side effect of the failure of automatic speech recognition was a deep-seated disenchantment with the central role assigned to the phoneme in the process of speech perception. The phoneme, generated initially through years of analyses by the auditory systems of expert phoneticians, did present a deceptively simple picture of the way in which the auditory system reconstructs concatenations of individual sounds into intelligible speech. The efforts at automatic recognition, along with the frustrating ambiguity of "visible speech" spectrograms showed unmistakably that speech perception by the auditory system is only in part a phoneme-by-phoneme process.

But even though we now know phoneme recognition fails to account for the complete process of speech perception, it is also apparent that it is an inherent part of the process. Consequently, one very fruitful area of intersection between phonetic theory and speech perception is the study of feature recognition. Feature recognition and feature extraction have been part of the data reduction scheme in general perception for years. In audition in general, as might be predicted from the "servile" nature of the auditory system, the search for pervading features beyond the relatively static loudness, pitch and duration has not been at all rewarding.[5,73]

In speech perception, however, distinctive feature models have now generated a comparative abundance of experimental work. Speech analysis through feature recognition begins with a treatise by Jakobson, Fant, and Halle.[40] A fairly recent listing of the features that according to the model serve to differentiate the sounds of English is shown in Table 1, from Chomsky and Halle.[13]

Even though the features are cast in a binary frame, most of the labels will be recognized to denote dimensions that could be considered to vary continuously—or at least to take more than the two values. The authors point out that this binary scheme is most convenient for phonemic classification, but for closer phonetic distinctions it would be possible to assign coefficients rather than settle for dichotomies. However, the simplest view of the operation of analysis-by-feature-detection would be a matrix of features by sounds with each sound (row) showing a different configuration of features present vs features absent.

Fant[25] has also fashioned a dictionary of features which should serve to classify speech sounds. He lists a total of twenty-one features, three of them vocal source features, seven vocal resonator features and eleven which he calls "segment pattern features," these latter having to do with place of articula-

Table 1

Feature	Description
CORONAL -	blade of the tongue raised from neutral
ANTERIOR -	constriction in front of palato-alveolar region
HIGH LOW BACK } -	placement of the body of the tongue
VOCALIC -	constriction does not exceed smallest vowel constriction folds in position for voicing
CONSONANTAL -	radical obstruction in midsaggital region
ROUNDED -	refers to lip orifice
TENSE -	configuration held in fixed position removed from neutral
VOICED -	folds close enough to vibrate when air flows
CONTINUANT -	air flow through the mouth is not blocked
NASAL -	velum lowered
STRIDENT -	noisiness contributed by turbulence of air stream

tion. My decision to give some greater priority to the scheme shown here springs from the much greater weight accorded the perceptual process in arriving at that features list, and the fact that the list is almost completely oriented toward articulatory dimensions. The reason for this latter preference will become clearer in a moment. How valid the feature orientation is must be tested by much more experimental work. Wang and Bilger[79] have expressed some doubts about the perceptual reality of the features; because they have shown that more than one small set of features can account for a large portion of the variance in an error matrix; but I believe their quarrel is really with the large number of interrelated features as opposed to the much smaller number of relatively independent ones it should require to account for the sounds of one language. This seems to me a legitimate complaint, though one can protest in turn that natural systems seldom work in an efficient manner, since the risk of error goes up with the complexity of the task.

Eventually, any list of identification features must be rated on how successfully perception can be tied to each feature extraction, but the more we learn of the nature of speech perception the less promising is the technique of isolating phonemes, or the subphonemic isolation of features in almost atomistic fashion. The reasoning behind this pronouncement will emerge more clearly as we explore further the interwoven nature of the three models of speech perception. But first we should develop further the reason for preferring articulatory features over acoustic ones for differentiating the sounds of speech perceptually.

Recognition of Speech Source Behavior

Over 20 years ago, the idea came independently from two sources that successful speech perception by the individual depended strongly on his knowledge of speech production. It is a fairly logical corollary of the principle of Source Identification and Source Behavior as the organizing rule of auditory perception. In 1950, in connection with his System Function Theory of Hearing, from which I have borrowed the Source Identification principle, Huggins asserted that "From an operational point of view, it seems altogether possible that the 'gestures' of the speaker's mouth are reconstructed within the ear and auditory pathways of the listener's brain. . . . "[38] At about the same time Lawrence[44] was perfecting a speech synthesizer which he presented in 1952. Lawrence's speech synthesizer was designed with only a few articulatorily-derived controls, and in explaining why this was feasible Lawrence remarked, "The interpretation of speech proceeds by inference. We hear a certain sound which we identify as speech and assume that it is made by a vocal mechanism similar to that which we use ourselves. We can then infer which of a small number of possible causes were operative to produce the sound heard at a given moment." And further: "The system function gives information relating to the mouth positions, and it is reasonable to suppose that the listener makes these distinctions by inferring, unconsciously, the mouth positions that could have produced the sounds he hears."[44]

This same general idea, put rather clearly, but only in germinal form by both Huggins and Lawrence, has been developed much more rigorously and has been tested experimentally in ingenious ways by the group at Haskins Laboratories. Their invaluable contribution has been to demonstrate conclusively that the sound-to-phoneme correspondence is not usefully viewed as a simple substitution, but rather should be considered a complex code, for which the receiver must have available a decoding dictionary containing rules for deciphering the message, and that such a stored dictionary must be available at more than one of the levels from phoneme to sentence. Some of our own work on Speech Discrimination Testing indicates that initial and final sounds, designated by the same phoneme, behave no more similarly than any other pair of sounds chosen at random; that is, their inter-item correlation on such tests is no higher than the average between other pairs.[69]

The availability of such a stored dictionary at the articulatory level appears on first glance to take a great load off the auditory system. Whether it really does, and whether the problem should be transferred from the auditory to the neuro-motor domain are questions that may be answered only by the appropriate experiments, but the existence of such questions need not vitiate the general usefulness of the principle. As I have suggested before, it is convincingly congruent with other supporting evidence for the Source Identification principle of auditory perception.

Regarding the degree of dominance of the auditory system in the process of speech perception, there is ample evidence, as I asserted earlier, that the auditory system is initially heavily dependent on other sensory inputs for assigning perceptual meaning to acoustic events, but, once this association has been made, retrieval may certainly be cued by the auditory system unassisted. Given enough experience, the auditory system is really quite an adequate performer. Miller and Tanis[56] set up an experiment to compare recognition of printed words, spoken words and familiar sounds. Their results show that the correct recognition scores were 84 percent for written words, 75 percent for spoken words and 69 percent for familiar sounds. In spite of a higher score for visual presentation, I interpret this result as a healthy endorsement of non-verbal acoustic memory considering the handicap necessarily imposed by acoustic presentation of such items. Also related to the non-linguistic storage capability of the system, Pollack, Pickett and Sumby[64] estimated their subjects could recognize 65 familiar voices, but this is admittedly restricted by the nature of the sample available. Most of us who are even marginally sociable can recognize a far greater number of familiar voices than can be presented in a practical experiment. Auditory recall in the absence of other extrinsic sensory input is difficult to experiment on, yet sufficiently well documented for us to question the need for a motor theory rather than a Source Identification theory. Certainly ample evidence has been amassed for the fact that there is a primarily acoustic component in the storage of verbal material. It is much more difficult to document the conclusion that this is *ipso facto* proof that it does not also reside in other domains, though on occasion this has been the inference drawn (see Wickelgren's discussion).[83]

But to return to the motor theory of speech perception: I would prefer to call it the Articulator Theory, since under that label it becomes more apparent that we are still ascribing to the auditory system primarily the ability to recognize the acoustic patterns resulting from the behavior of a familiar sound source. In that guise the theory is part of a more general one.

Development of Speech Perception

However, one huge difficulty with this otherwise attractive theory that speech perception is greatly aided by intimage knowledge of the behavior of the source is that it sorely magnifies the already baffling problem of how the child learns speech perception in the first place. The previously acceptable—or at least accepted—picture was that he proceeded from babbling sounds, an inherently pleasurable activity, to the accidental production and rewarded selection of linguistically useful sounds, then on to sound sequences and eventually spoken language. Lately, this view is more apt to lead to argument than agreement.[7,41,53,54,67] The evidence seems to be mounting that there is no reason to believe the child's motor speech production ever leads his language acquisition, in fact, quite the opposite appears to be the case. McNeill,[52] I believe, was the first to point out that the one-word utterances of the two-year-old signify the same underlying thought (deep structure if you like) that will later produce a complete conventional sentence. For example, it may be difficult to demonstrate rigorously, but certainly observation indicates that in some instances when the child points to the tricycle and says "Donald" the essence of that communication "That is Donald's tricycle" has previously been conveyed to the child verbally rather than solely through visual association of Donald and the object. Perception has definitely outstripped production. We must add to this the finding of Shipley, Smith and Gleitman[71] that children who are in the "telegraphic" stage of language production respond to linguistically well-formed commands more readily than they respond to telegraphic commands. Again, perception has outstripped production. The problem of ever understanding how speech perception evolves initially if it depends on the perceiver being a practiced producer is further exacerbated by the contention of Lieberman and his associates[47] that for some undetermined time after birth the articulatory mechanism of the child does not assume a shape suitable for forming human speech sounds. The inescapable conclusion is that speech perception must be learned without the benefit of first-hand knowledge of the role of the articulators in speech production. For the hard-shell empiricist who would still like to embrace the articulator theory of speech perception this looks like Scylla and Charybdis. If there is a safe channel between the two it is not immediately apparent.

If we agree to sidestep that controversy for the moment and recall that our major concern is the auditory system's speech-perceiving capability no matter what its genesis, then the work of Eimas, Siqueland, Jusczyk and Vigorito[24] and Cutting and Eimas[19] is most enlightening. Their results suggest that the infant auditory system exhibits evidence of the same boundary phenomena that influence adult categorical consonant perception. The technique is the one used by Siqueland and DeLucia.[73] The sucking response of the infant is used to trigger a sensory stimulus which in turn leads to a stronger and more frequent sucking response; and for some minutes the infant will sustain his own sensory stimulation by his sucking response. Specifically, in the work of interest here the infant's sucking response is used to trigger audible synthetic speech syllables—the sucking response produces the sound of the syllable about once per second for the infant. If the syllable remains the same over several minutes, the typical infant response is an intial increase in sucking rate and strength followed by what looks like an adaptation-curve decrease in sucking rate over as much as 6 to 8 minutes. Cutting and Eimas[19] used some pairs of syllables which are labeled as different sounds by adult listeners and some pairs that differ by the same physically measured amount, but are not heard by adults as different sounds. In the frame of categorical perception, these would be inter- and intra-category pairs respectively. Now the salient point is that the infant's sucking response adapts to an intra-category difference at about the same rate it adapts to an unchanged stimulus, but it responds to a between-category difference of the same physical size as though the stimulus has been changed. This closely resembles the responses of adult listeners to the same pairs of synthetic speech sounds.

Furthermore, if the formant-glide parts of these synthetic syllables are removed and used as the stimuli for a similar study, the infant responses again resemble those of the adult in that now both the between category and the within category are responded to as different when the rest of the acoustic signal is not simultaneously present.

Cutting and Eimas[19] take this as evidence for innate speech-sound discriminators. The empiricist view would be that these auditory characteristics, which later determine where we optimally choose our manageable articulated distinctions, are already in evidence at an astonishingly early age. Actually the larger principle is that an organism can aspire to evolve an elaborate communication system only to the degree that it can produce differentiable signals in the same range that its own sensory system can preserve the difference—a necessary, but not necessarily sufficient, condition. The question raised is whether the results reported by Cutting and Eimas[19] are necessarily unusual from an auditory point of view. There are perceptual discontinuities along the time-interval continuum, and only further experimentation will tell whether they are learned, and whether heightened differential sensitivity occurs at the boundaries. It is also quite generally true that parts of familiar sound complexes removed from their total context lead to different perceptual responses. What is astonishing is the demonstration that infants are already auditorily equipped to make the distinctions involved. Whether the infants were actually responding to speech sounds takes us back to an ancient problem in psychology about whether you and I really have the same sensation when we respond in the same way to the same physical stimulus. But the more practical question is whether these are speech perception phenomena or general auditory phenomena. Do they exist elsewhere in audition? Only a few relevant data are available.

Some generality is suggested when categorical behavior for non-speech sounds is reported by Cutting and Rosner[20] for subjects listening to systematically varied rise times of pure tones and sawtooth tones. On the slow-rise-time side of the category boundary the sounds sounded "bowed," and on the faster end of the continuum they sounded "plucked"; discrimination was heightened at the boundary. A similar phenomenon has been observed by workers with synthesized imitations of musical instruments who note that on gradually changing attack characteristics leaving the waveform unchanged one familiar instrument will quite suddenly shift to the sound of another, perhaps even of a different musical family. [14,31] Quite possibly certain time intervals in auditory processing behave as perceptual boundaries and thus make ideal points along a physical time-interval continuum to emphasize categorical differences in the sounds of speech, music, and conceivably in the less-explored auditory domain of environmental sounds. There does seem to be something special about timing patterns in speech production, as shown by the work of Eguchi and Hirsh[23] on variability in the speech production of children. They showed that in repetitions of the same short sentence, a given child's productions varied comparatively widely both in formant placement and in timing of consonantal blends. As the measurements were taken on older and older children, the variability decreased more dramatically for timing pattern than for formant placement. The course of the decrease in variability of formant placement is shown in Fig. 1a. The measurements were taken on two sentences: "He has a blue pen" and "I am tall." For an increase in the consistency of timing production, however, the sequence is as shown in Fig. 1b. Variability between repetitions was not appreciably greater than it is for the adult speaker when the children reached the age of about 8 years. It might be pertinent here that boundary effects have been shown for one of these variables, but not the other. In any event it is apparent that the elimination of variation in timing aspects, in repetition of the same phrase, is much more rapid than for formant placement.

Categorical perception is the rule along the fundamental frequency or the spectral placement continuum, but to my knowledge boundary effects have not been shown. In our culture, music has been organized in discrete steps for centuries. Until recently, the continuous glide was a fairly rare embellishment. And for most of our lifetime the tuning of these steps has been restricted to specific points anchored at A=440. Yet there is no evidence that musical pitch discrimination exhibits the boundary phenomenon that may permeate the time-pattern performance of the auditory system. This observation, combined with the boundary behavior exhibited by the infant subjects of Cutting and Eimas,[19] seems to inveigh against the view that category boundaries are learned. Only a thorough exploration of the perceptual responses to time intervals similarly imbedded in environmental sound will tell whether they are the peculiar province of speech-sound perception and eventually, possibly, whether they are earmarked (?) prenatally for phonemic feature discrimination. So, once again, as with the reliable identification of familiar sounds, the question seems to center on the kind of perceptual response the auditory system makes to very rapid timing patterns.

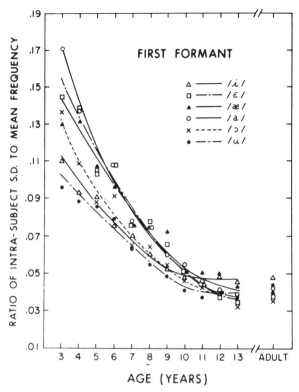

Figure 1. Variability in repeated productions of the same phrase as a function of age, for (a) formant frequency and (b) sound-sequence timing. (From Eguchi and Hirsh 1969)

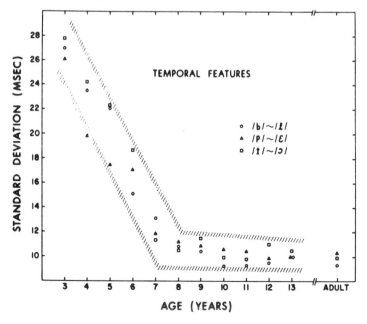

115

Auditory Perception of Patterns

In general, our realization of the importance of timing information to the auditory system has been rapidly growing in the last decade.[30] Because the ear can integrate sound energy over about a fifth of a second to make a faint sound more detectable in noise and because over about this same time an audible sound of constant amplitude gets louder as its duration increases, this rather long period (200 msec) has been referred to as the time constant of the ear. Now we know that the limit of time resolution of the auditory system is nearer to a period of a few thousandths of a second. This has been shown to be true for several kinds of signals. Gescheider[27] reported in 1966 that the sound of two clicks was perceptually different from the sound of one click when the separation between clicks was about 1.6 msec. His subjects were instructed to report when the sound of the pair became discernibly "rougher" than the sound of one click, so the particular response criterion may seem a little arbitrary. Ronken[65] was able to use a little tidier response and a more uniquely identifiable clue. Ronken investigated possibly the simplest pattern for temporal resolution, using a pair of closely-spaced clicks, one of which was weaker than the other. On a given trial Ronken's subjects heard two presentations of this click pair, and on the second presentation a strong-weak succession might either be kept the same or be reversed. In this way the energy spectrum of the compared signals is kept exactly the same—only the time pattern is changed. His subjects maintained a 75 percent correct Same/Different performance when the click spacing was between 1 and 2 msec. Even for tonal signals, the limits of temporal resolution fall into this same, roughly 2 msec, range. Patterson and Green[62] varied the time of onset of two very short tone bursts and found their subjects could hear a difference, dependent on which tone started first, when the time difference between onsets was only 1.5 msec. For signals of a different shape, Patterson and Green took advantage of the fact that signals may be constructed that have a different waveform but have precisely the same energy spectrum and the same duration. When such signals were only 2.5 msec long, their subjects could differentiate pairs of these signals at 75 percent correct in a 2AFC task; thus they must have been resolving time intervals of 2.5 msec or less.

More recently, Efron[22] demonstrated essentially the same phenomenon with very brief tonal stimuli having both onset and offset disparity. Efron's conclusion is sensibly the same: Subjects can readily distinguish a reversal of temporal order when the temporal onset and offset discrepancies are only 2 msec. Efron's statement that this is "unequivocally below the threshold for temporal order judgments" is very misleading. As has been amply demonstrated, the auditory system reliably hears the difference between the two orders. The only remaining step, then, is to identify which of the two differentiable sounds denotes one order and which the other. It is true that working without feedback, the system has only a 0.5 chance of being correct, but a system working without feedback is seldom a useful part of an adaptive perceptual system; and, as we have seen, this is especially applicable to the auditory system. It makes no sense, then, to say that resolvable differences are below the threshold of the system. The fact that the nature of the auditory percept changes when the judgments are made in the absence of any useful context is mostly of interest in studying the limits of the system; by itself it tells us only indirectly about the operation of the auditory analyzer as part of a larger perceptual system. Actually the fact that the auditory system can make such discriminations but can assign perceptually useful meaning to them only with cooperation of the other senses has some profound implications for the kind of models that should be deemed acceptable for auditory perception.

Whenever one talks about auditory perception of order, it is worth noting that ability to decipher the order of sound patterns is strongly dependent on the nature of the sounds presented. The Hirsh[36] study of the temporal order of different auditory signals is well known. Hirsh found that about a 17 to 20 msec difference in onset time was required for a correct perception of order.

But we get an entirely different estimate if we present a more complex auditory temporal pattern as shown by Warren et al.[80] They presented their subjects with various orders of hisses, buzzes and tones, and discovered that correct identification of the order of these signal patterns required a starting-time difference of nearly three-quarters of a second for naive listeners, and almost a third of a second for practiced listeners. Obviously there is something different about these results in a system which can resolve intervals of a few milliseconds. Some clarification comes from a part of the study by Patterson and Green[62] (see their Appendix C) in which the experimenters made a direct comparison of their 10-msec tonal signals and the Hirsh tonal signals which were a half-second long. You will recall that the order of the Patterson and Green short signals could be determined when the starting separation was only about 1.5 msec. But for the long Hirsh signals they too got the Hirsh value of nearly 20 msec before the order could be reliably determined. Apparently when auditory temporal order results are quoted the signals and method ought to be specified. Similar signal-dependent disparities in results are reported by Broadbent and Ladefoged.[8]

There is little reason to doubt, then, that the auditory system registers a difference even when the physical waveform difference is encompassed within an interval as small as one or 2 msec. What is the importance of this finding for auditory perception? It must be vital to an auditory operation that for the moment I will call "waveform storage" for reasons that I hope will become clear. The ear behaves as though it stores a segment of the sound waveform in an operation that must be one of the earliest steps in auditory processing—necessarily peripheral to the "echoic" storage of Neisser[59] or the "precategorical" storage of Crowder and Morton.[18] The closest sensory analogue would be the iconic storage of the eye, but there is no way of achieving truly iconic storage of the evanescent time pattern of an essentially aperiodic sound wave. Nevertheless, the auditory system behaves as though something like the raw waveform were available for a period of something like 20 msec after its occurrence, and if this is the first level of storage in the system it is of considerable import. Let me cite the evidence for its existence.

The most understandable and convincing evidence takes the form of the suppression of an echo perception when a waveform follows itself within a short time at the input to the auditory system. If the ear can resolve time interval differences of the order of a few msec as we have just seen, then failure to hear two sound images (an echo) when the same waveform occurs tens of milliseconds later must be attributed to a suppression of the second one or at least to a fusing of it with the first. Classically, Haas[34] receives credit for exploring the effects of the single echo. He demonstrated that if the repeated waveform is separated from the original by less than 30 msec it is not apt to be heard as a separate image. Even more dramatic, and pertinent to the same point is Cherry's demonstration[12] that if one listens through phones and puts the same speech wave into the two ears but with the waveform in one ear lagging behind the other by some interval, say, under the control of the experimenter, the system will report a single image at the leading ear until the waveform interval between ears is about 20 msec at which time an interaural echo will be heard. Now from these two studies and the fact that a repeated click waveform breaks up into two images either monaurally or binaurally when the time separation is only about two milliseconds, one might conclude that the Cherry and the Haas results have to do with the fact that their signals were speech, and that therefore we are not dealing with anything resembling waveform storage at all. However, Blodgett, Jeffress, and Wilbanks[6] put a meaningless waveform—namely a random noise—in the two ears, and got essentially the same result as Cherry: A noise image only at the leading ear until the interaural time separation was about 17 msec. How does a system which can recognize differences in waveform within intervals of a few milliseconds present only a single image when the same waveform recurs separated by 20 msec or more? It does so, of course, by recognizing that that same sequence has just occurred. I emphasize this because I believe at all levels this delayed processing is characteristic of the auditory system even though it is capable of reacting to extremely rapid time patterns; and that it is the same sort of mechanism that analyzes characteristic transient onset and decay patterns and makes Source Identification possible. Instrumentation has now reached the point where we can attempt to ascertain how this storage capability is affected when the following waveform is not an exact copy of the original but differs in some selected ways. Among other things this should tell us whether the "waveform storage" label is at all reasonable.

Actually this period of roughly 20 msec does appear to have some basic connotation in auditory processing. Not only does it appear in the determination of order in dissociated pairs of long signals as in the Hirsh study; it is also about the period of the lower limit of musical pitch[33] and the lower limit of spectral analysis[68] or the beginning of intraperiod analysis for repeated waveforms.

I have said that all of these periods listed are of the order of 20 msec. Failure to fix the exact length of this segment is no reason for concern, since it does not appear reasonable to view the operation as analogous to abrupt gating for some discrete moment, akin to the perceptual moment once proposed by Stroud.[77] The fact that it pervades the repertoire of auditory signals indicates to me that it is an early process more nearly akin to the running window of the Licklider dual theory of pitch perception,[46] its time-decay function being most likely exponential or Gaussian, and the measured length therefore being dependent on the depth (down from peak) to which the subsequent specific processing follows the continuously decaying trace. There is little reason to expect it to exhibit, for the perceptual output measurements available, a $1/e$ or a one-sigma width.

Now, as we have seen, immediate, or preperceptual, storage has assumed additional importance but from the results of the experimentation on auditory processing, this is, so far, the only relatively fixed storage period experimentally established. All others appear to be specific to the kind of signal being processed. Guttman and Pruzansky[33] set the lower limit of non-musical pitch at about 50 msec. Their non-musical pitch region is a region in which variation in the period of the signal (a pulse train) seems to parallel perceptual variation in pitch, but octave judgments are much less repeatable than in the musical range. A number of scholars signify the value of 60 msec as an important auditory interval,[2, 60, 78] but I have been unable to uncover the requisite experimental evidence. Massaro[51] shows than an auditory tonal stimulus is susceptible to interference for a period up to 250 msec as though it were in something like buffer storage. He does not, however, indicate whether 250 msec is the temporal length of the segment held in such a buffer, nor, I believe, does he consider it to be a peripheral operation. Guttman and Julesz,[32] using repeated sections of waveforms of random noise, labeled three distinguishable classes of perception related to duration of repeated segments. When the repeated waveforms were shorter than 50 msec the perception is that of a signal having pitch height (but not necessarily the characteristics of musical pitch, as Guttman and Pruzansky [33] showed). When the repeated waveforms are between 50 and 250 msec long (up to 1/4 second) they described the effect as "motor-boating." (This is likely an essentially obsolete term. It denotes a sound occasionally heard from faulty audio circuits. I mention it as another interesting example of resorting to source similarity rather than making an attempt at an abstract description of a sound. In discussing the Guttman and Julesz[32] study, Neisser[57] changes the term to "putt-putt".) When the repeated waveforms have a length greater than a quarter second but less than one second the sound is described as "whooshing." This one, I suspect, is sufficiently ono-matopoeic that any other description would be superfluous. With rates slower than 1 per second the repetitious nature of the sound can be discerned only with difficulty, but repetitions can be detected.

This study has been cited by both Neisser[59] and Crowder[17] as evidence for a peripheral storage period of one or two seconds. Guttman and Julesz [32] report that high pass or low pass filtering does not affect the periods at which the perceptual changes occur, hence either waveform storage is not the suitable label or else these particular temporal divisions are endemic audi-torily. But does the Guttman and Julesz demonstration actually mean the auditory system has the capability of storing as much as a second's worth of pre-category detail? Before we accept this as suitable pre-memory storage two questionable points make it necessary to look more closely at what Guttman and Julesz actually did. The first point is that their repeated segments were repeated more than one time. We do not know whether one immediate repetition could be detected, and this is what is required for the storage postulated by Neisser[59] and Crowder.[17] Secondly, neither do we know how much detail of the one-second waveform has been registered. No one has done the experiments which would tell what degree of change in the repeated sequence is discernible. For any one of these sequences longer than those that produce pitch, how much of the detail can be changed before the difference is perceptible? Simple short pulses repeated once per second also sound repetitious. I can present you with a one-second rhythmic click pattern, and you can store it and recognize it even though it might, on repeated presentations be immersed in, or nearly masked by, a background random noise. Is this all that happens on repeated presentations of such long patterns—the digging out of an almost masked rhythmic pattern? How much detail is registered for a single presentation of these sequences longer than the lower limit of pitch? Schubert and West[70] made a start at answering this question while trying to compare certain waveform parameters for immediate auditory storage. We discovered that, for signal lengths of between 100 and 200 msec subjects could recognize a single repeat, but not 100 percent of the time, and only for waveforms with sufficient variation—not for quasi-periodic ones. Further, the storage was not a very stable one, in that insertion of a short silent gap tended to degrade recognition appreciably, whereas insertion of a random noise burst of comparable length had less effect.

But in any event, the experiment of presenting single repetitions of this kind of waveform to subjects and ascertaining how long a segment can be recognized as completely identical in pattern has not been done.

We began this inquiry into the time-following capabilities of the auditory system to judge whether it could record the detail necessary for making delayed decisions about speech-sound identification. Inspection of the available data shows the system's time-interval resolution is certainly adequate, but the question of the locus and nature of precategorical storage is still wide open.

More information about what differences can be detected in previously unencountered waveforms would tell a great deal about the generality of the first stage of acoustic storage. Is there a different level or type of storage than the one that appears to govern echo suppression, binaural and monaural image fusion, and perhaps intraperiod homogeneity? This is central to understanding the auditory system's role in speech perception.

Analysis-by-Synthesis

What has become abundantly clear in work on both speech productions and speech reception is that neither the speaker in generating his utterances nor the listener in processing them operates phoneme by phoneme, except under quite artificial circumstances. Even from a strictly mechanical view, the work on coarticulation[45,61] implies that syllables are the smallest operational unit from the speech production standpoint. Similarly, a great deal of

evidence has been accumulating recently that speech perception is more likely
to be understood if our attempts to understand it are structured linguistically
rather than simply phonologically. One peculiarly auditory kind of evidence,
for example, comes from the work of Bever and associates[4, 26] showing that
clicks that are physically imbedded inside a syntactic unit are perceived
instead as being at a syntactic juncture (see also Ladefoged and Broadbent).[43]

Miller[55] voiced some years ago the same conviction that the decision
units in speech processing are of phrase or even sentence length by reasoning
that the usual pattern in complex behavior of the organism is to make larger,
more meaningful decisions first and then pursue the details only insofar as is
necessary. The potentially operational model of speech perception that em-
bodies these principles is the analysis-by-synthesis scheme, also born of the
attempt to computerize (mechanize) speech recognition. A recent version of
the postulated sequence of events when speech analysis is accomplished by
trial synthesis is shown in Figure 2, taken from a recent discussion by
Stevens.[75]

First of all, note that we go through two auditory operations before we
come to the "preliminary analysis" block. The first of these could be taken to
be synonymous with the output of the cochlea. Stevens designates the
"preliminary analysis" block as the locus of a partial feature analysis. The
"control" component, as Stevens explains, is the heart of the model. As
indicated, it receives the results of previous analysis and the output of the

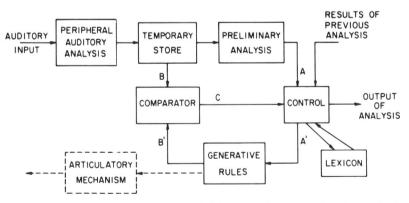

*Figure 2. Block diagram for accomplishing speech recognition by analysis-
by-synthesis. See text for description. (Reprinted from* Language by Ear and
by Eye, *by JF Kavanagh and IG Mattingly [eds.], by permission of the MIT
Press, Cambridge, Mass.)*

contemporary preliminary analysis, the error signal from the comparator and information from the stored lexicon. On the basis of all these data it forms a hypothesis about the utterance and, in my version at least, passes this on to another similar loop.

One interesting question, if one postulates more loops than are shown here, is whether the most peripheral loop should include an output to the articulatory mechanism as shown. This depends on how rigid, or essentially reflex-like, one considers the connection to be. It ought to be noted that auditory-monitoring does have its immediate effects on one's own speaking performance. The practiced speaker can produce quite acceptable—or at least quite intelligible—speech with the mouth cavities encumbered by food, with a pipe clenched in the teeth or, as Cotton[16] showed, with a small water-filled balloon in the vocal tract. Articulatory patterns are not so rigidly set that they cannot be rapidly modified and speech kept reasonably intelligible through auditory monitoring.

Obviously, analysis-by-synthesis is not exclusively an auditory operation, but our interest here is primarily in the performance of the auditory system if such a model is at all appropriate. What is quite apparent from studying the diagram is that again considerable burden is put on the temporary storage of the incoming signal, since, in order for this type of analysis to be possible, either pre-categorical options must be left open or a number of alternative partial analyses must be carried out and held in a form suitable for channeling to the control at the appropriate time. Considering the complexity of the total speech processing system and the tenuous nature of our knowledge of it, no decision is advisable about what level of segmentation is reasonable for this type of analysis—it could—in fact it is useful to assume that it does—go on at a number of processing levels simultaneously with something like error-signal feedback loops between levels.

What is the nature of auditory processing in the first loop of an analysis-by-synthesis model, if linguistically-carried decisions are to be postponed? Does the system routinely construct and continuously scan a running feature matrix, accepting only those feature-mediated decisions compatible with decisions already made about the linguistic content of the message? One can then suppose analogous comparisons are progressing in parallel at the level of the phoneme, the syllable and on to more linguistically-determined segments.

Let me digress for a moment to note that there are two aspects of my multi-loop view of analysis-by-synthesis that do not fit well with psycho-physical theory. The first is that the input operations implied are best accomplished by broadband processing of acoustic signals rather than the time-smeared output following the critical-band filtering; yet that filtering seems to move further toward the periphery as evidence accumulates. However, I see a great deal of rational evidence for the existence of broadband processing in the system and at least two good pieces of neurophysiological evidence,[9,42] so for the moment I believe firmly in the existence of both modes of processing in the system.

Secondly, the processing model implied is not a parsimonious one. However, there is little evidence that human sensory systems are, or need to be, parsimonious systems. James G. Miller's exposition of principles for living systems is of immediate relevance here. One of his hypotheses is that "Use of multiple parallel channels to carry identical information which farther along the net can be compared for accuracy is commoner in more essential components of a system than in less essential ones."[57] A hint of this same rationale is contained in Siebert's assertion that the designer of a natural-information-processing system "would have avoided the information losses associated with any attempt to replace the stimulus early in the system by a set of characteristic features and would instead have tried to construct a more-or-less continuous, analog, information-preserving type of system, at least in its peripheral parts."[72]

In an attempt to put something like the analysis-by-synthesis model into practice on a manageable scale, Neely[58] set up a computer chess-playing routine controlled both ways by vocal commands. Even with this restricted vocabulary he found it necessary to include three separate interacting loops involving an acoustic, syntactic and semantic dictionary. In deciding what had been said to the computer, all tentative decisions in the shorter-segment loops were held and scanned, weighted with conditional probabilities, until the most likely match to the stored lexicon was arrived at by the semantic controller.

To a large extent this seems to fit what we observe informally of speech perception, i.e., ample anecdotal evidence can be enlisted for this mode of operation. Sometimes in listening under difficult conditions one receives an entire sentence before the intact long segment suddenly springs seemingly full blown from the semantic output of something like the analysis-by-synthesis processor. It is possible when engrossed in another activity—it might even be reading, and it is traditionally behind the morning paper—to be aware that a previously unattended reception can be completely resurrected under duress. Conversely, the "phonemic restoration" of the Warrens[81] —the failure of the listener to detect the absence of deleted sound in a phrase-length message would also be predicted by the model as long as the message is a grammatical one.

During easy reception of speech by the practiced listener, linguistic decisions may be made far ahead of the phonemes being received, and possibly only the most cursory check takes place at the feature, phoneme or syllable level.

Perhaps, too, the reason we are currently blessed with so many names for interim storage is indicative of the reasonableness of a number of loops operating in something like an analysis-by-synthesis processor. Bryden[11] presented subjects with simultaneous dichotic words, with instructions to attend only to one ear, but later his subjects resurrected some of the unattended material, which he called "preperceptual". From very similar operations Glucksberg and Cowen[29] emerge with "nonattended" material, and Crowder and Morton[18] have been studying "precategorical" acoustic storage. We have already mentioned also Neisser's "echoic" storage. All these appear to me to be central to the boundary line I would like to establish operationally between raw auditory storage and perceptually stored entities.

One factor that makes the search difficult is the specificity of auditory processing. Studies of other auditory processing, like the Massaro study[50] of tonal identification tell us little or nothing about the pre-decision processing of speech. Deutsch's demonstration[21] of the independence of tonal memory and memory for spoken digits certainly reinforces this impression. Furthermore, although identifying the source of a tone is a common task of the auditory system, remembering the specific frequency placement of a tone out of context is not. Even when we do recall melodies, we remember the melodic form, not the specific frequency placement, or the same notes of the scale, as Attneave and Olson[1] have shown.

But the problem may be difficult because actually there is no such identifiable boundary. Perhaps the auditory system never stores in preprocessed form more than the 20 to 50 msec necessary to fuse echos into one image, accomplish spectral analysis of complex tones with low fundamentals and separate simultaneously present signals, and perhaps decide whether the source is a speech or a non-speech source. These seem to be the basic preperceptual tasks. There may be no reason for constructing pre-processed segments longer than, say, 50 msec before the information is passed to the most likely channel or channels for tentative perceptual assignment. Given that the main task of the auditory system is categorization of sounds and sound sequences of varying length, the main difference I see between environmental sound perception and speech sound perception is in the length of the dependent sound sequences. Analysis-by-synthesis is a perfectly suitable model for the processing of environmental sound events, but seldom does it require the complexity of dictionary storage demanded for the processing of continuous speech. One difference we have dwelt upon here is that whereas unifying rules are difficult in the environmental domain and categorization is paramount, the opposite is true for the processing of speech. Rules initially seemingly as far removed as the rules of grammar appear to govern even the purely auditory reception of speech sounds. But this, it seems to me, holds some warning about the proper direction of generalization from experimental findings to speech perception theory. Because of the interactive nature of analysis-by-synthesis-processing at different levels we risk evolving a different argument about speech perception for each level of processing. A finding, for example, that consonants are stored in one locus and vowel sounds in another may say more about the lack of generality of the method used than it does about the nature of speech perception. For the most part, this suggests that the proper study of speech reception is speech. Unhappily, the most likely outcome of such a state of affairs is that in the practical world, auditory perception and speech perception are destined for some time to go their separate ways. For the time being, at least, the methods of auditory perception are not suitable for answering the questions of highest priority in speech perception—questions at the level of word, phrase and sentence perception.

In brief, the following principles present a useful thumbnail sketch of the role of the auditory system, particularly pertinent to its assignment as a speech processor:

(1) Identification of sound sources, and behavior of those sources, is the primary task of the system. This same capability may well also be of great assistance in the processing of speech sounds.

(2) The system is capable of registering comparatively fine time discriminations and may be able to accomplish almost analog waveform storage for as long as 30—50 msec. Larger preperceptual storage than this could be possible, but has not been conclusively demonstrated.

(3) The system is highly dependent on the visual system for meaningful identification of environmental acoustic sequences other than speech or music.

(4) Even for the acoustic aspects of speech processing, the organizing principles are linguistic—the larger the units perceivable, the easier the task—all other things being equal.

That the processing of language is one of man's most intricate skills is axiomatic. The capture and preprocessed storage of the audible verbal message is likewise the most ambitious accomplishment of the auditory system. In this relatively brief perusal many facets have necessarily been neglected, but the portrayal of the inchoate nature of our knowledge of language processing is essentially accurate. Having attempted a "state of the art" paper on auditory perception, I recognize, on closer scrutiny, I have achieved but a state of the start of an understanding of auditory processing.

References

1. Attneave F, Olson RK: Pitch as a medium: a new approach to psychophysical scaling. Am J Psychol 84:147–166. 1971
2. Békésy G von: Auditory backward inhibition in concert halls. Science 171:529–535, 1971
3. Berger KW: Some factors in the recognition of timbre. J Acoust Soc Am 36:1888–1891, 1964
4. Bever TG, Lackner JR, Kirk R: The underlying structures of sentences are the primary units of immediate speech processing. Perception Psychophysics 5:225–234, 1969
5. Bismarck G von: Timbre of steady sounds: a factorial investigation of its verbal attributes. Acustica 30:146–159, 1974
6. Blodgett HC, Wilbanks WA, Jeffress LA: Effect of large interaural time differences upon the judgment of sidedness. J Acoust Soc Am 28:639–643, 1956
7. Bloom L: Language Development: Form or Function in Emerging Grammars. Cambridge, Massachusetts, MIT Press, 1970
8. Broadbent DE, Ladefoged P: Auditory perception of temporal order. J Acoust Soc Am 31:1539, 1959
9. Brugge JF, Anderson DJ, Hind JE, et al: Time structure of discharges in single auditory nerve fibers of the squirrel monkey in response to complex periodic sounds. J Neurophysiol 32:386–401, 1969
10. Bruner JS: On perceptual readiness. Psychol Rev 64:123–152, 1957
11. Bryden MP: Attentional strategies and short-term memory in dichotic listening. Cognitive Psychol 2:99–116, 1971
12. Cherry EC, Taylor WK: Some further experiments upon the recognition of speech, with one and with two ears. J Acoust Soc Am 26:554–559, 1954
13. Chomsky N, Halle M: The Sound Pattern of English. New York, Harper & Row, Publishers, 1968
14. Clark M Jr, Luce D, Abrams R, et al: Preliminary experiments on the aural significance of parts of tones of orchestral instruments and on choral tones. J Audio Eng. Soc. 11:45–54, 1963
15. Clark M Jr, Robertson P, Luce D: A preliminary experiment on the perceptual basis for musical instrument families. J Audio Eng Soc 12:199–203, 1964
16. Cotton JC: Tongue movements and vowel quality. Speech Monogr 4:38–42, 1937
17. Crowder RG: Visual and auditory memory. In Language by Ear and by Eye. Edited by JF Kavanagh, IG Mattingly. Cambridge, Massachusetts, MIT Press, 1972
18. Crowder RG, Morton J: Precategorical acoustic storage (PAS). Perception Psychophysics 5:365–373, 1969
19. Cutting JE, Eimas PD: Phonetic Feature Analyzers and the Processing of Speech in Infants. Haskins Laboratories Status Report SR-37/38, 1974, pp 45–64
20. Cutting JE, Rosner BS: Categories and Boundaries in Speech and Music. Haskins Laboratories Status Report SR-37/38, 1974, pp 145–158
21. Deutsch D: Tones and numbers: specificity of interference in immediate memory. Science 168:1604–1605, 1970
22. Efron R: Conservation of temporal information by perceptual systems. Perception Psychophysics 14:518–530, 1973
23. Eguchi S, Hirsh IJ: Development of speech sounds in children. Acta Otolaryngol Suppl 257, 1969

24. Eimas P, Siqueland E, Jusczyk P, et al: Speech perception in infants. Science 171:303–306, 1971
25. Fant G: Speech Sounds and Features. Cambridge, Massachusetts, MIT Press, 1973
26. Fodor J, Bever T: The psychological reality of linguistic segments. J Verbal Learning Verbal Behav 4:414–420, 1965
27. Gescheider GA: Resolving of successive clicks by the ears and skin. J Exp Psychol 71:378–381, 1966
28. Gibson JJ: The Senses Considered as Perceptual Systems. New York, Houghton Mifflin Company, 1966
29. Glucksberg S, Cowen GM Jr: Memory for non-attended auditory material. Cog Psychol 1:149–156, 1970
30. Green DM: Temporal auditory acuity. Psychol Rev 78:540–551, 1971
31. Grey JM: On the Perception of Synthesized Music Instrument Tones Having Time-Variant Harmonic Spectra. Doctoral Dissertation, Stanford University, 1974
32. Guttman N, Julesz B: Lower limit of auditory periodicity analysis. J Acoust Soc Am 35:601, 1963
33. Guttman N, Pruzansky S: Lower limits of pitch and musical pitch. J Speech Hear Res 5:207–214, 1962
34. Haas H: Über die Einfluss eines Einfachechoes aud die Hörsamkeit von Sprache. Acustica 1:49–52, 1951
35. Helmholtz HLF: Sensations of Tone. New York, Longmans, Green & Co., Ellis translation, 1930
36. Hirsh IJ: Auditory perception of temporal order. J Acoust Soc Am 31:759–767, 1959
37. House AS, Stevens KN, Sandell TT, et al: On the learning of speech-like vocabulaties. J Verbal Learning Verbal Behav 1:133–143, 1962
38. Huggins WH: System function analysis of speech sounds. J Acoust Soc Am 22:765–767, 1950
39. Huggins WH: A theory of hearing. In Communication Theory. Edited by W Jackson. London, Butterworth & Co., Publishers, 1953
40. Jakobson R, Fant CGM, Halle M: Preliminaries to Speech Analysis: The Distinctive Features and Their Correlates. MIT Technical Report no. 13, 1952
41. Kaplan EL, Kaplan GA: The prelinguistic child. In Human Development and Cognitive Processes. Edited by J Eliot. New York, Holt, Rinehart & Winston, 1970
42. Kiang NY, Moxon EC: Tails of tuning curves of auditory fibers. J Acoust Soc Am 55:620–630, 1974
43. Ladefoged P, Broadbent DE: Perception of sequence in auditory events. Q J Exp Psychol 12:162–170, 1960
44. Lawrence W: The synthesis of speech from signals which have a low information rate. In Communication Theory. Edited by W Jackson. London, Butterworth & Co., Publishers, 1953
45. Liberman AM: The grammars of speech and language. Cognitive Psychol 1:301–323, 1970
46. Licklider JCR: The duplex theory of pitch perception. Experientia 7:128–137, 1951
47. Lieberman P, Crelin ES, Klatt DH: Phonetic ability and related anatomy of the newborn and adult human, Neanderthal man, and the chimpanzee. Am Anthropol 74:287–307, 1972
48. Luce D, Clark M: Physical correlates of brass instrument tones. J Acoust Soc Sm 42:1232–1243, 1967
49. Luce DA, Clark M: Duration of attack transients of nonpercussive orchestral instruments. J Audio Eng Soc 13:194–199, 1965
50. Massaro DW: Preperceptual auditory images. J Exp Psychol 85:411–417, 1970
51. Massaro DW: Stimulus information vs processing time in auditory pattern recognition. Perception Psychophysics 12:50–56, 1972
52. McNeill D: Developmental psycholinguistics. In The Genetics of Language: A

Psycholinguistic Approach. Edited by F Smith, GA Miller. Cambridge, Massachusetts, MIT Press, 1966
53. McNeill D: The Acquisition of Language. New York, Harper & Row, Publishers, 1970
54. Menyuk P: The Development of Speech. New York, Bobbs-Merrill Co., 1972
55. Miller GA: Decision units in the perception of speech. IRE Trans Inf Theory, IE-8, 1962, pp 81–83
56. Miller JD, Tanis DC: Recognition memory for common sounds. Psychon Sci 23:307–308, 1971
57. Miller JG: Living Systems: structure and process. Behav Sci 10:337–379, 1965
58. Neely RB: On the Use of Syntax and Semantics in a Speech Understanding System. Doctoral Dissertation, Stanford University, 1973
59. Neisser U: Cognitive Psychology. New York, Appleton-Century-Crofts, 1967
60. Norman DA: The role of memory in the understanding of language. In Language by Ear and by Eye. Edited by JF Kavanagh, IG Mattingly. Cambridge, Massachusetts, MIT Press, 1972
61. Öhman SEG: Coarticulation in VCV utterances: spectrographic measurements. J Acoust Soc Am 39:151–168, 1966
62. Patterson JH, Green DM: Discrimination of signals having identical energy spectra. J Acoust Soc Am 48:894–905, 1970
63. Pfafflin SM, Matthews MV: Detection of auditory signals in reproducible noise. J Acoust Soc Am 39:340–345, 1966
64. Pollack I, Pickett JM, Sumby WH: On the identification of speakers by voice. J Acoust Soc Am 26:403–405, 1954
65. Ronken DA: Monaural detection of a phase difference between clicks. J Acoust Soc Am 47:1091–1099, 1970
66. Saldanha EL, Corso JF: Timbre cues and the identification of musical instruments. J Acoust Soc Am 36:2021–2026, 1964
67. Savin H: What the child knows about speech when he starts to learn to read. In Language by Ear and by Eye. Edited by JF Kavanagh, IG Mattingly, Cambridge, Massachusetts, MIT Press, 1972
68. Schubert ED: Some factors in pitch perception for complex tones (to appear in J Acoust Soc Am)
69. Schubert ED, Owens E: CVC words as test items. J Aud Res 11:88–100, 1971
70. Schubert ED, West RA: Recognition of repeated patterns: a study of short-term auditory storage. J Acoust Soc Am 46:1493–1501, 1969
71. Shipley EF, Smith CS, Gleitman LR: A study in the acquisition of language: free responses to commands. Language 45:322–342, 1969
72. Siebert WM: Stimulus transformations in the peripheral auditory system. In Recognizing Patterns. Edited by PA Kolers, M Eden. Cambridge, Massachusetts, MIT Press, 1968
73. Siqueland ER, DeLucia CA: Visual reinforcement of non-nutritive sucking in human infants. Science 165:1145–1146, 1969
74. Solomon LN: Search for physical correlates to psychological dimensions of sounds. J Acoust Soc Am 31:492–497, 1959
75. Stevens KN: Segments, features, and analysis by synthesis. In Language by Ear and by Eye. Edited by JF Kavanagh, IG Mattingly. Cambridge, Massachusetts, MIT Press, 1972
76. Strong W, Clark M: Perturbations of synthetic orchestral wind-instrument tones. J Acoust Soc Am 41:277–285, 1967
77. Stroud JM: The fine structure of psychological time. In Information Theory in Psychology. Edited by H Quastler. Glencoe, Illinois, Free Press, 1955
78. Studdert-Kennedy M, Liberman AM, Harris KS, et al: The motor theory of speech perception: a reply to Lane's critical review. Psychol Rev 77:234–249, 1970
79. Wang MD, Bilger RC: Consonant confusions in noise: a study of perceptual features. J Acoust Soc Am 54:1248–1266, 1973

80. Warren RM, Obusek CJ, Farmer RM, et al: Auditory sequence: confusion of patterns other than speech or music. Science 1644:568–587, 1969
81. Warren RM, Warren RP: Auditory illusions and confusions. Sci Am 223:30–36, 1970
82. Webster JC, Woodhead MM, Carpenter A: Perceptual constancy in complex sound identification. Br J Psychol 61:481–489, 1970
83. Wickelgren WA: Auditory or articulatory coding in verbal short term memory. Psychol Rev 76:232–235, 1969

PERSPECTIVES IN VISION: CONCEPTION OR PERCEPTION?

Michael T. Turvey

From what cloth shall we cut the theory of visual perception? For most scholars over the centuries the answer has been singularly straightforward: conception. The official doctrine is that our visual perception of the world depends in very large part on our conception of the world. To paraphrase: knowing the world perceptually rests on knowing about the world conceptually. The inquiry into visual perception is dominated by this thesis of *conception* as primary, and the first charge of this paper is to examine in elementary but reasonably detailed fashion the manifestations of this thesis in current theory and research.

But there is another and contrasting point of view to which this paper will turn in due course; one that asserts the primacy of *perception*. From this standpoint, information about the visual world is obtained without the intervention of conceptual processes. On this view, conceptual knowledge is the offspring of perception. To declare the independence of perception from conception is to declare the dependence of perception on stimulation. The second charge of this paper is to examine the meaning and implications of these declarations.

Indirect Perception:
Constructivism and the Primacy of Conception

Introduction

Only relatively superficial differences divide the various theories of visual perception with which we are most acquainted. With respect to the basic postulates on which each is founded there is an overwhelming consistency of

The preparation of this manuscript was supported in part by a John Simon Guggenheim Fellowship awarded to the author for the period 1973–1974 and by the National Institute of Child Health and Human Development Grant HD-01994.

opinion: they all concur to a greater or lesser degree that perception begins with retinal data that related imperfectly, even ambiguously, to their source—the world of objects, surfaces, and events.

Consequently, it is customary to liken the task of the perceiver to that of a detective who must seek to determine what transpired from the bits and pieces of evidence available to him. Extending this metaphor, we have supposed that there are "cues" or "clues" to be read from the retinal image and to a very large extent the endeavors of students of perception have been directed to isolating these cues and inquiring about how they are used. The impression is that a large discrepancy exists between what is given in the retinal image and what is perceived; we wonder, like Gregory[39] how so little information can control so much behavior. From necessity we argue that the perceiver must engage in a large stock of inferential and hypothesis-generating and testing procedures that rely heavily on memory—on internal models of reality established in the course of prior experience of both the individual and the species.

This general approach to the theory of visual perception has a long tradition. Recall that John Locke drew a distinction between primary qualities as given and secondary qualities as inferred, and that Helmholtz coined the phrase "unconscious inference" to represent this theoretical persuasion. Currently it is given expression through the term "constructivism," which will be used in this paper for any theory which proposes that in order to perceive one must go beyond what is given in stimulation. Thus, we understand constructivism to mean that perception cannot be achieved directly from stimulation (one might say that stimulation underdetermines perceptual experience). On the contrary, perceptual experience is constructed or created out of a number of ingredients, only some of which are provided by the data of the senses. Other ingredients in a perception recipe are provided by our expectations, our biases, and primarily by our conceptual knowledge about the world. The gist of the constructive interpretation is conveyed in the following remark: ". . . perceptions are constructed by complex brain processes from fleeting fragmentary scraps of data signalled by the senses and drawn from the brain's memory banks—themselves constructions from snippets of the past."[38] Helmholtz,[51] in response to the ambiguity of retinal stimulation, might have said: we perceive that object or that event that would normally fit the proximal stimulus distribution.[55]

Internal Modeling of the Relation Structure of External Events

The view of the brain as a complex information-processing mechanism that internally models the world is of central importance to theories of the constructivist persuasion. This view, represented best by Kenneth Craik,[19] can be stated explicitly: neural processes or mental operations symbolically mirror objects, events, and their interrelationships.

The advantage of internal modeling is that outcomes can be predicted. Mental processes allow us to proceed vicariously through a pattern of motions or a succession of events much as an engineer determines a reliable design for a bridge *before* he begins building. In short, we can try out mentally what would occur without actually performing the test, the outcome of which may be useless or even harmful. There would seem to be little reason to debate this property of mind with respect to thought and language, but can we with the same confidence regard visual perception analogously as a modeling, imitative, predictive process? The constructivist answer is an unequivocal, "Yes." We may conceptualize visual perception as the task of creating a short-term model of contemporary distal stimuli out of, on the one hand, the contemporary but crude proximal stimulation and on the other, from the internalized long-term model of the world.   This is a significant feature of constructivism: it encourages us to examine the possibility that psychological processes such as thought, language and seeing, are more similar than they are different. The kinds of knowledge, heuristics, algorithms, and so on, that permit thought may not differ significantly from those that permit language, and these in turn may be equivalent to those that yield visual perception. Paraphrasing Kolers,[72] Katz,[65] Sutherland[137] and others, there is nothing that would suggest to a constructivist different kinds of intelligence underlying these apparently different activities.

That brain mechanisms can model the world in the sense of exhibiting processes that have a similar relational structure to sets of physical events, is an intuition that is currently receiving some measure of support in the laboratory. Echoing Craik's[19] hypothesis, Shepard[124,125] proposes a second-order isomorphism between physical objects and their internal representations. This isomorphism is not in the first-order relation between a particular object and its internal representation (as Gestalt psychologists used to have it), but rather in the relation between (1) the relations among a set of objects and (2) the relations among their corresponding internal representations. To quote Shepard and Chipman, "Thus, although the internal representation of a square need not itself be a square it should (whatever it is) at least have a closer functional relation to the internal representation of a rectangle than to, say, a green flash or a taste of persimmon."[125]

There are two experiments that speak favorably for the notion of a second-order isomorphism. In the first experiment,[125] 15 states of the United States—ones that did not differ too greatly in size—were selected for similarity judgments. One hundred and five pairings of members of this set were presented in name form and ranked by the subjects according to similarity. The same subjects then ranked the same 105 pairs of states presented in picture form. The structure of similarity relations among the shapes was virtually identical whether the states compared were there to be perceived (pictorial presentation) or could only be imagined (name presentation). Moreover, for both name and pictorial presentation, the similarity judgments corresponded to identifiable properties of the actual cartographic shapes of the states (see also Gordon and Hayward[37]).

In the second experiment,[47] a second-order isomorphism is implied between the structure of color space as represented in memory and the structure of color space as given in perceptual experience. The question asked was whether two people who differed markedly in color terminology (the Dani of New Guinea and Americans) actually structured the color space in markedly different ways. There were two tasks: in one, subjects from the two populations named colors; in the other, they matched colors from memory. Through multidimensional scaling, it was determined that the structure of the color space was remarkably similar for the two populations when derived from the memory data but, as expected, quite dissimilar when derived from naming. The important comparison here lies between the relational structure of colors in memory, and the relational structure of colors in perception.[50,123] On the available evidence, the two structures appear to be virtually the same.[47]

One may argue from these experiments that memory preserves or mimics the structural relations among perceptual properties. But the notion of brain mechanisms modeling external events suggests something more: an isomorphism between external and internal *processes*. We turn, therefore, to an experiment examining the following proposition as a corollary of the second-order isomorphism theorem: when one is imaging an external process, one passes through an orderly set of internal states related in a way that mimics the relations among the successive states of the external process.[126]

Suppose that you are shown a pair of differently oriented objects pictured in Figure 1 and that you have to determine whether the two objects are the same or different. I suspect that you would reach your decision by manipulating the objects in some way, say, by rotating one of them and comparing perspectives. But suppose that you are shown a pair of two-dimensional portrayals of the three-dimensional objects (which, of course, is what Figure 1 is) and that your task is to decide as quickly as possible (and obviously without the aid of manipulation) whether one of the objects so depicted could be rotated into the other. In an experiment of this kind, [127] it was shown that the decision latency was an increasing linear function of the

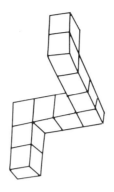

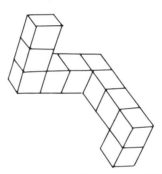

Figure 1. Are these two perspectives of the same object? (After Shepard and Metzler, 1971)

angular difference in the portayed orientation of the two objects. At 0° difference the latency was one sec., while at 180° difference the latency was 4 or 5 sec. Each additional degree of rotation added approximately 16 milliseconds (msec) to the latency of recognition. This was essentially so whether the rotation was in the plane of the picture or in depth.

This example illustrates the capability of neural processes to model the relational structure of external happenings. For further instances, the reader is referred to Cooper and Shepard[17] and Shepard and Feng. [126]

What Presupposes Indirect Perception?

What is behind the assumption that stimulation underdetermines perception and that to perceive visually one must go beyond what is given in the light to an ocular system? What is the *given*? History's answer is that the reference is to the stimuli for the receptors or to the sensations provided by the senses. Clearly, the need to suggest that a brain must guess, infer, or construct will have its roots primarily in the attributes that tradition has adduced for stimuli and/or sensations.

We can begin with the notion that they are given and given directly. Construction presupposes some basic materials and therefore all constructive theories concede a preliminary stage whose output is not guessed or created. And the degree to which a theory conceives perception as indirect is inversely related to the elaborateness of the evidence deemed to be directly detectable. The point sensations which occupied this preliminary stage in the thinking of the structuralists have given way to the oriented lines and angles imposed upon us by an impressive neurophysiology[56, 57] and the pragmatics of building workable computer programs for pattern recognition.[90]

A current idea is that preliminary to object recognition is a stage which detects primitive features. It is assumed as a matter of principle that there is a finite number of such features which poses the problem of how an indefinitely large number of objects can be discriminated and recognized. In order that infinite usage may be made of a limited number of features, subsequent processes in perception must instantiate knowledge about relations among features and must, perhaps, be capable of generating a variety of object representations.[90] As one theorist has remarked: "Perception must, it seems, be a matter of seeing the present with stored objects from the past."[40]

The assumption that what is given directly in perception is a finite set of *punctate* elements necessitates a search beyond the stimulus for an explanation of the perception of objects and of the fact that we experience optical events as spatially unified. The assumption of stimuli as punctate demands a theory of indirect, constructed perception.

It is curious that the circumscribed feature set, so far uncovered by neurophysiology, has been adopted energetically and somewhat uncritically as the departure point for much of current visual perception theory. The experimental evidence is that there are neural units which are selectively sensitive to simple spatial relations (e.g. a line in a given orientation). Does this evidence delimit the list of feature detectors? Clearly, there is no *a priori* reason for believing that future research will not reveal detectors, or more aptly, systems, selectively sensitive to more complex optical relations. The growing evidence for selective sensitivity to spatial frequency[116] corroborates this suspicion.

But whatever our misgivings, we should not lose sight of the important and instructive fact that the above "simple" spatial and spatial-temporal relations are characterized as being directly given. In using the term "direct" with respect to the detection of features, we intend the following. First, the course of detection does not involve establishing an internal representation of the feature which is then matched by some separate process against a stored representation. Second, and related, the pick-up of these features does not depend upon information other than that currently available in the stimulation; that is to say, their detection is not underdetermined.

Closely allied with the interpretation of stimuli as punctate elements, is the prevailing assertion that stimuli are temporally discrete. If stimuli are momentary, then there must be routines for combining stimuli that are distributed in time. This is exemplified in the familiar problem of how scenes are perceived through a succession of eye movements. An aim of the fovea corresponds to the reception of a sample of the available stimuli. Thus a succession of aims yields a succession of retinal images and therefore a succession of different sets of punctate elements. For the observer who moves or scans, the fitting-together operations performed on each set of adjacent punctate elements must be supplemented by processes which collect together and synthesize the products of these operations over time.

Hochberg[53,54] and Neisser[94] have emphasized the distinction between the information in a single glance and the integration of information from a succession of glances. They argue that a panoramic impression cannot be specified by a single fixation, for in general a single fixation provides the observer with only local information about the three dimensional structure of a scene. Moreover, only in the foveal region of a fixation is the information detailed. Thus to perceive a scene an observer must integrate several fixations. Evidently panoramic perception is constructed, but how this construction-through-integration takes place remains very much a mystery and to date there are no viable accounts of how it might occur.

The characterization of stimuli as punctate and momentary supplies the backdrop for one of the more heralded reasons for claiming that perception goes beyond what is given. The well-known phi phenomenon provides a case in point. If two lamps are lit in alternation with an appropriate interval elapsing between successive lightings, one perceives a single lamp moving back and forth. Punctate and momentary characterization of stimuli would indicate that there are actually two stimuli separate in space and time, although perceptually the impression is of a single stimulus moving from one point in space to another. Thus, we appear to have a compelling reason for the notion that perception goes beyond what is given: perceiving a stimulus where it is not.

One particularly dramatic variant of the phi phenomenon which would seem to dictate rather than invite the constructive interpretation is provided by Kolers.[69] When a Necker cube is set into oscillating apparent motion an observer under the appropriate conditions will see the cube as rotating in "midflight." In similar circumstances one can also see circles elastically transformed into squares and upward pointing arrows rigidly transformed into downward pointing arrows.[74] We see a changing form where there is no form changing. Moreover, the particular transformation experienced befits the forms involved. Based on these observations, seeing mirrors thinking.

If perception is indirect, we may ask: what do perception by eye and perception by hand have in common? We might answer "very little" on the assumption that an eye delivers to a brain sensations or features that are radically different from those that a hand delivers. So how is it that I can often perceive by eye that which I can also perceive by touch? Traditionally, the answer to this question has been sought in a mediating link—frequently association—which relates visual impressions to tactile impressions, and vice versa. In this view, the data of one sense are rationalized—given meaning—by the data of another.

Where we conceptualize the senses as yielding distinctively different data we are forced into assuming that cross-modality correlation is an essential feature of perception. This is especially so where we believe that data of one sense are intrinsically less meaningful than the data of another. Since the time of Bishop Berkeley, vision has been construed, repeatedly, as parasitic upon touch and muscle kinesthesis.

Let us now turn to pictures, for they would appear to provide prima facie evidence that perception must go beyond what is given in the stimulation. Pictures are flat projections of three dimensional configurations and they can be visualized in either way. Further, it is quite obvious that we can "see" the three dimensional structure which a picture represents even when the information is peculiarly impoverished, as witnessed by outline drawings. We can also "see" the appropriate three dimensional arrangement, even though the picture is ambiguous in the sense that the same projected form could arise from an infinite variety of shapes. In Goodman's[36] view, pictorial structure is an arbitrary conventional language that must be learned in a way that corresponds to how we learn to read. For Hochberg[53] the resolution of the problem of picture processing is sought in the schematic maps stored in one's memory banks and evoked by features. Similarly, Gregory[40] has looked to object-hypotheses as the tools by which we disambiguate a two dimensional portrayal of a three dimensional scene. Though none of these authors provides anything like an account of how "other knowledge" is brought to bear on picture processing, the task has been taken up in earnest by workers in Artificial Intelligence. It is worth noting that there are students of perception who, contrary to the above points of view, suspect that the perception of pictures need not be indirect.[31, 43]

Finally, there is the idea that the environment is broadcast to the observer as a set of visual cues or clues which are intrinsically meaningless. Here the claim is that the relation between clues and assigned meaning is homomorphic: one clue may be assigned many meanings, many clues may be assigned the same meaning. The perceiver, therefore, is assumed to possess a memory-based code which rationalizes the complex of clues read off the retinal image. In sum, where the stimuli are considered as only clues to environmental facts, there is a need for positing mediating constructive activity as the means by which these facts are determined.

Information Processing: A Methodology for Constructivism

Closely cognate with the constructivist philosophy is an approach to problems of perception that is currently in vogue and which may be loosely referred to as "information processing."[42] Implicitly, it takes as its departure point the assumptions as noted above. More explicitly it defines perception not as immediate but as a hierarchically organized temporal sequence of events involving stages of storage and transformation. Transformations occur at points in the information flow where storage capacity constraints demand a recoding of the information. Such recoding must exploit long-term memory structures—or internal models of the world—and, in keeping with a fundamental constructivist belief, perceiving cannot be divorced from memorial processes. Guided by these assumptions, information processing seeks methods that will differentiate the flow of visual information on the nervous system; that is, methods which will decompose the information flow into discrete and temporally ordered stages. In the main, backward masking,[131, 141] delayed partial-sampling,[130] and reaction-time procedures,[106, 135] singly or in combination have provided the requisite tools.

An example will provide an elementary illustration of the information processing approach: the simple task introduced by Sternberg. [133, 135] A display of one to four characters is presented briefly to an observer who must press a key to indicate whether a subsequently presented single character was or was not a member of the previously displayed set. In general, as the number of items in the memory set increases from one to four, the latency of the observer's response to the probe increases linearly. The linear plot, of latency against number of items, has two characteristics: slope and intercept. We might assume that the slope of the function identifies the process of comparing the probe character with the representations of the characters in memory. But what of the intercept? Does it signify a perceptual/memorial operation or just simply the time taken to organize the response?

Suppose that we now degrade the probe character in some way. Does the degrading affect the memory comparison or some other process? If it affects memory comparison, then we should expect the slope to alter, assuming the validity of our original interpretation. An experiment of this kind reveals that degrading the probe essentially leaves the slope of the function invariant but it does raise the intercept.[134] We can now argue that the intercept reflects, at least in part, the processes of normalizing and perceiving the probe prior to memory comparison. In short, in the performance of this simple task we can identify two independently manipulable and successive stages. Witness to the potential usefulness of this distinction is the observation that with words as both memory items and probes, poor readers differ from good readers only in the height of the intercept.[66]

Though it is true that information processing as an approach often provides an elegant framework and set of procedures for examining perceptual processes, it is also the case that the descriptions it yields are for the most part crude and approximate. It is not unjust to say that the information-processing methodology is limited to a broad identification of stages; and is inherently insufficiently powerful to supply sophisticated descriptions of perceptual procedures and their complex interrelationships. For the achievement of a more rigorous account of the *how* of perception, constructivism may have to look elsewhere.

Scene Analysis by Machine: Formalized Constructivism

It is by now evident to the reader that constructivism conceives perception as an act involving a potentially large variety of knowledge structures. To gain a purchase on the form of such structures, to discover effective representations[14] and how they could relate, is in part the task of research and theory in Artificial Intelligence. It will prove instructive for our purposes to look at systems sufficiently intelligent to infer the three dimensional structure of objects from two dimensional line portrayals of opaque polyhedra of the type depicted in Figure 2.

The early work in pattern recognition by machine was dominated by models which held that patterns could be classified by a procedure that listed feature values and then mapped these values onto categories through statisti-

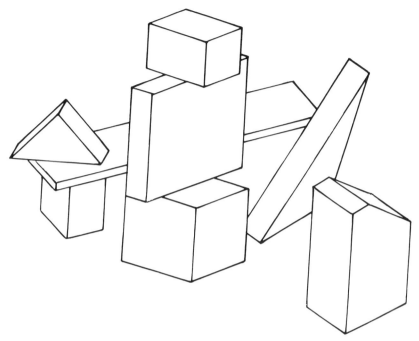

Figure 2. A scene consisting of polyhedral objects. (After Guzman, 1969)

cal decision processes. [117] Contemporary work follows the principle that pattern classification systems must possess the ability to articulate patterns into fragments and to specify relations among the articulated fragments. [90] Consequently, Artificial Intelligence research has been attracted to the structural models which have proved successful in linguistics and the focus of the enterprise has switched from the problem of pattern *recognition* to the problem of pattern *description*. The search is for structural grammars which describe the relationships among the parts of a pattern.

As a preliminary to our discussion, let us conjecture on the types of stages that might intervene or mediate between a picture and the resulting three dimensional description. First, we can assume that a picture is projected onto the retina as an array of points that can be partitioned into sets as a function of brightness. The three dimensional properties of a picture cannot be inferred from this initial points representation. The endeavor, then, of early visual operations must be that of recovering from these patches of brightness, the lines which make up the picture and from these lines, the regions into which the picture may be parsed. (For the purposes of computation, a region may be defined as a set of points with the property that a path drawn between any two elements of the set does not cross a line.) We can usefully refer to these three representations—points, lines, and regions—as being in the *picture domain,* for as yet they are indifferent to the three dimensional structure which the picture represents. But what we want is a three dimensional account, a description of a scene. Having recovered regions, the next constructive operation is to map the regions description onto a surfaces description and this in turn onto a description of the bodies to which the surfaces belong. To facilitate the discussion that follows, we will refer to these two representations—surfaces and bodies—as being in the *scene domain* and recognize that most of Artificial Intelligence research on intelligent picture processing has been concerned with the mapping between the picture and scene domains. The final representation and domain—the *objects domain*—is obtained by identifying the objects that the bodies represent. This task probably requires knowledge of a higher order such as permissible real-world relations among surfaces and the functional capabilities of variously described bodies (e.g. cups are for containing liquids but they could also be used as effective paper weights).

Thus, arriving at a three dimensional description of a picture may be interpreted as the construction of a number of representations in an orderly fashion from less to more abstract. A representation is said to consist of those entities and the relationships existing among them. [137] We can now provide an elementary description of computer methods for analyzing complex configurations of objects presented pictorially. The computer is programmed to begin by detecting local entities or features of a given picture. Then it searches for relationships among entities that indicate the presence of particular subpatterns. The determination of specific relationships of subpatterns allows for the detection of more global patterns, i.e. for the establishment of a higher-order representation, and so the procedure continues until a satisfactory structural description of the scene has been obtained.

Let us examine in an approximate way a few representative programs for scene analysis. We are indebted to Sutherland's [137] lucid clarification of these complex programs.

We begin with Guzman's [41] well-known program partly because it is relatively simple and partly because it provides the jumping-off point for many subsequent programs. Guzman's program takes an input which has already been parsed into regions and seeks to discover from this description how many separate bodies are present in the two dimensional portrayal. The goal of the program is quite modest: it aims only at specifying which groups of regions are the faces of a single body—a preliminary step to arriving at a three dimensional account. The inferences are based on the properties and implications of vertices of the kind shown in Figure 3, with each vertex being classified on the basis of how many lines meet at the vertex and their respective orientations. Essentially, the program having classified the vertices into types, establishes links between regions which meet at vertices. Consider the arrow type of vertex. This would normally be caused by an exterior corner of an object where two of its plane surfaces form an edge. Consequently, the two regions which meet on the shaft of an arrow—that is, those that are bounded by the two smaller angles—are linked; those regions that meet these regions at the barbs of the arrow, however, are not. Similarly, a vertex of the Fork type depicts three faces of an object so that links may be inserted across each line. By linking the regions as a function of where they meet, it is possible to separate the bodies represented in Figure 2. The final stage of the program consists of grouping together regions connected directly by a link or indirectly by a chain of links with other regions.

Where a region is connected by only a single link to the members of a connected collection of regions, it is not identified as a member of that collection. Additionally, the program incorporates a policy of examining in a limited fashion neighboring vertices in order to determine whether links should indeed be made at a given vertex.

It is evident that the more closely and formally we examine the question of how a picture is decomposed into separate bodies the more sensitive we become to the complexity of the problem. Guzman's program, though primitive, hints at the type of heuristics that may have to be employed by a human observer in arriving at a description of a picture. Of special importance is the suggestion that the figure-ground or segmentation problem which is often discussed airily in a single sentence of a text on visual perception is not likely to be solved by the nervous system in any simplistic manner. In this context one is reminded of Hebb's[46] distinction between primitive and

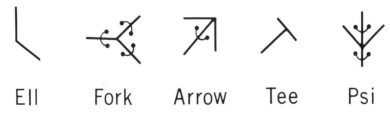

Ell   Fork   Arrow   Tee   Psi

Figure 3. Examples of vertices and the links they imply.

nonsensory unity. Segmentation in the former case could be done on the basis of brightness differentials, in the latter it could only be achieved, so Hebb argues, through an application of knowledge of patterns and objects.

Guzman's program is not an especially successful program. In a significant number of instances it fails to achieve a correct decomposition of a scene. It is obvious the program is insufficiently knowledgeable. What is needed is knowledge of what is permissible and what is not in the structuring of real-world objects.

To map from regions to surfaces asks that we describe lines in the picture domain as entities in the scene domain. In the general case, a picture line can represent a number of different scene entities, e.g. edge or boundary of a shadow and so on. How may object edges be recovered from line drawings? It turns out that vertices provide a useful basis for the edge interpretation of picture lines. Regions that meet at a line will correspond to surfaces in the scene domain which meet at a convex or concave edge; certain arrangements of adjacent regions will correspond to the occlusion of one surface by another. Fortunately, with respect to edges each vertex type identifies a limited set of three dimensional interpretations. Furthermore by mapping vertices in the picture domain onto corners in the scene domain it becomes possible to eliminate ambiguous edge interpretations through the systematic examination of vertices arranged around regions, and checking for consistency in the set of edge interpretations.[14]

Limiting his problem to that of pictures with no more than three lines meeting at a point, Clowes[14] draws up an exhaustive classification of corners into four types. The classification is based on the concave/convex relationship between surfaces and the visible/invisible properties of surfaces. A Type I corner is defined as one in which the three edges meeting at the corner are all convex; a Type II is one in which two of the edges are convex and concave; a Type III corner has two concave edges and one convex edge; and a Type IV corner is one where three concave edges meet. The corners are further subcategorized according to the number of visible surfaces.

Table I. The mapping of vertex types onto corner types

Vertex Type	Corner Type
ELL	I_1, II_1, II_2, III_2
ARROW	I_2, II_3, III_3
FORK	I_3, II_2, IV_3
TEE	I_2, II_2

How may we construct a representation of a picture in terms of surfaces (three dimensional entities) and their relationships? In part the solution lies in defining the mapping of vertex type onto visible corner type. First, the Clowes program recovers regions and associated with each region the lines and vertices bounding the region. Then the vertices are classified and for each vertex recovered the program lists the possible corner interpretations. The problem now is to arrive at an unequivocal description of corners and hence of the manner in which the surfaces present in the picture articulate. To do this the program asks: Which set of corner interpretations is compatible with the structure of three dimensional bodies? Obviously, the program must instantiate knowledge about the physical structure of polyhedra in order that it may answer this question and reach a satisfactory three dimensional description of the scene. It turns out that the following single fact proves sufficient to eliminate impossible combinations of corner interpretations: where two surfaces meet at an edge, that edge must be invariant (either convex or concave or implicate one surface behind another) throughout its length. Thus, given two vertices connected by a line, one could not interpret one vertex as being of Type I and then interpret the other as being of Type IV, for this would mean that the edge corresponding to the connecting line changes from convex to concave which is contrary to the structure of possible polyhedra. It is important to recognize that where this injunction imposes constraints on the interpretation of a pair of connected vertices it automatically restricts the corner interpretations of neighboring vertices. Through iteration it will lead to the discovery of sets of compatible corner interpretations.

Thus, the Clowes' program exceeds the proficiency of Guzman's by constructing a three dimensional description of the bodies present in a scene. It successfully differentiates holes from bodies and rejects impossible polyhedral structures. Its limitations include that it accepts only pictures with three or fewer lines converging on a point, and it accepts these pictures only when the lines have been specified beforehand. We may say of Clowes' program that it starts upstream avoiding the problem of recovering lines from points.

Although this may not appear to be overly serious, consider that in naturally illuminated scenes it is often the case that faces of different bodies may reflect the light equally, which means that some edges will not yield a brightness differential or if they do it is below some working threshold. How might such edges be recovered? How are lines missing from the picture domain detected?

Where programs have been written to take as their starting point the actual output from a television camera—i.e. an input of points—it has proved fruitful, even necessary, to introduce greater flexibility in the relations among representations and to extend the knowledge of the program to include descriptions (prototypes) of possible objects. This higher-order knowledge can be used to guide the construction of lower-level representations.

A program which makes modest use of these principles is that of Falk. [21] Here directly recoverable lines are assigned to different bodies by a variant of Guzman's program. Special heuristics beyond those specified by Guzman are needed, however, to achieve a segmentation into bodies given that certain lines are just not presented in the input. At all events, having obtained a rough decomposition of the scene into bodies the program then applies heuristics to fill in the missing lines. It is important to recognize that these low-level operations are meant only to provide a sketch—a working hypothesis—of what a representation of the bodies in the scene might look like.

But in order that we might better understand Falk's program, let us examine more closely the kinds of scenes the program is dealing with and some of the program's esoteric capabilities. There are nine permissible objects (polyhedra, as before) of fixed size which can be variously arranged on a table top such that some objects may be resting on the faces of others. The program possesses highly specialized knowledge about the three dimensional coordinates of the television camera relative to the table surface, and about the exact size and shape of each of the nine objects. The program will use its exact knowledge of the dimensions of the permissible objects in order to recognize them, but to apply this knowledge, it needs to be able to compute the lengths of at least some of the edges of a given body. Since it knows the position of the camera relative to the table top, it can infer the exact position of any point on the table in 3-space, and, in consequence, the lengths of those edges that contact the table can be determined.

The outcome is a determination of which base edges of which bodies contact the table and the program then calculates the lengths of the base edges of each body and the angles between them. These data are then subjected to operations which seek to match the bodies corresponding to the calculated base lengths and angles to the program's knowledge of permissible objects. Recognizing a body as a particular object carries the bonus of knowing fully the exact dimensions of the body—and that includes, of course, the faces that might be "invisible" in the picture. By recognizing which objects are in contact with the table, it is now possible to reassess the earlier conclusions about which bodies were supporting which bodies.

In the final stages of Falk's program, once supported bodies are isolated from those resting on the table, it maps the supported bodies into the object domain and is then in a position to provide a description of the entire scene in terms of objects and their relationships. But recall that the lines representation from which all else developed was incomplete and the bodies representation was constructed with a strong element of guesswork. To ensure that the description in the objects domain is accurate, a lines representation is *synthesized* from the objects representation and mapped onto the original lines representation. Where a significant mismatch occurs, the bodies and the objects representations may be revised guided by the now available knowledge about the global properties of the scene.

The latter provides the significant feature of the Falk program, namely, the introduction of a more flexible processing routine which permits less abstract descriptions to be reexamined and the information present there to be reinterpreted in the light of more abstract descriptions—thus the objects representation is used to reevaluate the lines representation. This mode of organization is becoming more of a necessity in writing computer programs to perform successful scene analysis.[91] We have seen that the program relies heavily both on exact knowledge of a limited number of objects and on the fact that no other objects than these will be pictured. But we should not be too seriously put off by this austerity and rather should view Falk's program as an illustration of how prototypes might be exploited in visual perception. This approach is represented more elaborately in the program of Roberts [110] which has knowledge both of prototypes and of their lawful perspectives on the argument that the computer program should assume, like the human observer, that a picture is a perspective of a scene which obeys the laws of projective geometry. In addition the Roberts program uses only three prototypes—a cube, a wedge, and a hexagonal prism—and is able to treat a large array of complex polyhedral objects as combinations of these prototypes. The idea that the structure of human memory for things seen may be described as prototypes together with transformation rules has received some measure of experimental support.[25]

If I have dealt at some length with these examples of Seeing Machines it has been owing to several reasons. In the first place, they foster an appreciation of the complexity of formalizing visual processes within the constructivist framework and yet at the same time suggest the directions this formalizing might take. In the second place, they rarely find their way into the psychological literature on visual perception and that, in my opinion, is a serious oversight from the point of view of constructive theory. Lastly, they permit the illustration of certain principles which may have significant implications for the general theory of vision.

Thus from the perspective of a Seeing Machine, the stuff with which a brain works is descriptions, and not images, of optical events. Efforts to explain how vision works ought to focus on computational or symbolic mechanisms rather than the physical mechanisms which have been the mainstay of traditional theories. The latter, as Minsky and Papert[91] point out, are inherently incapable of accounting for the influence of other knowledge and ideas upon perception.

The particular form of computational or symbolic mechanism currently being advanced is not hierarchical. It cannot be said to consist of parts, subparts, and sub-subparts that stand in fixed relation to each other. While a hierarchical label may be appropriate for a physical system, it is less so for a computational system. The latter often exploits the method of two different procedures using each other as subprocedures and thus what is "higher" at one time is "lower" at another. To capture the essence of nonhierarchical, highly flexible mechanisms, the terms "heterarchical"[87,91] and "coalitional"[118,119] have been suggested.

Through the formalization of coalitions is still very much in its infancy, we can identify in a rough and approximate way some fundamental features which distinguish the coalition (heterarchy) from the more familiar hierarchy. First, many structures would function cooperatively in the determining of perception although not all structures need participate in all determinations. Second, while it is certainly the case that a coalitional system has very definite and nonarbitrary structures, the partitioning of these structures into agents and instruments and the specifications of relations among them is arbitrary. In short, any inventory of basic constituent elements and relations is equivocal.

Perhaps the main emphasis of the coalitional formulation is the flexibility of relations among structures. Falk's program[21] is a very modest instantiation of these coalitional features. Winograd's celebrated Language Understanding System[160] is a more ambitious one. Contrary to much of current theoretical linguistics, Winograd's system is concerned more with the problems of representing the meanings conveyed by discourse than with the grammatical structure of discourse. The system is predicated upon the coalitional thesis that sentence comprehension necessitates an intimate and flexible confluence among grammar, semantics, and reasoning. In the Winograd system the sentence "parser" can search out semantic programs to determine if a particular phrase makes sense; semantic programs can exploit deductive programs to determine whether the proposed phrase is sensible in the context of the current state of the real world.[91,160] The fundamental principle of operation, though complex, may be stated simply: *each piece of knowledge can be a procedure and thus it can call on any other piece of knowledge.*

Perception at a Glance: The Contribution of the Information-Processing Approach

The preceding discussion has focused on the theory of seeing as a constructive act. In an elementary but sufficient manner, we have considered some of the principal notions, the scaffolding if you like, upon which theories of indirect perception are erected. Next let us examine experimental efforts to unravel the processes by which information to an eye is "transformed, reduced, elaborated, stored, recovered and used."[94]

Our initial focus is the analysis of perception at a glance. Much of information-processing research has revolved around tachistoscopic presentations and an interpretation of their perceptual consequences. Moreover, the materials briefly exposed have been for the most part letters, numbers, and words so that we might take the liberty of describing the analysis as that of "the stages underlying the perception of linguistic material in a single fixation." The dominant use of linguistic material inhibits the elaboration of tachistoscopic perception into a general theory of visual-perception-at-a-glance, but given the language processing interests of this conference that limitation is perhaps of no great consequence. Let us remind ourselves that on the constructivist view an understanding of perception in a single fixation is fundamental since normal everyday perception is construed as the fitting together of successive retinal snapshots.

Iconic and Short-term Schematic Representations

There is one thing which we can assume from the outset: if perception is a process over time, then in the cases of brief but perceivable optical events (say of the order of several milliseconds to provide an extreme instance) there ought to be a mechanism which internally preserves such events beyond their physical duration. It is upon this internally persisting representation that constructive operations are performed and in its absence we ought to suppose that the perception of brief displays would be well nigh impossible. Furthermore, we can suggest the following about this representation: it should be in an uncategorized form. Suppose that the mechanisms of perception were prefabricated in the sense of possessing knowledge about, and routines for, abstracting universal regularities, and that these regularities were automatically registered and classified. One consequence of this arrangement would be category blindness.[81] If a new category attained significance for the organism, the organism would not be able to grasp it. Obviously, the perceptual mechanisms, although partly prefabricated, must also be flexible. What we can imagine is that on the occurrence of an optical event prefabricated general procedures are brought to bear, and a variety of testings are carried out to determine how this event might fit into the current organization. This suggests[81] that there ought to be a region or "workshop" in the perceptual system which allows for hypothesis testing before categorization. We might anticipate, from the constructivist position, the existence of a transient memory for visual stimulation which preserves the raw data in a relatively literal form.

In many respects the pivotal concept in the information-processing account of perception-at-a-glance is a memory system which has the properties suggested above. The original evidence for a transient, high capacity, literal visual memory comes from the well known experiments of Sperling [130] and Averbach and Coriell.[2]

Brief visual storage, or iconic memory as Neisser[94] has termed it, was isolated through the use of a delayed partial-sampling procedure. Essentially, this procedure involves presenting simultaneously an overload of items tachistoscopically followed by an indicator designating which element or subset of elements the subject has to report. If the indicator is given soon after the display, the subject can report proportionately more with partial report than if asked for a report of the whole display. This superiority permits the inference of a large capacity store; the sharp decline in partial-report superiority with indicator delay permits the inference of rapid decay. Purest estimates of the decay rate reveal that the duration of this storage is of the order of 250 msec.[2,144]

The proof of the precategorical character of iconic storage is found in the kinds of selection criteria which yield efficient performance in the delayed partial-sampling task. Generally, superior partial report can be demonstrated when the items in a display are selected for partial report on the basis of brightness,[146] size,[146,147] color,[13,140,146,147] shape,[143] movement[139] and location.[130] Partial report performance, however, is notably poorer (i.e. not significantly better than whole report) when the letter/digit distinction is the basis for selection.[130,147] On these data we can conclude that one can select or ignore items in iconic storage on the basis of their general physical characteristics, but one cannot with the same efficiency select or ignore items on the basis of their derived properties. We might wish to argue, therefore, that the iconic representation is literal.

We can gain a richer purchase on the character of iconic storage by comparing it with another form of visual memory that arises quite early in the flow of information and which may be described as abstract or schematic. As we shall see, the longevity of this representation exceeds by a considerable degree that of the icon.

It has often been argued that the iconic representation of linguistic material undergoes a metamorphosis from a visual to a linguistically related form. One elegant expression of this view suggests that the raw visual data are cast rapidly into a set of instructions for the speech articulators for subsequent (and more leisurely) rehearsal and report. [132] However, as one would intuit, the transformation of the icon establishes not only a representation in the language system but, in addition, and we may suppose in parallel,[16] a further and more stable representation in the visual system. The first strong experimental hints that this might be so were provided by Posner and Keele [105] in an experiment which stood on the shoulders of an earlier series of now celebrated experiments by Posner and Mitchell.[106]

Consider a situation in which subjects are presented a pair of letters and asked to respond "same," if these letters have the same name, and "otherwise," if they are different. On some occasions the letters with the same name are also physically the same (e.g. AA) and on others the letters with the same name are physically dissimilar (e.g. Aa). It proves to be the case that "same" responses to AA are significantly faster than same responses to Aa, which suggests that AA-type pairs are not necessarily being processed on the basis of name but rather that their visual characteristics are being used to make the response. Adopting Posner's terminology, [103] we will refer to matches of physically identical letters as "physical matches" and matches of physically different but nominally identical letters as "name matches."

We now look at what happens when the two members of a pair are presented sequentially rather than simultaneously and the time elapsing between the appearance of the first and the appearance of the second is varied. Under these conditions, the latency of a name match is indifferent to the delay time, but the latency of a physical match increases with delay until it and the name match latency are virtually identical. The converging of physical- and name-match latencies identifies a decline in the availability of a visual code and an increasing dependence on the name of the letter with the passage of time. In the original experiment, [105] the estimated duration of the visual code isolated by the reaction time procedure was of the order of 2 sec; however, subsequent research has shown that it is considerably more durable than the original experiment would have us believe. [75, 99] At all events, the superior longevity of this visual code to that exposed by the delayed partial-sampling procedure (i.e. the icon) suggests that we are indeed dealing with two different visual, memorial representations, two different descriptions, of an optical event. But before elaborating upon this conclusion, we ought to be more explicit about the difference between the two procedures defining the two representations. In one, delayed partial-sampling, we are interested in the persistence of aspects of visual stimulation not yet selectively attended to; in the other, our concern is with the persistence of the visual description of stimulation that has enjoyed the privileges of selective attention.

Beyond the difference in persistence between the two visual representations we can note the following differences. In the first place, the iconic representation is perturbed by an after-coming visual mask, the schematic representation is not. [98, 103, 112, 131] In the second place, the capacity of the iconic representation is probably unlimited but that of the schematic representation is clearly constrained. [16, 98] In the third place, if during the existence of a representation demands are made concurrently on processing capacity, [92, 102] the persistence of the iconic representation seems to be unimpaired[20] in contrast to the persistence of the schematic representation which can be shown to be severely reduced. [103] The corollary to this latter distinction, however, is that the close dependency of the schematic representation on central processing capacity means that the persistence of this representation is indeterminate—it may persist for as long as sufficient processing capacity is devoted to it. [75, 103, 104]

One last difference is worth attention. The high capacity, maskable iconic representation is tied to spatial position; the low capacity, unmaskable schematic representation is not.[98] On the basis of the schematic representation, the perceptual system can match two succesive optical events when they are spatially separate as efficiently as it can when they are spatially congruent. On the basis of the iconic representation, however, a match of successive and spatially separate events is conducted less efficiently than a match of successive events which spatially overlap.[98]

For current theory, memory consists of two basic structures, termed "active" and "passive," or alternatively two basic models, the "short-term" and the "long-term." The relation of the iconic representation to these two structures is not perfectly obvious, although an appeal to the consensus of opinion[42, 94, 132, 141] informs us that the icon is a necessary precursor to active memory and that it interfaces visual stimulation with internal models. Thus in this view the iconic representation is a transient state which in the hands of long-term knowledge structures is molded into a variety of representations in active memory. On the foregoing account, we may identify the schematic visual code and the name code as examples of active representations so produced. Figure 4 captures these ideas.

Temporal Characteristics of the Iconic Interface

One tool that has proved reasonably successful for examining the fine temporal grain of events surrounding the iconic interface is visual masking. There are a number of renderings of this phenomenon, some of which are

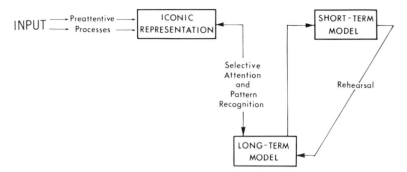

Figure 4. A typical information-processing scheme.

particularly significant to the discussion that follows. First, the influence of the second member of the pair on the first, which is referred to as "backward masking"; and the influence of the first, on the second, which is termed "forward masking." Second, the two stimuli may be presented binocularly (i.e. both stimuli are presented to both eyes) or monoptically (i.e., both stimuli are presented to one eye); or they may be presented dichoptically in which case one member of the stimulus pair is presented to one eye and the other member is presented to the other eye. Masking which occurs under conditions of binocular or monoptic viewing may originate in either peripheral or central visual mechanisms, but masking that occurs in dichoptic viewing is more likely due to central effects. Third, the two stimuli may or may not overlap spatially. We reserve the special term "metacontrast" for the case in which backward masking occurs with non-overlapping but spatially adjacent stimuli.

Essentially, there are two major interpretations of masking effects. If we refer to the stimulus to be identified as the target and the stimulus impeding perception as the mask then one interpretation, the ingetration hypothesis [64] stresses the effect that the mask has on the target representation. The idea is that the two stimuli in rapid succession are effectively simultaneous within a single "frame" of psychological time, analogous to a double exposure of a photographic plate. The result of this summation favors the higher energy stimulus; thus, if the mask is of greater energy, then the target will be reduced in clarity and its identification impeded. Closely related to this interpretation is the notion that where a greater energy mask follows a target, the neural response to the target is occluded. This view is often dubbed "overtake" and it may be thought of as an integration which emphasizes a nonlinear summation of responses rather than a linear summation of stimuli. [64]

A contrasting interpretation of masking is presented in the form of the interruption hypothesis:[64] if a mask follows a target stimulus after some delay, processing is assumed to have occurred during that delay but is terminated or interfered with by the mask. In the context of the iconic representation we can view the interruption hypothesis as saying that an aftercoming stimulus does not affect the accuracy of the iconic description of a prior stimulus, but rather interferes with its translation into active memory codes. In this same context it is evident that the stimulus version of the integration hypothesis is saying that the target and mask are dealt with as a composite, resulting in an iconic representation in which the target is unintelligible. The response version of the same hypothesis suggests that the iconic description of the target is never formed.

When looked at in terms of the icon, the two interpretations of masking do not appear as competing explanations; rather they seem to be interpretations of masking originating at different stages in the flow of visual information.[141]

We can provide some measure of proof for this point of view through an experiment of the following kind. A target stimulus, say a letter, is presented briefly ($<$ 10 msec) to one eye followed shortly afterward (say, 0 to 50 msec) by a similarly brief exposure of a masking stimulus to the other eye. A contoured mask with features in common with the target will seriously impair the perception of the target in this dichoptic situation but, by way of contrast, a non-contoured mask which bears no formal relation to the target, such as a homogeneous flash or a fine-grain random dot pattern, will not do so even if within limits its energy is made considerably greater than that of the target.[115,141] Yet if a non-contoured mask is presented to the same eye as the target, masking can be demonstrated. On these observations it may be argued that with respect to a contoured target, a contoured mask can exert a central influence but a non-contoured mask cannot. The influence of the latter is limited primarily to the peripheral processing of the target.

The gist of the whole matter is given in an experimental arrangement in which a contoured target and an after coming contoured mask are presented to separate eyes with a non-contoured higher-energy mask following shortly thereafter on the same eye as the contoured mask. The perceptual outcome of this apparently complex configuration of events is singularly straightforward; the target can be seen and identified against the unimpeding background of the non-contoured mask.[141] Although straightforward, the outcome is curious. It implies that the second arriving mask occluded the first arriving mask in the "peripheral" sequence of neural transformations from retina to cortex. That is to say, the first mask which could impede target perception centrally never in fact reached central processing mechanisms and the perceptibility of the target was thus unhindered. One might venture to propose that different kinds of masking obeying different principles originate at different stages in the flow of visual information on the nervous system.

Consider the monoptic masking of letter targets by a masker of equal or greater energy that is relatively ineffectual dichoptically. It has been demonstrated that in this situation the following principle relates target duration to the minimal interstimulus (target offset to mask onset) interval permitting evasion of the masking action: target duration X minimal interstimulus interval = a constant. [95, 141] We owe the first demonstration of this relationship to Kinsbourne and Warrington. [67]

When examined more closely, target energy rather than target duration emerges as the true entry into the relation. [141] Furthermore, it is of some importance that the relation holds for forward as well as backward masking, although the constant for the forward relation is higher than that for the backward; [68, 141] forward masking in the domain of the multiplicative rule extends over a greater range than backward masking.

My own treatment of the multiplicative function is that it characterizes peripheral processing. If we assume that there are a large number of independent and parallel networks detecting features and/or spatial frequencies, then the relation tells us, that the rate of detection is a direct function of target energy.

We should inquire as to the relation between target duration and the minimal interstimulus interval when the two stimuli are presented dichoptically and the masker is a contoured, effective dichoptic-masking agent. In this situation the relation proves to be additive: target duration + minimal interstimulus interval = a constant [95, 141] and here target duration *is* the proper entry. Indeed, this dichoptic or central principle tells us that the total time elapsing between stimulus onsets is what is significant. While the energy relation between target and mask is of major importance to peripheral processes it is of limited importance to central processes.

Perhaps the brunt of the peripheral/central difference is carried by the contrast of forward and backward masking. We recall that peripherally forward masking was greater than backward even though both obeyed the same principle. Contrapuntally, central forward masking is slight in comparison to central backward masking. [129, 141] We see that central masking is primarily backward and this may be an important comment on the nature of central information processing. [72]

To summarize: when two successive stimuli compete for the services of

the same central processes, it is the later arriving one which is more completely identified. On the other hand, when two stimuli compete for the same
peripheral networks, order of arrival is less important than energy. Peripherally the stimulus of greater energy, whether it leads or lags, will be the one
whose properties are likely to be registered.

We ought to ask how the two rules described above relate to each other.
On the hypothesis that the multiplicative rule relates to primarily peripheral
processes and the additive to central processes, our question becomes that of
how peripheral and central processes combine. At first blush we may think
that this relationship is successive and additive, that is to say, peripheral
processing is completed first, then central processes occur and total processing time is given by adding the two stages. It proves to be the case, however,
that a successive and additive interpretation will not do. [141] A more reasonable interpretation is that the output from peripheral networks is parallel and
asynchronous—different features are detected at different rates [71, 155] —and
that central processes, obviously dependent upon peripheral input, operate
simultaneously with peripheral processes. The relation is said to be concur-
rent and contingent. [141]

Identifying Feature-detectors in Human Information Processing

We noted earlier that "information processing" as a methodology for
examining transformations of neural states may not be able to give us a
measure of vision's structural grammars nor a sufficiently detailed account of
how representations commute. We may now turn to a particularly significant
contribution of the approach—its ability to suggest or demonstrate feature-
sensitive systems in human vision.

It is well known that there are cells in the visual cortex of the cat and
monkey that are selectively sensitive to the orientation of lines. How can we
reveal the presence of such units in human vision? A demonstration is
important because our constructive theories of human pattern and object
recognition presuppose the existence of these units.

A phenomenon well suited to this purpose is the "after effect." The logic
behind visual after effects as a technique is that prolonged viewing of a
stimulus consisting of a particular visual feature should selectively depress the
mechanism detecting that feature. We can take advantage of a fairly general
rule: if any form of stimulation is continued for a long time and then
stopped, one will tend to experience the reverse condition.

Orientation-specific systems in human vision are hinted at by the tilt
after effect. [35] Suppose that one is exposed for a period of time to a

high-contrast grating which is tilted slightly to the right of vertical. A subsequently exposed vertical grating (or vertical line) will then appear tilted slightly to the left. This is termed the "direct effect." The fact that exposure to a vertical grating tilted clockwise will cause a horizontal grating or line to appear counterclockwise from the horizontal is termed the "indirect effect."[15] An eminent example of this after effect is provided by Campbell and Maffei.[12] The evidence is that the human visual system exhibits a narrow orientational tuning of the type reported for units in the cat and monkey.[57]

A particularly intriguing aspect of the tilt after effect is that it can be color specific. If one is first exposed to red stripes tilted clockwise off vertical and green stripes tilted off vertical by the same amount but counterclockwise and then one examines a vertical test stripe, its apparent orientation will depend on the color of the light in which it is projected. Projected in red light, it will appear tilted counterclockwise; projected in the green light, it will appear tilted clockwise.[49] This orientation after effect specific to color should be contrasted with the now famous McCullough phenomenon[88] which is a color after effect contingent upon orientation. In the latter, viewing alternatively a vertical grating on a blue background and a horizontal grating on an orange background induces an orange after image when vertical lines on a white ground are inspected and a blue image when horizontal lines on a white ground are inspected.

A variety of contingent after effects has now been demonstrated. A representative but not exhaustive list would look like this: motion-contingent color after effects;[136] color-contingent motion after effects;[22] texture-contingent visual motion after effects[86, 148] and curvature-contingent color after effects.[108]

One further example of how the after effect phenomenon demonstrates that different characteristics of visual stimulation can be processed selectively. If one views a contracting simple arithmetic ("Archimedes") spiral for some period and then directs the eyes to another object, one experiences an equally great but opposite effect, i.e. the object will appear to expand. But suppose that the adapting spiral subtended only $4°$ of visual angle and that following prolonged viewing one looked at a large and regular 20×20 matrix of squares. A region of the matrix subtending about $4°$ will appear to enlarge and even to approach. The lines, however, will not look curved nor will there be any interruption between the growing part of the matrix and the remainder of the matrix. As Kolers[70, 72] remarks, a part of the figure seems to change in size and position without looking discontinuous with the remainder.

Although after effects are curious and engaging, their usefulness as a source of information about feature analyzers in human vision has not been endorsed uncritically by all students of perception. Weisstein[151] sees the principal weakness of the technique as that of examining what is left *after* adaptation. It is reasonable to conjecture, and indeed the contingent after effects bear this out, that the after effect manifests a pooling of many different types of analyzers. Moreover, a number of different populations of analyzers could give the same phenomenal result. Other students have raised similar doubts about the integrity and fruitfulness of after effect data for the exploration of feature detectors in human vision.[44,93]

An alternative strategy is one that is referred to as cross adaptation. The essential characteristic of cross adaptation is that one examines the loss of sensitivity to one pattern given a preceding exposure to another. The measure of change in sensitivity contrasts cross adaptation with the "after effect" which is concerned with the degree to which perception is reversed. When a grating is viewed for some period of time, the thresholds for the same and similar gratings are raised but thresholds for gratings differing in orientation and size are virtually unchanged.[8] This may be taken as evidence that different populations of neurons respond differentially to features of a stimulus.

There is an especially provocative application of this procedure which permits the opportunity of drawing together several strands of this discussion. Weisstein and coworkers[152, 154] were motivated by an aspect of the theory of object recognition which is prominent in scene analysis programs but neglected in psychological experiments. In scene analysis, constructing a representation involves abstracting certain entities, identifying their attributes, and specifying the relationships among them. Virtually all after effects and all cross adaptation experiments are directed toward isolating and defining entities. But of interest to Weisstein was the possibility of demonstrating relations among entities in the scene domain. She inquired whether one could selectively adapt the neural structures responsible for the relation "in back of." Her experiment was deceptively simple. Subjects inspected a vertical grating which was partially blocked from view by a perspective drawing of a cube. A subsequent vertical test grating was presented within the portion of the visual field where the prior grating was visible and also where it was not (i.e., in the region covered by the cube). A reduction in apparent contrast (adaptation) was found for both positions of the test grating. This means that a population of size-selective and orientation-selective systems that was adapted out by the original grating was also adapted out (although not to the same degree) by the cube. Yet it could be demonstrated that a cube by itself (i.e., not covering a grating) does not induce a significant adaptation effect nor does a hexagon outline drawing of a cube which partially occludes the same area of grating. [154] Apparently what is important to the effect is the impression of depth given by the *perspective* drawing of the cube, and one might interpret this result to mean that the relation "in back of" is specified by the firing of those cells which would have fired if the grating had been visible in the region covered by the cube. In Weisstein's view, this effect implies the involvement of neural mechanisms which separate a scene into its components—analogous perhaps to the operations involved in the computer programs described earlier.

Information Processing as a Coalitional Skill

Let me conclude this selective account of constructivism with an emphasis on the coalitional/heterarchical conception of how perceptual procedures are organized. What follows is a potpourri of curious experimental observations which implicate (but do not necessarily dictate) the form of organization encountered in our earlier discussion of Seeing Machines.

Oriented-line detectors play a significant role in theories of object recognition. Generally they are assigned to an early stage in a hierarchically organized processing scheme. However, their actual status within the scheme and the scheme's structure are less than obvious, as witnessed by an experiment of Weisstein and Harris. [153] They demonstrated facilitation of "feature" (line) detection by object context. This work is matched by a facilitation of "object" detection by scene context elegantly revealed in the studies of Bierderman and his colleagues. [5, 6, 7] An object is more accurately identified when it is part of a briefly exposed real world scene than when it is part of a jumbled version of that scene, exposed equally briefly.

These observations are puzzling on the assumption that the detection of fragments of a pattern predates the determination of the global structure and identity of a pattern. Thus, paradoxically, the identity of the whole depends on the identity of its fragments, but the perceptibility of a fragment is determined by the whole in which it is embedded as an integral part. Significantly, where a fragment is immaterial to the global structure its presence is more likely to be obscured than enhanced. [109]

This paradox is also apparent in the perception of linguistic material. It can be demonstrated that a letter is perceived more readily in the context of a word than in the context of a meaningless string of letters. [62, 107, 157] Though some have suggested that results of this kind can be interpreted solely in terms of the superior orthographic/phonologic regularity in the word,[4] others have sought to demonstrate the significance of meaning. Controlling for orthographic/phonologic regularity (as best one can), Henderson[52] has shown that meaningful letter strings (e.g. VD, LSD, YMCA) are compared faster in a binary classification task than meaningless strings (e.g. BV, LSF, YPMC).

There is some motivation for interpreting results of the latter kind in terms of a direct accessing of semantic knowledge. For example, it has been shown that the time needed to reject a meaningful consonant triplet as a word is longer than the rejection latency for a meaningless consonant triplet.[95] This observation contradicts the idea that an analysis of orthographic/ phonologic regularity precedes entry into the lexicon and suggests to the contrary that lexical access is temporally contiguous with structural analysis. One conception that may be useful here is that of Henderson:[52] feature analysis has parallel access to various memory structures or domains— grapheme knowledge, orthographic rules, a content-addressable semantic base—though consulted in parallel, the domains interact coalitionally through rules which map from one to the other. Presumably perceptual decisions are reached through this mutual cooperation among separate domains.

It is worth discussing the idea of a direct mapping between script and meaning. Several scholars have found this notion necessary to their accounts of skilled reading[9, 73] and there are a number of provocative clinical observations which speak in its favor. To take but one example, a paralexic error (though not a common one) is to read a word as a semantic relative; thus *hen* is read as "egg."[85] The reader in this instance cannot identify the word, nor can he give a phonetic rendering of it, but he can relate to its semantic structure. There are parallels to this clinical observation to be found in the visual masking literature, namely, experiments which suggest that an observer may have some knowledge of the meaning of a masked word even though he may be unable to report the actual identity of the word. [84, 159]

There is a second batch of curious results, much related to those just described. Suppose that one is asked to scan a list of items in search of a specified target item. As a first approximation we can say that the perceiver looks for the set of features (or an appropriate subset) that defines the target item. In this case nontarget items, or foils, which share many of the target's features will be a greater hindrance to the search than foils which are less closely related. Experimental evidence tends to bear this out.[94] Unfortunately, this first approximation is challenged by visual scan experiments in which the target is drawn from a conceptual category different from the foils—the target, say, is a letter and the foils are digits, or vice versa. Here the evidence is that the time to find *any* letter (digit) in a list of digits (letters) is less than the time it takes to find a particular digit (letter) in a list of digits (letters). [11, 58] The implication is that category discrimination can precede character identification: one can know that a character is a letter or digit before one knows what letter or digit it is. Our puzzle is: what are the features that define the *category* of letters on the one hand and digits on the other? This puzzle is compounded by the following experiment which plays on the ambiguity of the character "O" (it may be interpreted as either the digit zero or the letter "oh"). When "O" is embedded in a list of digits it can be more rapidly found if the observer is told that he or she is looking for a letter than if he or she is told that he or she is looking for a digit. Conversely when "O" is a member of a list of letters, latency of search is considerably shorter if one is looking for the digit zero than if one is looking for the letter "oh".[63] This result is not restricted to the digit/letter distinction, for research at the University of Belgrade reveals the same pattern of findings when the target is an ambiguous letter. That is, a letter which has one phonetic interpretation in the Cyrillic alphabet and another in the Roman alphabet (Lukatela, personal communication). (The popular use of two alphabets is an interesting feature of the Serbo-Croatian language.)

Though we cannot provide an explanation for the phenomena just described, we can appreciate their implications for the modeling of the human as an information processor. Whatever procedures are presumed to be involved in the processing of information, it can be hypothesized that their manner of interrelating is not obligatory. The nature of the task constrains the structure of the coalition with different tasks requiring different coordinations of procedures. In this sense information processing is a coalitional skill.

Perception as Primary and Direct:
The Gibsonian Alternative

Introduction

Since constructivism starts from the assumption that stimuli are informationally inadequate, then it is obvious why the primary concern of perceptual theory is taken to be the investigation of the *how* of perception. Constructivism encourages an inquiry into memory structures and cognitive operations which mediate cues, punctate sensations, features, or whatever, and the perceptual experience. On this view internal models enable adaptation to a world poorly signaled by the flux of energy. Thus it is the internal models, their acquisition and their usage, that we seek to understand.

In polar opposition to this strategy stands J. J. Gibson who suggests that we ask not what is inside the head—as the constructivists would have it—but rather what the head is inside of.[80] For Gibson the question of the *what* of perception has been given short shrift, and in his view we are burdened with excessive theoretical baggage relating to the how of perception for the very reason that what there is to be perceived has not been seriously examined. [119]

Gibson begins with the question: What do terrestrial environments look like? A departure point which has been curiously ignored by those who would build general theories of visual perception. Indeed, it can be argued that the constructivist approach to vision has not broken kinship with the school of thought which gave rise to Molyneux's premise in the seventeenth century.[97] By taking empty Euclidian space as the frame of reference, the intellectual predecessors of modern constructivism were forced into the position of arguing that distance, for example, could not be apprehended through vision. Distance could only be arrived at (constructed, inferred) through the supplementary information provided by past experience and represented in the form of kinesthetic and tactile images. A moment's examination of the classical exposition of space perception will stand us in good stead.

In the classical view the third dimension was construed as a straight line extending outward from the eye. But since physical space was interpreted as an empty Euclidean space, nothing existed between the eye and an object fixated. One might refer to the theory derived from this conception as the "air theory" of space perception,[26] for it implies an observer looking at unsupported objects hanging in mid-air. (We can readily admit to the unnaturalness of this characterization but our criticism must be held in abeyance for the time being; there is a great deal of modern theory which has been erected on this way of describing perceptual situations in the abstract and it is incumbent upon us to appreciate fully the point of view.)

On the "air theory" formulation, an object fixated by an observer projects a two-dimensional form on the retina which relates to the size and outline of the exposed face(s) of the object. What needs to be explained is how the object's distance is perceived. To grasp the nature of this problem, consider Figure 5 which portrays in traditional fashion a number of objects at varying distances from the observer. The size of each object's projection onto the retinal surface is a function of the visual angle formed by the light rays from the extremities of the object. We have chosen our objects and their

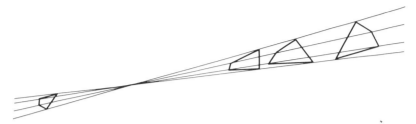

Figure 5. Different forms at different slants and distances from the eye can produce the same retinal image (the form at the left). Thus the retinal image is ambiguous for form, size and distance.

slants so that the visual angle projected by each is the same. Clearly, size on the retina does not unequivocally specify distance and we are led to conclude that retinal information, and thus vision, is insufficient for object-distance perception. It necessarily follows that for perceiving the distance of objects other information must be supplied, supposedly from the observer's memory banks. For instance, the transactionalists[59] looked to one's familiarity with objects (and thus with their actual dimensions) as the relevant memory material. But this left unsettled the problem of perceiving the distance of unfamiliar objects. For an alternative one could look to the information available in the converging of the two eyes.[39] Supposedly the angle set between the eyes when converging on an object is a cue to its distance. But there is a good reason to doubt the efficacy of convergence[96] and in any event such a cue is not at the disposal of many animals, namely, those with nonconverging eyes who do perceive object distance. Furthermore, we can readily imagine the problem pictured in Figure 5 as being that of the limited information to a single eye and we can, after all, perceive distance monocularly.

In his 1950 text Gibson[26] responded to the classical treatment of space perception in a way that was both elegant and simple. To begin with he translated the abstract question, "How is space perceived?" into the biologically and ecologically meaningful question of, "How is the layout of surfaces detected?" More especially Gibson asked, "How, from a point of observation, do we see continuous distance in all directions?" rather than the commonplace experimental question of "How do we judge the distance of these two objects?" The importance of an impression of *continuous* distance is that it underlies our capability to perceive the distances of *any number of objects* in a field of view.

In the next step he replaced the traditional conception of an isolated eye

viewing mathematical points in empty space with that of an eye attached to a
body in contact with a ground surface viewing points *attached to the surface.*
In this account of the problem it is evident that by the laws of linear
perspective the retinal image is structured in a way that corresponds unam-
biguously to the distribution of points. (Figure 6 contrasts the classical and
Gibsonian accounts.) Moreover, if we now replace the points with objects,
then it is similarly evident by the laws of linear perspective that the projection of these objects-on-a-surface will be such that near objects will be imaged
large and high up on the retina while far objects will be imaged smaller and
lower down.

Although what has been said so far does not do justice to Gibson's
current thinking (particularly the references to retinal image), it is clear that
on this reinterpretation of the space perception problem the information
coming to an eye is conceivably richer than traditional theory would have us
believe. Indeed, one might venture to say that the light to an eye could be
structured in a way that *corresponds* to the layout of points and objects on a
ground surface.

Let me return to the classical view in order that I may illustrate its
pervasive influence on vision theory. Earlier we examined the motivation for
assuming that perception goes beyond what is given, that is, the view of
perception as indirect. In the classical theory of space perception the third
dimension is lost in the two-dimensional retina. The immediate theoretical
consequence of this "loss" is already obvious: the retinal image is held to be a

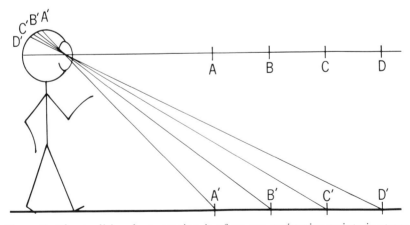

*Figure 6. The traditional conception is of an eye registering points in space
(ABCD). Gibson's conception is of an eye attached to a body registering
points on a surface (A'B'C'D').*

flat patchwork of colors, more precisely of colored forms, to which one can add a third dimension by using available clues, some of which are given directly and some of which are themselves constructions (e.g. superposition).

Of the many conceptual progeny sired by the classical story the following two are among the most significant. First is the notion, now inviolate, that the two-dimensional retinal image is the proper starting point for any theory of seeing. It is this notion which legitimizes, among other things, the enterprise of building theories of visual perception on the shoulders of experiments in picture perception. Moreover, since perceiving begins with a flat patchwork of colored forms, it gives to the theories of form perception and color-patch perception a special status. They are, as it were, introductory to the theory of visual perception.

Second is the idea that one should examine the retinal image for *copies* of environmental aspects and where copies are not found those aspects are said to be inferred, guessed at, or created. For instance, the third dimension does not have a copy in the retinal image and so it must be constructed; similarly the shape of an object (its structure in 3-space) is not replicated in the image and so it must be constructed or inferred from the two-dimensional outline of the object which *is* replicated in the image; and by the same token the arrangement of flashes for the phi phenomenon does not produce a retinal copy of physical movement defined as object displacement in space—so the impression of movement in this situation must be a mental creation.

Gibson's contention then is that this way of conceptualizing visual perception, that is, along the lines suggested in the classical theory of space perception, is blatantly in error. Among his reasons for this contention, the following bears directly on the classical position. For Gibson there is no such problem as the problem of depth or space perception. The very concept of "space" as empty Euclidean space is irrelevant to discourse on perception, and its use in psychology, he argues, is confused and confusing. Animals, he will tell us repeatedly, do not perceive space. We have misconstrued the problem: what animals perceive is the layout of surfaces. And the significance of this restatement of the problem is that in the light there is information for the perception of surface layout—thus surface layout may not have to be created or guessed at, it can be sensed in the meaning of detected.

If Gibson's point of view is valid, then many concepts which evolved with the attempts to solve the space perception problem, and which were perpetuated by its classical solution, may have to be discarded. Let us therefore proceed to the question of what terrestrial environments look like.

Ecological Optics

The tenor of Gibson's denunciation of classical theory is that evolution did not devise visual systems to operate in a vacuous Euclidean space but to detect and interact with the properties of cluttered environments. The environments of animals and man induce inhomogeneities in reflected light, and it is Gibson's principal, guiding intuition that environmenal events structure light in ways which specify their properties. The proof of this intuition rests with "ecological optics"[29] an enterprise which seeks to determine what is contained in the light: if it can be demonstrated that the light is structured by environmental events in a specific fashion, then it is said that the light contains information for these events. In Gibson's view we should look for tighter corespondences between environmental facts and the light as structured by those facts. But all of the above is by way of a summary and to be appreciated it requires that we reexamine the conception of light with reference to visual perception.

The terrestrial environment is manufactured from solids, liquids, and gases of various chemical composition. The interfaces between these phases of matter are what we normally refer to as surfaces. Surfaces can be said to have structure, that is to say, they are textured, where the texture (or grain) consists of elements of one kind or another which are duplicated over the entire surface. The "signature" of a surface is given by the cyclicity or periodicity of these textural elements.

But significantly the terrestrial environment as a whole posseses structure at all levels of size—at one extreme it is structured by mountains; at the other, by pebbles and grass.[30] And equally significantly the structure at one level of size is nested in the structure at the next higher level of size. Each component of the environment can be said to consist of smaller components; facets are nested within faces, and in the most general of senses, forms are nested within forms. Thus the texture of the individual brick is nested within the texture of the wall as given in the arrangement of bricks. We see that it is considerably more apt to treat the structure of the environment as hierarchic, than as mosaic.

The natural environment receives its illumination from the sun, although our living and working environs are mostly illuminated by man-made sources of radiant light. Not all surfaces are directly illuminated by radiant light; some, occasionally most, are illuminated by the light reflected from other surfaces. Natural surfaces tend to be opaque rather than transparent which means they reflect light rather than transmit it. More precisely, opaque surfaces reflect some portion of incident light and absorb the remainder as a function of their chemical composition. A significant feature of natural surfaces is that they do not reflect light like a mirror; they scatter it. This scatter-reflectance is of two kinds: selective for wavelength and unselective for wavelength. In combination, gradations in these two kinds of reflectance, and complex differences in reflectivity—in scattering—due to a textural difference, mean that each different surface modifies light idiosyncratically.

Surfaces, of course, articulate at various angles to each other and when illuminated reflect light among themselves in multiple fashion. The consequence of this is a "flux of interlocking reflected rays in all directions at all points,"[30] and, therefore, the light which impinges upon an observer in the transparent medium of an illuminated environment is primarily indirect, reflected light.

We need a term to distinguish this light from the radiant light with which we have become most acquainted through physics. Gibson[29,30] suggests the term "ambient" for radiant light which has been modulated by an arrangement of surfaces, that is, by an environment.

There are several significant distinctions to be drawn between radiant and ambient light. Ambient light is in reference to an environment and radiant light is not. Also, ambient light converges to a point of observation, while radiant light diverges from a source of energy. In an illuminated room, wherever one stands there is a sheaf of rays converging at that point. This is a consequence of the multiple reflection (reverberation) of radiant light from the walls, ceiling, and floor. An illuminated medium therefore is said to be packed with convergence points, or points of observation.[29,30]

To the bundle of light rays converging to a point of observation we give a special name—the optic array.[29,30] Now because surfaces differ in the amount of incident light falling upon them and in inclination, reflectance, and texture, the optic array at a point of observation will consist of different intensities (and different spectral values) in different directions. Radiant light has no structure and is simply energy, while ambient light has structure and is potentially information.

What is implied by the radiant/ambient distinction? Assuming that one does not find the distinction quixotic, the foremost implication is that light as stimulation for the ocular equipment of man, animal and insect has not been properly described by physics. Radiant light has been lucidly portrayed, but not ambient light; and if the preceding is to be respected, it is ambient light which permits perception of the environment.

However if, following tradition, we remain true to the persuasion that radiant light is the valid and only starting point for the theory of visual perception, then we must conform to the task of explaining how the richness and variety of the visual experience is derived from intensity and wavelength, the variables of radiant light to which brightness and hue correspond as the basic variables of perception. With radiant light as the starting point, we are virtually condemned to a theory of indirect perception.

What befalls us when we take ambient light as the point of departure? To begin with, we lose the security of physics, for the stimulus variables of an optic array are not readily couched in the fundamental physical measures. We gain, however, a new perspective on the problem of visual perception, for with ambient light the variables of stimulation are potentially as rich as the variables of experience. Let us dwell, therefore, a little longer on the concept of the optic array.

An especially useful description of the optic array is that it consists of a finite (closed) set of visual solid angles with a common apex at the point of observation and with a transition of intensity separating each solid angle from its topological neighbors.[32] A component solid angle of an array corresponds to a component of the environment—and just as the environment is hierarchically structured, so it is with the optic array: visual solid angles are nested within visual solid angles, and more generally, forms are nested within forms. A few of the variables of the optic array can now be noted: abruptness and amount of intensity transition between visual solid angles; density of intensity transitions within a visual solid angle and change of density across visual solid angles; rates of change, or gradients, in the density of intensity transitions and, with movement, rates of rates of change. This truncated inventory should suffice to suggest that the variables of ecological stimulation are both much richer and of a higher order than those normally adduced for the energy impinging upon an organism.

In summary, explanations of visual perception have traditionally been proposed with reference to the limited variables of radiant light. It would seem, however, that ambient light, that is, radiant light as structured by an environment, is the proper reference. The variables of ambient light are complex and probably limitless. Moreover, there should be a strict correspondence between an ambient optic array and the environment responsible for it. This suggests the following hypothesis: for any isolable property of the environment there should be a corresponding isolable property of the stationary or flowing optic array, however complex. It is this hypothesis, relating to the *what* of perception, which constitutes the concern of ecological optics. If true, this hypothesis has profound implications for perceptual theory. For if the structured light to the visual system can specify the world and if it is only rarely equivocal (contrary to hundreds of years of studied opinion), then we can imagine that visual systems evolved to be sensitive to its structure, i.e., to the higher-order variables of the optic array. Such being the case, visual perception need not be constructive—it need not be a guessing game—it could be direct. The latter is Gibson's working hypothesis on the *how* of perception and it may be stated more formally: for every visual perceptual experience there is a corresponding property of the stationary or flowing optic array, however complex.[28,30]

The Concept of Invariance

What then is the nature of the correspondence between the optic array and environmental properties?

Recall that tradition opted for replication as the form of the correspondence between environment and retinal image. One consequence of this has been dealt with, namely that because the third dimension is not registered in the retinal image, it therefore must be constructed. The upshot of the Gibsonian analysis is that the correspondence is correlative (in the sense of analytic geometry and not in the sense of statistics) and that our search should be for correlates of environmental properties, and not for copies. Moreover, one should look for these in the ambient optic array rather than in the retinal image. Where a property of the static or changing optic array corresponds in this sense to a persistent property of the environment it is referred to as an invariant.

The Stationary and Flowing Optic Array

In the current scheme the natural stimulus for an ocular system is the optic array. This contrasts with the earlier discussed view of stimuli as punctate and momentary, because an optic array by definition is extended and persistent. Furthermore, stimuli are traditionally conceived to be at the retina (hence the primacy of the retinal image) whereas the optic array clearly is not. Indeed, we can mathematically describe the optic array at a point of observation in an illuminated environment without assuming that the position is occupied by an observer.[30] A significant feature of Gibson's conception of a point of observation is that it is stationary only as a limiting case. The motivation for this lies in the fact that observation generally accompanies movement (i.e., the observer is often in motion).

A moving point of observation means a changing optic array: component visual solid angles will be transformed, some will even cease to exist. But the surrounding layout of surfaces which is responsible for the optic array at a stationary point of observation must also be responsible for the flowing optic array at a moving point of observation. There ought to be abstract optical relations which persist during the course of change, and these relations ought to be specific to the persisting or permanent properties of the environment. On the other hand the nonpersisting features of the optic array are due to the motion of the point of observation, that is, to locomotion itself. Of the changes in the optic array we will say that they specify locomotion, and herein lies a significant insight.

Briefly, the gist of the preceding may be conveyed in this fashion: the invariant structure of the changing optic array is information about the environment, that is, it is exterospecific; the variant structure, on the other hand, is information about the observer and therefore may be referred to as propriospecific. We proceed from here with the notion of invariant structure (drawing a comparison between invariant information in the changing and in the unchanging, stationary optic array) leaving to a later moment the ego-specific character of variant optical structure.

Consider a problem encountered earlier, that of perceiving continuous distance. From a stationary point of observation, a receding textured surface projects a gradient of optical texture density. (By "gradient" is meant nothing more than an increase or decrease of some measured quantity along a given dimension or axis.) For two identical (but hypothetical) visual solid angles, the one which corresponds to a region of the surface close to the point of observation will be less densely packed with intensity transitions (produced by the surface's textural elements scattering the light) than the one which corresponds to a region farther away. And, of course, for each identical visual solid angle sandwiched between these two the density of transitions would increase with the distance of the region to which the visual solid angle corresponded.

In the case of a moving point of observation we can suppose that the impression of distance is given by a dynamic transformation of texture, more precisely, by a gradient of flow velocities: the rate of textural flow for "close by" would be greater than that for "far away." In sum, there are correlates of distance in both the flowing and stationary optic array. The impression, however, is that the flowing optic array is less equivocal in its specification of distance, and of surface variables such as slant.[24] But this is only an instance of what is a most general rule, namely, the superiority of changing optic arrays over stationary optic arrays as information about an environment.[30] We should not be surprised by this observation. After all, if a stationary point of observation is a limiting case of a moving point of observation, then it follows that the structure of the optic array at a stationary point is but a special case of the structure of the optic array at a moving point. One can contrive stationary perspectives to fool an observer; to fool a moving observer is an incomparably more difficult task. The notorious Ames room—a distorted room with unpatterned walls and floors—is a case in point. Limited to a stationary perspective, the observer is fooled, but he detects the ruse once he is allowed to move.

It is already understood that the ambient optic array as the natural stimulation for vision has structure: it has some degree of adjacent order and some degree of successive order. What we now understand is that, concurrently, it has components of change and nonchange. For Gibson the import of change is that it reveals what is essential, namely, invariance. We can put this another way: structural variation reveals structural nonvariation. In this conception, movement on the part of the organism serves a singularly important geometric function. There is structure which can be detected in a frozen array, but there is considerably more structure to be detected in a changing array, and the organism can effect the change. In short, the movements of the observer transform the ambient optic array and thereby enhance the detection of invariants.

The Visual Perceptual System

The above reasoning motivates the conception of the mechanism of vision as an actively exploring system. Traditionally, however, a sense system is conceived more conservatively as a well specified anatomical route which delivers sensations to identifiable centers; integration and cross-correlation of sense data then follow as circumstance demands. But in an ecological perspective, the system responsible for seeing ought to be described in ascending levels of activity; for example, mobile eye-mobile eyes in a mobile head-mobile eyes in a mobile head on a mobile body. A hierarchy of levels of activity constitutes the visual perceptual system with each level of activity, from lesser to greater, permitting increasingly more complex transformations of the optic array and, concomitantly, the detection of increasingly higher-order invariants. This conception, of course, does not deny that an eye is for light, but it does question the assumption that seeing is entirely an act of the brain and can be understood solely as such. Seeing, Gibson would say, is an act of the organism.

Consider if you will what transpires when an observer is confronted with an interesting but imperfectly clear object at some distance from him. What does he do to increase the clarity of his perception? He could, of course, adjust the lenses of the eyes, but an eminently more significant improvement would follow upon his walking up to the object. The moral is simple. Locomotion is not immaterial to vision and an eye is all the better for having legs.

It is instructive in this context to consider what is meant by visual information processing. From the traditional interpretation of vision as a sense system, the meaning is clear: there are signals emanating from the environment yielding neural signals to be interpreted. But for Gibson, processing cannot mean this. Quite to the contrary, processing resides in the activities of the perceptual system, in its adjusting, orienting, exploring, and optimizing of information about the environment that is external to the perceiver.[33] On this view, processing is not in the brain as such but pervades the continual cybernetical loop of afference—efference—reafference that defines the synergistic relation between the perceiver and his ecology.

Equivalence of Perceptual Systems

Let us now return to the characteristics of the optic array in order that we may touch upon a further aspect of the concept of invariance with respect to the notion of perceptual system. We commented above that the optic array as the natural stimulation for the visual perceptual system consisted of order and change of order. What we now recognize is that these characteristics are not modality specific and may be taken as intrinsic to stimulation for any perceptual system. This being the case, one may conjecture that the same structure and thus the same environmental event can be equally available to more than one perceptual system. For example, the pattern of discontinuity formed by rubbing or scraping the skin with an object might have the same abstract description as the pattern of acoustic discontinuity in the air determined by rubbing and scraping the same object against other objects.

Experiments into seeing with the skin speak to this very issue.[158] The "observer" in these experiments is attached to a system which uses a television camera as its eye where the camera is quite mobile and can be variously aimed by the observer. The video image is electronically transferred and delivered to a 20 by 20 matrix of solenoid vibrators that stimulate an area of approximately 10 inches square on the observer's back. Each solenoid vibrates when its locus is within an illuminated region of the camera field; thus the matrix as a whole yields a pattern of discontinuity on the skin that corresponds essentially to the arrangement of intensity transitions in the optic array.

Of the many intriguing results reported, the following are the most significant to our concerns. First, properties of the environment are specified in the tactile array. Second, there is no qualitative difference between blind observers and blindfolded normal seeing observers; nor are there any quantitative differences of any great significance. Both blind and sighted (but blindfolded for testing) observers learn to detect the environmental properties specified in the tactile array with virtually equal facility. Third, the tactile array specifies the layout of surfaces and the whereabouts and identity of objects significantly better when it is changing than when it is static. In brief, the observer's ability to detect environmental facts is enhanced when he can move the camera, that is, when he can transform the tactile array. As with the optic array, variation in the tactile array *reveals* nonvariation, it permits the isolation of what is essential from what is not.

That a changing tactile array can yield information about the three-dimensional structure of an environment, more precisely, the surface layout, and that its pick-up does not require prodigious training [158] is most favorable to Gibson's position and embarrassing to the traditional one. The fact that the tactile array at a moving point of observation contains the same adjacent and successive order—the same abstract mathematical structure—as is contained in the transforming optic array means that the same invariants are there to be detected. On this account, the tactile stimulation does not have to be cross-correlated with information detected by other perceptual systems, or compared with memorial information, in order to be rationalized—to the contrary, the tactile arrangement affords the same meaning as the optical arrangement.

At this juncture it is appropriate to draw a further contrast between the constructivist perspective, in particular the information-processing approach, and the Gibsonian. The emphasis upon transforming arrays in the preceding discussion implies that perception is easier, in some sense of the word, when the input variation is greater. But common to a great deal of information-processing modeling is the principle that the nervous system is severely limited in its information-handling capabilities; the implicit assumption is that the fewer the sensory events to be handled per unit of time, the more proficient is the nervous system as an information processing device. The contrast between the two perspectives, the information-processing/constructivist and the Gibsonian, is highlighted in the following comments by White and his colleagues: "Visual perception thrives when it is flooded with information, when there is a whole page of prose before the eyes, or a whole image of the environment; it falters when the input is diminished, when it is forced to read one word at a time, or when it must look at the world through a mailing tube. . . . The perceptual systems of living organisms are the most remarkable information-reduction machines known. They are not seriously embarrassed in situations where an enormous proportion of the input must be filtered out or ignored, but they are invariably handicapped when the input is dramatically curtailed or artificially encoded. Some of the controversy about the necessity of preprocessing sensory information stems from disappointment in the rates at which human beings can cope with discrete sensory events. It is possible that such evidence of overload reflects more of an inappropriate display than a limitation of the perceiver." [158]

Let us consider one further example of the equivalence of perceptual systems. Consider an object on a collision course with an observer. Optical concomitants of this event consist, in part, of a symmetrically expanding radial flow field kinetically defined over the texture bounded by the object's contours and, simultaneously, the occlusion and disocclusion of texture at the contour edges. If this mathematically complex change or some reasonable facsimile of it is simulated on a screen the observer will involuntarily duck or dodge. [113,114] And he will do so whether he is human (adult or infant), or animal (e.g. monkey, chicken, crab).

For simplicity, we may say that the acceleration in symmetrical expansion, referred to as "looming," [114] specifies impending collision. Now it is the case that the participants in the seeing with the skin experiments would often give startled ducks of the head when the part of the tactile array corresponding to an object was suddenly magnified by a quick turn of the zoom lever on the camera. [158] One anticipates the Gibsonian interpretation of this curious fact: the mathematical description of the changing optic array and of the changing tactile array corresponding to looming are identical. That is to say that even though there are obvious qualitative differences between visual and tactual experience, both perceptual systems detect the same information specifying the event of looming.

And consider now the acoustic array as structured by a car that is on a collision course with you. Again we will have to entertain the hypothesis that the mathematical description of this looming is the same as that for vision and touch. In sum, perceptual systems as different modes of attention sample the same world, and when the same event is detected this is because of an abstract identity in the available structure to which each system is sensitive. Looming as an environmental event structures the optic array, the tactile array, and the acoustic array in the same fashion.

But what then becomes of the notion of sensation in this scheme of things? For Gibson, sensation is largely divorced from perception, in contrast to the more traditional orientation which classifies sensation as the necessary precursor to perceptual experience. Gibson's stance on this point is very similar to that of Heider,[48] who distinguishes between thing (message?) and medium. The human perceiver may attend to either. If he attends to the way in which the medium is structured by the environment, then he perceives; if, on the other hand, he attends to the medium itself, then he is said to have sensations. Given our current understanding of infant vision,[10] which suggests that infants see objects in definite ways and at determinate distances, we might be led to conjecture that attending to the way in which light is structured by the environment, i.e., attending to the message, is ontogenetically prior to the ability to attend to the medium itself. On this conjecture, sensitivity to the medium and interpreting the medium reflect a later-day sophistication whereas at the outset the visual perceptual system is geared to detecting messages.

The reader may be of the opinion that I am belaboring a somewhat arbitrary and even meaningless distinction. Or he may feel more simply that a discussion of the sensation/perception distinction is out of place in a treatment of current thought on visual perception. For myself, however, I am convinced that much of current theory acknowledges implicitly the view that sensation is prior to perception. As hinted earlier, constructivism has departed little from the structuralist notion of discrete sensations as the sum of what is directly accessible. Fundamentally, all that has been done is to substitute the term "feature" for "sensation." And whether antiquated sensations or modern features are taken as directly given (with all else as inference or construction) Ryle's [111] prisoner-in-the-cell parody is still fashionable. [142] As the parody goes, a prisoner has been held in solitary confinement since birth. His cell is devoid of windows but cracks in the walls provide occasional flickers of light, and through the stones occasional scratchings and tappings can be heard. On the basis of these snippets of light and sound, our hapless prisoner apprehends the unobserved happenings outside his cell such as football games, the Miss America Pageant, and audiences at the World Congress on Dyslexia. But we should ask, as Ryle does, how could our prisoner ever come to know anything about, say, football games, except by having *perceived* one in the first place?

Information about One's Self

We recall the conclusion drawn about the flowing optic array at a moving point of observation: the change is propriospecific in contrast to the nonchange which is exterospecific. Having deliberated upon the contrast between perceptual systems and information about the environment, on the one hand, and sense systems and sensations on the other, we are now in a better position to appreciate the implications of the egospecific nature of vision.

On the classical Sherringtonian view, [128] each sense or receptor system performed a unique function—it was said to be exteroceptive, proprioceptive, or interoceptive. This view was buttressed by an older and more sacred doctrine, namely, Johannes Müller's law of specific nerve energies, which holds that sensation is specific to the receptor initiating it. Müller's doctrine argues that one's awareness is of the state of the nerves; thus, by implication, an awareness of movements of the self is an awareness of the states of a specialized receptor system. Tradition referred to this awareness as proprioception/kinesthesis and localized the specialized receptor system in the muscles and joints.

Gibson's rebuttal to these conceptions is by now quite evident. If by exteroceptive we mean detecting information about events extrinsic to the organism and if by proprioceptive we mean detecting information about the animal's own bodily activities, then clearly vision is as capable of the latter as it is of the former. The classical dichotomy of exteroceptive and proprioceptive systems is wrong. Thus we may speak meaningfully of "visual proprioception" in reference to the visual perception of bodily movement[30, 77, 78] to emphasize that proprioception is not the prerogative of a specialized receptor system or sense organ. Indeed, one can make an argument that visual proprioception is the more reliable and, oftentimes the only reliable source of information about movements of the self (egomovement). For example, muscle-joint kinesthesis is uninformative when I am traversing an environment by car or by train. But the flowing optic array would appear to specify locomotion of the observer, be he passive or active. And what of the fish swimming upstream or the bird flying against a head wind? Muscle-joint kinesthesis would specify movement in the sense of change of location, where there is none.

For a locomoting observer the flow-pattern ought to provide information for getting about in an environment, that is, for guiding or steering one's movements. The principal feature of the flowing optic array concomitant to locomotion is that it is a *total* transformation of the projected environment. The array expands ahead and contracts behind. The projection of the place in the environment to which the observer is heading is the focus of expansion in the ambient optic array, while the focus of contraction is the direction from which the observer has just come. Thus there is information about the direction of movement, and to steer toward a particular object means essentially to keep that object—as a closed internally textured contour in the optic array—as the focus of optical expansion.[27, 61] In a detailed mathematical analysis of the transforming optic array at a moving point of observation, Lee[76] develops a proof of the availability of body-scaled information about the size and shape of potential obstacles to locomotion. Relatedly, the claim can be made that there is body-scaled information relevant to the amount of thrust needed to leap over an obstacle and to the time at which the thrust is to be applied. In sum, for an animal capable of registering the optical velocity field and its derivative properties, there is directly specifiable optical information for the guidance of locomotion in a cluttered environment.

But do I need to view the focus of expansion in order to know in which direction I am moving? We know, of course, that we can perceive our direction of movement when the head is turned sideways. Is it possible therefore that samples of the total optical flow pattern, samples that do not contain the focus of expansion, can specify the direction of one's motion? The answer is provided through the use of computer-generated motion pictures depicting various flow patterns for egomotion over an endless textured plain.[150] Samples of optical flow patterns can be generated which give specific impressions of movement toward specific locations which are not contained in the samples. Aside from highlighting the broad egomovement specificity of the changing optic array, a particularly significant feature of this demonstration is that a sample of the total ambient array can specify the total ambient array. Or, to put it somewhat differently, the flow pattern of the field of view specifies characteristics of the ambient optic array outside the field of view. On this point, Warren[150] reminds us of Merleau-Ponty's claim that: "We see as far as our hold on things extends, far beyond the zone of clear vision, and even behind us. When we reach the limits of the visual field we do not pass from vision to nonvision. . ."[89]

The proprioceptive role played by the visual perceptual system enjoys further elaboration in the demonstration that the human infant's ability to maintain a stable posture is very much under visual control. More generally, it is believed that the principal information about body sway is broadcast by receptors in the vestibular canals and in the muscle/joint complexes—mechanoreceptors as they are often called. However, it can be shown that balance is perturbed by transformations of the ambient optic array in a direction that is specific to the transformations.[77] From the foregoing account, an expanding optic array specifies forward egomovement, a contracting optic array specifies backward egomovement. An infant standing on a stationary floor in a room can be caused to sway forward or fall forward when the walls and ceiling of the room move away from him (i.e. contraction of the optic array) and to sway backward or fall backward when the "room" moves toward him (expansion of the optic array). Though not as pronounced, the same relation between standing and optical change can be observed in adults.[77]

To a very large extent this section and those preceding it have assumed a "frozen" environment. Our analysis has concentrated on the stationary and the moving point of observation in respect to an illuminated environment which was described tersely as a fixed arrangement of textured surfaces. Of course, implicitly it was assumed that the environment was cluttered with objects—themselves arrangements of surfaces—but little comment was made about them or about their activities with the exception of a passing reference to "looming." In the sections that follow, this omission is partially remedied as we direct our attention, in measured steps, to objects and the changes they undergo. In what follows, we unfreeze the environment.

Object-Structure Correlates in the Optic Array and Fourier Analysis

A brief consideration of the information about a nontransforming object at a stationary point of observation is in order. (The object in mind is one that is detachable from the ground plane; it is moveable.) Expressed roughly, an object's concomitant in the optic array is a visual solid angle corresponding to the exposed face(s) of the object packed with smaller (and nested) visual solid angles corresponding to the facets or grain of the exposed face(s). One might say for simplicity that the concomitant is a closed contour with internal texture.

We can raise two elementary but instructive questions. First, what kind of ordered discontinuity in the arrangement of ambient light separates the visual solid angle corresponding to an object from the other visual solid angles in which it is nested? More precisely, what is the mathematical invariant for contour? Second, what kind of ordered discontinuity in the optic array is specific to the type of articulation between surfaces comprising an object? More bluntly, what is the mathematical invariant for edge type?

We are reminded that both of these questions were raised earlier in a different way and in a different context, that of Seeing Machines, where the concern is with line drawings of variously arranged polyhedral bodies and how a three-dimensional description of them can be recovered. It is important in that connection to devise heuristics for separating bodies from bodies and for identifying the quality of the joint between surfaces. In the current context we are assuming a natural environment, as opposed to a line drawing, and ecological optics, as opposed to image optics. Our current intuition is that the light to an eye should specify unequivocally the presence of contours and the type of edge. The following is meant only as a hint of how this intuition might be substantiated.

Solid objects are composed of textured surfaces whose gradients relative to some stationary point of observation are correlates of their shape and slant. For example, as the slant of a surface varies in continuous or stepwise fashion, then the projected gradient ought to do likewise.[26, 30] In the instance of an object-surface bending or of two surfaces of a polyhedral object joining, the abrupt change in slant will yield an abrupt change in the gradients of optical texture density. Precisely, a concave bend or joint(edge) is specified by an abrupt transition from one rate of change in intensity transitions to a slower rate; a transition to a faster rate specifies a convex bend or joint. These mathematical discontinuities exemplify the form of invariant for edge type. An invariant for contour can be a more simple mathematical discontinuity—a sudden transition in optical texture density.

The above is but a rough account of the optical specification of edge and contour in a frozen array. (For a fuller account dealing with transforming arrays, see Mace.[79]) It is instructive though in the following senses: first, it highlights the principle that the optical structure uniquely specifying environmental properties is "... defined not over parameters of radiant light rays such as intensity, but over relations of *change* in intensity";[79] second, it expresses the mathematically abstract nature of invariants—an edge type is given by a particular change in rates of change; third, it strongly implies that the perception of object relations in a scene is predicated upon optical variables and mechanisms quite different from those currently envisioned by Artificial Intelligence research.

The last point is well worth elaborating upon. In most scene analysis programs there has to be a method for mapping lines in the picture domain onto edges in the scene domain. But in the Gibsonian view lines are not primitive entities from which all else is constructed. The organism is confronted by mathematical relations in the light, relations across changes in intensity transitions, which are specific to edge types. If he can pick up on these higher-order relations, he has no need for lines nor for line-to-edge mapping rules.

Mackworth[82] has described a computer program for interpreting line drawings of polyhedral scenes which does not rely on knowledge of specific object prototypes[21] nor does it appeal to the technique of mapping vertices onto corners.[14] The kernel feature of Mackworth's program is the mapping of surfaces into a gradient space and the use of this representation to determine (through the use of "coherence" rules that articulating surfaces must satisfy) the properties of the scene. Of course, Mackworth's program is designed for line drawings (i.e., textureless regions) and therefore requires the use of heuristics to determine the pattern of surface orientations. But one is motivated by this program to ask how computationally more straightforward scene analysis programs would be if they worked upon natural scenes instead of line drawings, and were equipped with the means to determine density and discontinuities of texture. Gibson for a long time has argued that picture perception is not a simpler version of natural scene perception. His suspicion is that, on the contrary, an account of the latter is more readily forthcoming than an account of the former.

The tenor of the immediately preceding comments suggests that it would be useful to grasp, if only in a rough and approximate way, the kind of mechanism permitting the detection of textural variables. Understandably little effort has been directed to the determination of how surface structure is perceived because most investigators interested in the *how* of perception are firmly entrenched in retinal image optics. Consequently, they have been satisfied with inquiries into two dimensional outline forms and features. However, research in computer vision has not been so remiss[45] and one recent report is especially interesting: Bajcsy[3] points to the special advantages of surface texture descriptions derived in the Fourier domain. Why this should be thought interesting becomes evident when one considers a rather peculiar version of the cross-adaptation experiment described earlier.

Consider a grating of vertical dark bars of equal width on a light background such that the plot of luminance against spatial location yields a regularly repeating square wave. Now consider a further grating in which the relation between bars and background yields a sinusoidal plot of luminance against spatial position. Most clearly we could generate an indefinitely large number of gratings yielding square waves and sinusoids of different spatial frequencies as measured in cycles per degree of visual angle. The use of gratings such as these in cross-adaptation (and related) experiments suggests that the visual system is selectively sensitive to spatial frequency—that it performs a spatial frequency analysis.[18, 116]

A stronger inference but one that is not dictated by the data[116] reads as follows: there is a set of independent channels each sensitive to a particular spatial frequency band whose overall behavior may be characterized as that of performing an analysis into Fourier components.[101] By way of illustration, Blakemore and Campbell[8] demonstrated that adapting to a high contrast square wave grating of frequency F raised the threshold for sinusoidal gratings of frequency F and (to a lesser degree) sinusoidal gratings of frequency 3F. If the visual system is performing a Fourier analysis, then the square wave grating ought to be "decomposed" into its fundamental and odd harmonics. And, consequently, there ought to be a change in the sensitivity of the system to sinusoidal gratings at the fundamental and odd harmonic frequencies. In this respect, the Blakemore and Campbell finding fits the Fourier model. A further fit is a demonstration by Maffei and Fiorentini[83] of Fourier synthesis: a perceptual impression of a square wave grating of frequency F results when two sinusoidal gratings, one of frequency F and one of frequency 3F, are presented separately, one to one eye and one to the other.

Though discoveries like the above have aroused considerable interest and are proliferating at an enormous rate,[116] investigators have yet to concern themselves seriously with the role played by frequency analysis in visual perception. But surely Gibson's ecological analysis and Bajcsy's[3] insight suggest the role: natural environments consist of surfaces, natural surfaces are textured in the sense of repeating patterns of varying spatial frequency and the detection of surface properties, static and kinetic, is mandatory for a being that must adapt to its world.

Event Perception: Structural and Transformational Invariants

Let us now come to an examination of objects undergoing change. The examination remains in relation to a stationary point of observation.

Shaw, McIntyre, and Mace[120] have remarked: "The environment of any organism is in dynamic process such that the smallest significant unit of ecological analysis must be an *event* rather than a simple stimulus, object, relation, geometric configuration or any other construct whose essence can be captured in static terms." "Event" is the term most befitting a change in an arrangement of surfaces, and rolling, opening, falling, rotating, and aging are examples of events. Nonchange is but a special case of change; consequently resting, standing, being supported, etc., are legitimate events. However, the concept of an event cannot be meaningfully construed in the absence of a subject; thus events are more accurately exemplified by: "the ball rolls," "the door opens," "the rock falls," and "Bill grows old." The last is particularly instructive because it reminds us that the events we perceive can be of varying duration—the "slow" event of Bill aging contrasts with the "fast" event of rocks falling.

In concert with the fundamental hypothesis of ecological optics, the light is structured by an event in a fashion that is specific to that event. An event is said to modulate the light in a way which specifies the identity of the participant in the event and the dynamic component of the event, the form of the change. Consequently, for event perception it is conjectured that the visual perceptual system must detect the *structural invariant* specifying the structure undergoing the change and the *transformational invariant* specifying the nature of the change undergone. [122]

A demonstration by Gibson and Gibson[34] provides an appropriate instance. The observer viewed a screen onto which was projected the shadow of one of the following: a regular form (a solid square), an irregular form (ameboid shape), a regular pattern (a square group of dark squares), an irregular pattern (an ameboid group of ameboid dark shapes or spots). Each silhouette was semirotated cyclically and the observer had to report on the degree of change in slant. For both the regular and irregular silhouettes the observer's experience was of a rigid constant surface changing slant and he was able to judge the slant most accurately. The implication of this simple demonstration is quite paradoxical as Gibson and Gibson[34] realized: a change of form yields a constant form together with a change of slant. The paradox originates, in part, in the two uses of the term 'form.' When we speak of "change of form," we are referring to the abstract geometrical projected form, or silhouette; when we refer to "constant form," we are speaking about the rigid substantial form. The traditional way to interpret kinetic depth effects, such as that just described, is to say that the currently perceived static and flat projected form is combined with the memories of the preceding static and flat projected forms to yield, through an act of construction, the substantial form-in-depth.[149] And it is evident that this interpretation is motivated by the two assumptions of (a) stimuli as momentary frozen slices in time and (b) retinal image optics as the proper departure point for speculation. Quite to the contrary is the Gibsonian interpretation which follows from ecological optics with its notion of an enduring ambient optic array: a lawful transformation of the optic array specifies both an unchanging rigid object and its motion. The emphasis here is on the event's modulation of the structure of the ambient light.

The implication of this interpretation for the understanding of object-shape perception is quite radical and exceedingly difficult to grasp on initial reading. In any event let me take the liberty of spelling it out relying upon subsequent discussion for its clarification. *The shape of an object is not given by a set of frozen perspectives but by a unique transformation of the optic array. Or, synonymous, object-shape perception is not based on the perception of static forms but on the perception of formless invariants detected over time.* [120] This hypothesis denies that shape can be captured by the formal descriptions of classical geometry; that static forms are unique entities (to the contrary, a form is not a thing but a variable of a thing); that static forms are primary sources of data for perception and that shape is an isolable physical property of objects. On the latter point, we may comment that shape is perhaps better conceived as a property of events. [120,122] Before further examination of this hypothesis let us consider an example of a transformational invariant.

The sensibility of the observer to the form of change in a changing optic array is demonstrated in a singularly elegant fashion by von Fieandt and Gibson. [145] Consider the contrast between rigid and nonrigid (elastic) motions. An observer peers at a screen onto which is projected the shadow of an irregular elastic fishnet. The fishnet is attached to a frame which is manipulatable in the following ways: one end of the frame can be slid in and out, compressing and stretching the shadow (an elastic transform) or the whole frame can be semirotated back and forth subjecting the shadow to foreshortening and its inverse (a rigid translation). All the observer witnesses on the screen is the changing textured shadow, that is, he does not see the shadow of the frame, only the changing motion of the textural elements which are virtually quantitatively identical for the two transformations. Yet the observer readily perceives a distinct elastic (topological) transformation, in the one case, and a distinct rigid transformation, in the other. In short, he is sensitive to the quality of change, i.e., to the transformational invariants in the ambient optic array which specify elastic and rigid happenings.

Now the explicit and implicit strands of the currently developing thesis can be woven together. At a stationary point of observation, a detached object, as a surface arrangement, has specifiable structural concomitants in the ambient optic array. If the object is caused to move, or if it is squashed, or if it grows, or if it disintegrates, the ambient optic array will be transformed, that is to say, its structure will be disturbed. The onset and offset of this transformation or disturbance will be identical to the beginning and termination of the event and since the duration of ecologically significant events ranges from milliseconds to scores of years so it is with the event-related optical disturbance. Though the form of the disturbance does not copy the event, it does correspond mathematically to the event and is said to do so in two ways: it corresponds to the kind of change (transformational invariant) and to the structure whose identity persists in the course of change (structural invariants). Visual perceptual systems are assumed to sense (detect) these invariants.

Objects that participate in events are said to have shape, but it is argued here that shape is more accurately a property of the events into which the objects enter as participants than of the objects themselves. Shape, we have said, is a formless invariant over time and to this proposition we now turn.

Symmetry Groups and Shape Perception

Intuitively a circle and square both have symmetry but they do not have the same symmetry. How might we describe the idea of symmetry so that we can capture this difference? The mathematician's answer is that symmetry is concerned with certain rigid mappings (referred to as symmetry operations or automorphisms) which leave sets of points unchanged. Thus mathematically any rotation in the plane about its center leaves the circle, as a set of points, invariant. On the other hand, only certain rotations (i.e., the integer multiples of $\pi/2$) map the square to itself. Evidently the properties of circle and square could be revealed and contrasted in the symmetry operations which leave them unchanged. Moreover, we can recognize the synonymity of the concepts of symmetry and invariance: paraphrasing Weyl,[156] a thing is symmetrical if there is anything we can do to it so that after we have done it, it appears the same as it did before.[23, 120] For the mathematician, those symmetry operations which leave an object unchanged form a group, and this group describes exactly the symmetry (invariance) possessed by the object. Though we cannot draw an exact parallel between the mathematician's notion of symmetry and Gibson's notion of invariant we can use the mathematician's insights as a guideline. Ideally, the reader will find this particular guideline useful for understanding the ideas expressed in the last section.

To illustrate, consider the symmetry of a square. There are eight operations which leave the square invariant (i.e., map the square into itself): the null operation (no change), the clockwise rotations through $\pi/2$, π, and $3\pi/2$; and the reflections in the horizontal axis, vertical axis, and the two diagonal axes. Now the composition of any two symmetry operations is itself a symmetry operation, thus reflection in the horizontal axis and the clockwise rotation by π is the same as reflecting in the vertical axis. A table therefore can be constructed of the composition of each symmetry operation with each other symmetry operation. This table, or more accurately the mathematical structure of this table, describes the symmetry of the square and it has certain interesting properties which are possessed by all symmetry tables.

(i) if a and b are symmetry operations, then a o b is a symmetry operation where o is some principle of combination. This is the property of closure.

(ii) if a, b, and c are symmetry operations then (a o b) o c = a o (b o c). This is the property of associativity.

(iii) there is a symmetry operation e such that a o e = a = e o a. e is the identity symmetry operation.

(iv) given any symmetry operation a we can always find a symmetry operation b such that a o b = e. For every operation there is an inverse.

These four properties define what is referred to mathematically as a group.

We can now return to our hypothesis on shape perception remarking after Shaw et al. [120] that rigid shape is the structural invariant of an event whose transformational invariant is formally equivalent to a symmetry group, that of rotations. A partial substantiation of this notion is given in a demonstration in which a wire cube is rotated at constant speed on each of its axes of symmetry and strobed at appropriate rates. [120] When rotated on a face, self-congruence is achieved every $90°$; when rotated on a vertex; positions of self-congruence occur every $120°$. It follows that the group description of the cube's symmetry will differ as a function of the axis of rotation.

For rotation on a face, the period of symmetry is four; for rotation on a vertex, the symmetry period is three. In the demonstration, the strobe rate is either synchronous, or asynchronous with the period of symmetry (i.e., the strobe rate is either an integer multiple or not an integer multiple of the symmetry period). When the strobe rate is synchronized with the symmetry period, a cube is seen, when the strobe rate is not synchronized with the symmetry period, the shape of the object is no longer recognizable as "cube." And significantly a strobe rate which permits the perception of cube-shape when the cube is rotating on a face does not permit that perception when rotation is on a vertex, and vice versa.

This demonstration is significant in the following respects. First, it is evident that shape is not specified by *any* arbitrarily chosen set of variant perspectives. On the contrary, it appears that rotational symmetry must be preserved in the variant perspectives projected to the eye. Asynchronous strobing annihilates this symmetry and results in a set of ordered perspectives which specify some other shape. In short, different successive orderings of perspectives specify different shapes of the same physical object and we can now understand what it means to say that shape is a property of events rather than of objects. Second, it is clear that not all perspectives are needed to specify shape, only a special ordered subset of those perspectives. There is reason to believe that the "special ordered subset" may be well defined mathematically; Shaw and Wilson [122] conjecture that it is the generator set of the group. All in all, there is some justification for Gibson's claim that shape perception is based on the perception of formless invariants detected over time.

We can gain a further purchase on the conception of formless invariants by considering an event which, quite unlike the rotating cube, can be said to transpire slowly.

Of some considerable significance to our everyday living is the ability to determine the relative age-level of faces. All things considered we manifest this ability rather well. In the light of our current discussion of events we might venture to say that this ability reflects our sensitivity to a particular class of symmetry operations—those that characterize aging. For most assuredly when we speak of the face aging we are speaking of a remodeling of the head which leaves invariant the structural information specifying the species and the more specialized structural information affording recognition of the individual.

The biologist D'Arcy Thompson [138] had the insight that transformations of a system of spatial coordinates permits the characterization of the remodeling of plants and animals by evolution. The particular advantage of the method of coordinate transformation lies in the fact that one can uncover the appropriate symmetry operations in the absence of a complete mathematical description of the object to be transformed. Pittenger and Shaw [100] applied this insight to aging. They inscribed a profile in a space of two coordinates and then subjected the coordinate space to the affine transformations of *strain* (a transformation which maps a square into a rectangle) and *shear* (a transformation which maps a square into a rhomboid). These symmetry operations—for with appropriately chosen parameters, they preserve the identity of the individual and the species—suitably described the transformational invariant of aging: the original profile could be mapped into younger and older versions whose relative age levels could be accurately ranked by observers. Of the two transformations, strain was the more significant.

The argument emerges that the perception of aging is not necessarily based on the discrimination of local features but rather upon the perception of global invariant information of a higher order that is detected over time. Indicative of the higher-order nature or abstractness of this information is the fact that when the strain transformation is applied to the profile of an inanimate object, such as a Volkswagen "Beetle," it generates a family of profiles that can be rank ordered for age commensurate with the rank ordering of faces. [121] The implication is that the transformational invariant for aging is independent of the features common to all animate things that grow—just as it is most obviously independent of the features of any single face, or of the features common to all faces.

Indirect and Direct Perception: A Brief Comparison and Summary

The purpose of this paper is to provide an overview of perceptual theory as it relates to vision, together with a liberal sprinkling of empirical facts. To this purpose I have dealt at length with what I take to be the two major and contrasting perspectives; that visual perception is indirect and a derivitive of conception; that visual perception is direct and independent of conception. The focus of this final statement is that the distinction between the two perspectives turns on the issue of what order of physical space is the proper basis for the theory of visual perception.

In the main, conjectures on the nature of visual experience derive from a framework which takes as its departure point a bidimensional description of the environment and which seeks to explain how descriptions in three and four dimensions are achieved through mental elaboration. A consensus is that these higher-order accounts are the result of inference and memory, and it is evident how the doctrine of a two-space world as the sum of what is given dictates an attitude of visual perception as constructed. We have remarked earlier on the centuries old hegemony of this doctrine.[97]

In opposing the official doctrine, the view of perception as primary takes kinetic events rather than static two-dimensional images as the proper point of departure.[30, 60, 120] More precisely, it is argued that the theory of seeing ought to be anchored in four-dimensional space rather than in the two-dimensional space favored by tradition. We may suppose that for naturally mobile animals and primitive man the instances of pure, static perception are rare. Moreover, "the structuring of light by artifice"[30] —the representation of environments and events by picture—is a relatively recent addition to man's ecology. The argument, in principle, is that the variety of visual perceptual systems evolved by nature are incomparably better suited to the transforming optic array—to the mathematically abstract, optical concomitants of three-dimensional structures transformed over time—than to the static two-dimensional pattern.

On this argument there should be several consequences of reducing the dimensionality of the space in which the visual perceptual system operates. First, the sum total of environmental properties mapped by the ambient optic array is reduced. Second, there is a nontrivial change in the class of invariants—spaces of fewer dimensions are accompanied by invariants of a lower order. Third, perceptual equivocality relates inversely to order of invariant; thus, given the second consequence, equivocal perceptions are more likely when the visual system operates in spaces of fewer dimensions. As one might suspect, these consequences have implications for learning.

It is quite obvious that in both perspectives one must learn to perceive.

But the kind of learning implied by the traditional perspective differs radically from that which is implied by the Gibsonian perspective. In the former case, one must know in advance something about the environment in order to perceive it properly; thus one must come tacitly to understand a variety of rules and to register a variety of facts so that one can make sense of the inadequate deliverances of his visual system. The alternative, of course, is that one cannot know anything about the environment except as he perceives it, or has perceived it. On the alternative view, we should not treat perceptual learning as a matter of supplementing inadequate data with information drawn from memory. Rather we should see perceptual learning as a matter of differentiating the complex, nested relationships in the dynamically structured medium—of tuning into invariants.

But given the above, we may conjecture that perceptual learning is a function of the dimensionality of the physical space in which the visual perceptual system operates. The frozen array, the limiting case of continuous nontransformation, provides a less than optimal set of conditions for visual perception; the invariants are fewer, more difficult to tune into, and less reliable. Distinguishing bidimensional information poses a more difficult problem for the visual perceptual system than distinguishing information of higher dimensions; learning in the former case should be slower and more devious. On this line of reasoning we may conjecture that reading, the distinguishing of information in the "letter array," is not a task to which the visual perceptual system is especially suited, despite its necessary involvement in the process.

References

1. Arbib MA: The Metaphorical Brain: An Introduction to Cybernetics as Artificial Intelligence and Brain Theory. New York, John Wiley & Sons, 1972
2. Averbach E, Coriell AS: Short-term memory in vision. Bell System Tech J 40: 309–328, 1961
3. Bajcsy R: Computer Description of Textured Surfaces (Third International Joint Conference on Artificial Intelligence). Menlo Park, California, Stanford Research Institute, 1973
4. Baron J, Thurstone I: An analysis of the word superiority effect. Cognitive Psychol 4:207–208, 1973
5. Biederman I: Perceiving real-world scenes. Science 177:77–79, 1972
6. Biederman I, Glass AL, Stacy EW Jr: Searching for objects in real-words scenes. J Exp Psychol 97:22–27, 1973
7. Biederman I, Rabinowitz JC, Glass AL, et al: On the information extracted from a glance at a scene. J Exp Psychol 103:597–600, 1974
8. Blakemore C, Campbell FW: On the existence of neurons in the human visual system selectively sensitive to the orientation and size of retinal images. J Physiol (Lond) 203:237–260, 1969

9. Bower TGR: Reading by eye. *In* Basic Studies in Reading. Edited by H Levin, J Williams. New York, Basic Books, 1970
10. Bower TGR: The object in the world of the infant. Sci Am 225:30–38, 1971
11. Brand J: Classification without identification in visual search. Q J Exp Psychol 23:178–186, 1971
12. Campbell FW, Maffei L: The tilt after-effect: a fresh look. Vision Res 11:833–840, 1971
13. Clark SE: Retrieval of color information from the preperceptual storage system. J Exp Psychol 82:263–266, 1969
14. Clowes M: On seeing things. Artif Intelligence 2:79–112, 1971
15. Coltheart M: Visual feature-analyzers and after-effects of tilt and curvature. Psychol Res 78:114–121, 1971
16. Coltheart M: Visual information processing. *In* New Horizons in Psychology. Vol 2. Edited by PC Dodwell, Hammondsworth, Penguin Books, 1972
17. Cooper LA, Shephard RN: Chronometric studies of the rotation of mental images. *In* Visual Information Processing. Edited by WG Chase. New York, Academic Press, 1973
18. Cornsweet TN: Visual Perception. New York, Academic Press, 1970
19. Craik KJW: The Nature of Explanation. Cambridge, Cambridge University Press, 1943
20. Doost R, Turvey MT: Iconic memory and central processing capacity. Percept Psychophysics 9:269–274, 1971
21. Falk G: Interpretation of imperfect line data as a three-dimensional scene. Artif Intelligence 3:101–144, 1972
22. Favreau O, Emerson VF, Corballis MC: Motion perception: a color-contingent after-effect. Science 196:78–79, 1972
23. Feynmann R: The Character of Physical Law. Cambridge, Massachusetts, MIT Press, 1967
24. Flock HR: Some conditions sufficient for accurate monocular perceptions of moving surface slants. J Exp Psychol 67:560–572, 1964
25. Franks JJ, Bransford JD: Abstraction of visual patterns. J Exp Psychol 90:65–74, 1971
26. Gibson JJ: The Perception of the Visual World. Boston, Houghton Mifflin Company, 1950
27. Gibson JJ: Visually controlled locomotion and visual orientation in animals. Br J Psychol 49:182–194, 1958
28. Gibson JJ: Perception as a function of stimulation. *In* Psychology: A Study of a Science. Vol 1. Edited by S Koch. New York, McGraw-Hill Book Company, 1959
29. Gibson JJ: Ecological optics. Vision Res 1:253–262, 1961
30. Gibson JJ: The Senses Considered as Perceptual Systems. Boston, Houghton Mifflin Company, 1966
31. Gibson JJ: The information available in pictures. Leonardo 4:27–35, 1971
32. Gibson JJ: On the concept of the "visual solid angle" in an optic array and its history. Unpublished manuscript, Ithaca, New York, Cornell University, October 1972
33. Gibson JJ: What is meant by the processing of information. Unpublished manuscript. Ithaca, New York, Cornell University, February 1973
34. Gibson JJ, Gibson EJ: Continuous perspective transformations and the perception of rigid motion. J Exp Psychol 54:129–138, 1957
35. Gibson JJ, Radner M: Adaptation, after-effect and contrast in the perception of tilted lines. I. Quantitative studies. J Exp Psychol 20:453–467, 1937
36. Goodman N: Languages of Art: An Approach to a Theory of Symbols. Indianapolis, Bobbs-Merrill, 1968
37. Gordon IE, Hayward S: Second-order isomorphism of internal representations of familiar faces. Percept Psychophysics 14:334–336, 1973
38. Gregory R: Seeing as thinking: an active theory of perception. London Times Literary Suppl, June 23, 1972, pp 707–708

39. Gregory RL: On how so little information controls so much behavior. *In* Towards a Theoretical Biology. Vol 2. Edited by CH Waddington, Chicago, Aldine Publishing Co., 1969

40. Gregory RL: The Intelligent Eye. New York, McGraw-Hill Book Company, 1970

41. Guzman A: Decomposition of a visual scene into three-dimensional bodies. *In* Automatic Interpretation and Classification of Images. Edited by A Grasseli. New York, Academic Press, 1969

42. Haber RN: Information processing analyses of visual perception: an introduction. *In* Information Processing Approaches to Visual Perception. Edited by RN Haber. New York, Holt, Rinehart & Winston, 1969

43. Hagen MA: Picture perception: toward a theoretical model. Psychol Bull 81:471–497, 1974

44. Harris CS, Gibson AR: Is orientation-specific color adaptation in human vision due to edge detectors, afterimages or "dipoles"? Science 162:1506–1507, 1968

45. Hawkins JK: Textural properties for pattern recognition. *In* Picture Processing and Psychopictorics. Edited by BS Lipkin. New York, Academic Press, 1970

46. Hebb DO: The Organization of Behavior. New York, John Wiley & Sons, 1949

47. Heider ER, Oliver DC: The structure of the color space in naming and memory for two languages. Cognitive Psychol 3:337–354, 1972

48. Heider F: On perception and event structure and the psychological environment. Psychol Issues 1 no. 3, 1959

49. Held R, Shattuck SR: Color and edge-sensitive channels in the human visual system: tuning for orientation. Science 174:314–316, 1971

50. Helm CE: Multidimensional ratio scaling analysis of perceived color relations. J Opt Soc Am 54:256–262, 1964

51. Helmholtz H von: Treatise on Psychological Optics. (Translated from the Third German Edition, 1909–1911. Edited by JP Southall) Rochester, New York, Optical Society of America, 1925

52. Henderson LA: A word superiority effect without orthographic assistance. Q J Exp Psychol 26:301–311, 1974

53. Hochberg J: In the mind's eye. *In* Contemporary Theory and Research in Visual Perception. Edited by RN Haber. New York, Holt, Rinehart & Winston, 1968

54. Hochberg J: Attention, organization and consciousness. *In* Attention: Contemporary Theory and Analysis. Edited by DI Mostofsky. New York, Appleton-Century-Crofts, 1970

55. Hochberg J: Higher-order stimuli and inter-response coupling in the perception of the visual world. *In* Perception: Essays in Honor of JJ Gibson. Edited by RB MacLeod, HL Pick Jr. Ithaca, New York, Cornell University Press, 1974

56. Hubel DH, Wiesel TN: Receptive fields and functional architecture in two non-striate visual areas (18 and 19) of the cat. J Neurophysiol 30:1561–1573, 1967

57. Hubel DH, Wiesel TN: Receptive fields and functional architecture of monkey striate cortex. J Physiol (Lond) 195:215–243, 1968

58. Ingling N: Categorization: a mechanism for rapid information processing. J Exp Psychol 94:239–243, 1972

59. Ittleson WH: Visual Space Perception. New York, Springer-Verlag, 1960

60. Johansson G: Projective transformations as determining visual space perception. *In* Perception: Essays in Honor of James J Gibson. Edited by RB MacLeod, HL Pick Jr. Ithaca, New York, Cornell University Press, 1974

61. Johnston IR, White GR, Cumming RW: The role of optical expansion patterns in locomotor control. Am J Psychol 86:311–324, 1973

62. Johnston JC, McClelland JL: Perception of letters in words: seek not and ye shall find. Science 184:1192–1194, 1974

63. Jonides J, Gleitman H: A conceptual category effect in visual search: O as a letter or a digit. Percept Psychophysics 12:457–460, 1972

64. Kahneman D: Method, findings and theory in studies of visual masking. Psychol Bull 70:404–426, 1968

65. Katz JJ: The Underlying Reality of Language and its Philosophical Import. New York, Harper & Row, Publishers, 1971
66. Katz L, Wicklund D: Word scanning rate in good and poor readers. J Educ Psychol 62:138–140, 1971
67. Kinsbourne M, Warrington EK: The effect of an after-coming random pattern on the perception of brief visual stimuli. Q J Exp Psychol 14:223–234, 1962
68. Kinsbourne M, Warrington EK: Further studies on the masking of brief visual stimuli by a random pattern. Q J Exp Psychol 14:235–245, 1962
69. Kolers PA: Apparent movement of a Necker cube. Am J Psychol 77:220–230, 1964
70. Kolers PA: An Illusion that Dissociates Motion, Object, and Meaning. Quarterly Progress Report No. 82, Research Laboratories Electronics, Cambridge, Massachusetts, MIT Press, 1966, pp 221–223
71. Kolers PA: Comments on the session on visual recognition. In Models for the Perception of Speech and Visual Form. Edited by W Wathen-Dunn. Cambridge, Massachusetts, MIT Press, 1967
72. Kolers PA: Some psychological aspects of pattern recognition. In Recognizing Patterns. Edited by PA Kolers, M Eden. Cambridge, Massachusetts, MIT Press, 1968
73. Kolers PA: Three stages of reading. In Basic Studies in Reading. Edited by H Levin, J Williams. New York, Basic Books, 1970
74. Kolers PA, Pomerantz JR: Figural change in apparent motion. J Exp Psychol 87:99–108, 1971
75. Kroll NEA, Parks T, Parkinson SR, et al: Short-term memory while shadowing: recall of visually and of aurally presented letters. J Exp Psychol 85:220–224, 1970
76. Lee DN: Visual information during locomotion. In Perception: Essays in honor of James J Gibson. Edited by RB MacLeod, HL Pick Jr. Ithaca, New York, Cornell University Press, 1974
77. Lee DN, Aronson E: Visual proprioceptive control of standing in human infants. Percept Psychophysics 15:529–532, 1974
78. Lishman JR, Lee DN: The autonomy of visual kinaesthesis. Perception 2:287–294, 1973
79. Mace WM: Ecologically stimulating cognitive psychology: Gibsonian perspectives. In Cognition and the Symbolic Processes. Edited by W Weimer, DS Palermo. Hillsdale, New Jersey, Lawrence Erlbaum Associates, 1974
80. Mace WM: James Gibson's strategy for perceiving: ask not what's inside your head, but what your head's inside of. In Perceiving, Acting and Comprehending: Toward an Ecological Psychology. Edited by RE Shaw, J Bransford. Hillsdale, New Jersey, Lawrence Erlbaum Associates (in press)
81. MacKay DM: Ways of looking at perception. In Models for the Perception of Speech and Visual Form. Edited by W Wathen-Dunn. Cambridge, Massachusetts, MIT Press, 1967
82. Mackworth AK: Interpreting Pictures of Polyhedral Scenes (Third International Joint Conference on Artificial Intelligence). Menlo Park, California, Stanford Research Institute, 1973
83. Maffei L, Fiorentini A: Processes of synthesis in visual perception. Nature 240:479–481, 1972
84. Marcel AJ: Perception with and without awareness. Read at the meeting of the Experimental Psychology Society, Stirling, Scotland, July 1974
85. Marshall JD, Newcombe F: Patterns of paralexia. Read at the meeting of the International Neuropsychology Symposium, Engelberg, Switzerland, 1971
86. Mayhew JEW, Anstis SM: Movement aftereffects contingent on color, intensity, and pattern. Percept Psychophysics 12:77–85, 1972
87. McCulloch WS: A heterarchy of values determined by the topology of nervous nets. Bull Math Biophys 1:89–93, 1945
88. McCullough C: Color adaptation of edge-detectors in the human visual system. Science 149:1115–1116, 1965

89. Merleau-Ponty M: Phenomenology of Perception. (Translated by C Smith, 1947) New York, Humanities Press, 1962
90. Minsky M: Steps toward artificial intelligence. In Computers and Thought. Edited by AE Fergenbaum, J Feldman. New York, McGraw-Hill Book Company, 1963
91. Minsky M, Papert S: Artificial Intelligence Memo, 252. Cambridge, Massachusetts, MIT Press, 1972
92. Moray N: Where is capacity limited? A survey and a model. Acta Psychol (Amst) 27:84–92, 1967
93. Murch GM: Binocular relationships in a size and color orientation after-effect. J Exp Psychol 93:30–34, 1972
94. Neisser U: Cognitive Psychology. New York, Appleton-Century-Crofts, 1967
95. Novik N: Developmental Studies of Backward Visual Masking. Unpublished Thesis, University of Connecticut, 1974
96. Ogle KN: Perception of distance and of size. In The Eye. Vol 4. New York, Academic Press, 1962
97. Pastore N: Selective History of Theories of Visual Perception: 1650–1950. New York, Oxford University Press, 1971
98. Phillips WA: On the distinction between sensory storage and short-term visual memory. Percept Psychophysics 16:283–290, 1974
99. Phillips WA, Baddeley AD: Reaction time and short-term visual memory. Psychonomic Sci 22:73–74, 1971
100. Pittenger JB, Shaw RE: Aging faces as viscal-elastic events: implications for a theory of nonrigid shape perception. J Exp Psychol Hum Percept Performance (in press)
101. Pollen DA, Lee JR, Taylor JH: How does the striate cortex begin the reconstruction of the visual world? Science 173:74–77, 1971
102. Posner MI: Components of skilled performance. Science 152:1712–1718, 1966
103. Posner MI: Abstraction and the process of recognition. In Psychology of Learning and Motivation. Vol 3. Edited by GH Bower, JT Spence. New York, Academic Press, 1969
104. Posner MI, Boies SJ, Eichelman WH, et al: Retention of visual and name codes of single letters. J Exp Psychol Monogr 79:1–17, 1969
105. Posner MI, Keele SW: Decay of visual information from a single letter. Science 158:137–139, 1967
106. Posner MI, Mitchell RF: Chronometric analysis of classification. Psychol Rev 74:392–409, 1967
107. Reicher GM: Perceptual recognition as a function of meaningfulness of stimulus material. J Exp Psychol 81:275–280, 1969
108. Riggs LA: Curvature as a feature of pattern vision. Science 181:1070–1072, 1973
109. Rock I, Halper F, Clayton T: The perception and recognition of complex figures. Cognitive Psychol 3:655–673, 1972
110. Roberts LG: Machine perception of three-dimensional solids. In Electro-optical Information Processing. Edited by JT Toppitz et al. Cambridge, Massachusetts, MIT Press, 1965
111. Ryle G: The Concept of Mind. London, Hutchinson Publishing Group, 1949
112. Scharf B, Lefton LA: Backward and forward masking as a function of stimulus and task parameters. J Exp Psychol 84:331–338, 1970
113. Schiff W: Perception of impending collision: a study of visually directed avoidance behavior. Psychol Monogr 79: whole no. 604, 1965
114. Schiff W, Caviness JA, Gibson JJ: Persistent fear responses in Rhesus monkeys to the optical stimulus of "looming." Science 136:982–983, 1962
115. Schiller PH: Monoptic and dichoptic visual masking by patterns and flashes. J Exp Psychol 69:193–199, 1965
116. Sekuler R: Spatial vision. In Annual Review of Psychology, 1974. Palo Alto, Annual Reviews, 1974
117. Selfridge OG, Neisser U: Pattern recognition by machine. Sci Am 203:60–68 (Aug) 1960

118. Shaw RE: Cognition, simulation, and the problem of complexity. J Structural Learn 2:31–44, 1971
119. Shaw RE, McIntyre M: Algoristic foundations to cognitive psychology. In Cognition and the Symbolic Processes. Edited by W Weimer, D Palermo. Hillside, New Jersey, Lawrence Erlbaum Associates, 1974
120. Shaw RE, McIntyre M, Mace W: The role of symmetry in event perception. In Perception: Essays in Honor of JJ Gibson. Edited by RB MacLeod, HL Pick Jr. Ithaca, New York, Cornell University Press, 1974
121. Shaw RE, Pittenger J: Perceiving the face of change in changing faces: toward an event perception theory of shape. In Perceiving, Acting and Comprehending: Toward an Ecological Psychology. Edited by RE Shaw, J Bransford. Hillsdale, New Jersey, Lawrence Erlbaum Associates (in press)
122. Shaw RE, Wilson BE: Generative conceptual knowledge: how we know what we know. In Cognition and Instruction: Tenth Annual Carnegie-Mellon Symposium on Information Processing. Edited by D Klahr. Hillsdale, New Jersey, Lawrence Erlbaum Associates (in press)
123. Shepard RN: The analysis of proximities: multi-dimensional scaling with an unknown distance function. I and II. Psychometrika 27:125–140; 214–246, 1962
124. Shepard RN: Studies of the form, formation, and transformation of internal representations. In Cognitive Mechanisms. Edited by E Galanter. Washington, Winston & Sons (in press)
125. Shepard RN, Chipman S: Second-order isomorphism of internal representation: shapes of states. Cognitive Psychol 1:1–17, 1970
126. Shepard RN, Feng C: A chronometric study of mental paper folding. Cognitive Psychol 3:228–243, 1972
127. Shepard RN, Metzler J: Mental rotation of three-dimensional objects. Science 171:701–703, 1971
128. Sherrington CS: The Integrative Action of the Nervous System. New York, Cambridge University Press, 1906
129. Smith MC, Schiller PH: Forward and backward masking: a comparison. Can J Psychol 20:337–342, 1966
130. Sperling G: The information available in brief visual presentations. Psychol Monogr 74: whole no. 498, 1960
131. Sperling G: A model for visual memory tasks. Hum Factors 5:19–31, 1963
132. Sperling G: Sperling G: Successive approximations to a model for short-term memory. Acta Psychol (Amst) 27:285–292, 1967
133. Sternberg S: High-speed scanning in human memory. Science 153:652–654, 1966
134. Sternberg S: Two operations in character-recognition: some evidence from reaction-time measurements. Percept Psychophys 2:45–53, 1967
135. Sternberg S: Memory scanning: mental processes revealed by reaction time experiments. Am Sci 57:421–457, 1969
136. Stromeyer CF, Mansfield RJ: Colored aftereffects produced with moving images. Percept Psychophys 7:108–114, 1970
137. Sutherland NS: Intelligent picture processing. Read at the Conference on the Evolution of the Nervous System and Behavior, Florida State University, Tallahassee, 1973
138. Thompson DW: On Growth and Form. Second edition (original edition, 1917). Cambridge New York, Cambridge University Press, 1942
139. Treisman A, Russell R, Green J: Brief visual storage of shape and movement. In Attention and Performance V. New York, Academic Press, 1974
140. Turvey MT: Some aspects of selective readout from iconic storage. (Haskins Laboratories Status Report on Speech Research, 1972, SR-29/30, 1–40.) New Haven, Haskins Laboratories, 1972
141. Turvey MT: On peripheral and central processes in vision: inferences from an information processing analysis of masking with patterned stimuli. Psychol Rev 80:1–52, 1973
142. Turvey MT: Constructive theory, perceptual systems and tacit knowledge. In

Cognition and the Symbolic Processes. Edited by W Weimar, D Palermo. Hillside, New Jersey, Lawrence Erlbaum Associates, 1974

143. Turvey MT, Kravetz S: Retrieval from iconic memory with shape as the selection criterion. Percept Psychophys 8:171–172, 1970

144. Vanthoor FLJ, Eijkman EGJ: Time course of the iconic memory signal. Acta Psychol (Amst) 37:79–85, 1973

145. Von Fieandt K, Gibson JJ: The sensitivity of the eye to two kinds of continuous transformation of a shadow-pattern. J Exp Psychol 57:344–347, 1959

146. Von Wright JM: Selection in immediate memory. Q J Exp Psychol 20:62–68, 1968

147. Von Wright JM: On selection in visual immediate memory. Acta Psychol (Amst) 33:280–292, 1970

148. Walker JT: A texture-contingent visual motion aftereffect. Psychonomic Sci 28: 333–335, 1972

149. Wallach H, O'Connell DN: The kinetic depth effect. J Exp Psychol 45:205–207, 1953

150. Warren R: The Perception of Egomotion. Unpublished Thesis, Ithaca, New York, Cornell University, 1975

151. Weisstein N: What the frog's eye tells the human brain: single cell analyzers in the human visual system. Psychol Bull 72:157–176, 1969

152. Weisstein N: Neural symbolic activity: a psychophysical measure. Science 168: 1489–1499, 1970

153. Weisstein N, Harris CS: Visual detection of line segments: an object-superiority effect. Science 186:752–754, 1974

154. Weisstein N, Montalvo F, Ozog G: Differential adaptation to gratings blocked by cubes and gratings blocked by hexagons: a test of the neural symbolic activity hypotheses. Psychonomic Sci 27:89–92, 1972

155. Weisstein NA: W-shaped and U-shaped functions obtained for monoptic and dichoptic disk-disk masking. Percept Psychophys 9:275–278, 1971

156. Weyl H: Symmetry. Princeton, New Jersey, Princeton University Press, 1952

157. Wheeler DD: Processes in word recognition. Cognitive Psychol 1:59–85, 1970

158. White BW, Saunders FA, Scadden L, et al: Seeing with the skin. Percept Psychophys 7:23–27, 1970

159. Wickens DD: Characteristics of word encoding. In Coding Processes in Human Memory. Edited by AW Melton, E Martin. Washington, Winston & Sons, 1972

160. Winograd T: Understanding natural language. Cognitive Psychol 3:1–191, 1972

CROSS-MODAL DEVELOPMENT AND READING

Peter E. Bryant

We can perceive most of the objects around us and most of the events that happen near us through more than one sense. We see the shape and texture of an object in our hands, and we also feel this shape and texture by touch. We hear the results of an event like a door slamming and we see what is going on as well.

That we often have more than one sensory source of information about the same thing is interesting, but even more intriguing is the fact that we often know exactly when these different types of information are equivalent. We usually seem to realize when tactual and visual information, or auditory and visual information mean the same thing. We have, for example, only to feel a shape tactually to have a pretty clear idea what its visual appearance will be, and, *mutatis mutandis,* we can anticipate how an object will feel tactually from our visual impression of it. We can, then, translate information from one sensory modality into another.

Cross-modal organization is the term currently used to describe the fact that we can make these connections between modalities. The fact that this organization unquestionably does exist in human adults adds, no doubt, as much to the interest as to the complexity of the task facing the psychologist bent on discovering the basic rules of perception. But its existence also concerns psychologists involved with other problems as well.

Reading is an example. To be able to read one has to make some connection between visual and auditory information. The child must learn that written, and therefore visually presented, letters and words signify particular sounds which themselves are spoken letters, and words. If therefore he simply cannot associate visual with auditory information he just will not be able to learn to read.

Of course, simply to say that cross-modal organization of some sort is essential to reading does not, on its own, mean that this is a subject which people concerned with reading must know about. A child presumably has to be able to breathe to be able to read, but no one, I think, has put breathing forward as a crucially important topic in the study of backwardness in reading.

The question really is whether cross-modal organization is ever a limiting factor in learning to read. Can any of the difficulties which children have in learning to read be traced back to an inability to link visual with auditory patterns? This is the question which I shall try to answer.

There are, as we shall see, a host of experiments which try to tackle this problem directly by comparing backward with normal readers in tasks which in one way or another are "cross-modal." However I do not think it possible to assess these properly without first having a general idea about the way in which humans manage to make links between different modalities. In fact, the literature in this area raises a number of quite serious conceptual and experimental problems which apply in the end, as much as anywhere, to the experiments concerned with reading.

Visual and Tactual Connections

We can start with an experimental problem. How does one establish how good someone is at making connections between patterns perceived through different sensory modalities? More specifically, since we are primarily concerned with children at the time they learn to read, how do we establish how good children are at it, and whether their cross-modal ability changes as they grow older?

At first the answer seems essentially a simple one. Simply present children with tasks in which they have to detect when objects presented through different modalities are the same. This kind of task has often been given to children. It is usually described as cross-modal matching, and it takes one of two forms. In the first type, two objects which may be the same as each other or dissimilar are presented, one in each modality. The child is asked whether they are the same or different. In the second type, the child is presented with one object (the standard) in one modality. Then two other objects, one of which is the same as the standard, are offered in the other modality. The child has to say which of these two choices is the same as the standard.

Obviously a child who succeeds in these tasks must possess some sort of cross-modal organization. Suppose that I give a child a series of pairs of shapes, allowing him only to see one of the objects in each pair and only to touch the other. Suppose also that he always can say whether they are the same or not. Then I can be sure that he can equate visual and tactual information about shapes, at least to some extent. If I then find that children get better at this task as they grow older, it might seem just as obvious that their cross-modal ability improved with age.

Here we meet our first snag. Perhaps the best way to illustrate it, is to describe one of the first experiments in which children of different ages were asked to match visual with tactual shapes.

This was a study which Piaget and Inhelder[33] carried out in the late forties. They gave young children aged between three and eight years a series of shapes to hold but not to see, one at a time. At the same time, they showed the child visually a whole series of shapes. Each time that he was given a shape tactually he had to point to the visual shape which he thought was most like the object in his hands. This then was a cross-modal task. What it showed was that the younger children tended to make some characteristic errors, such as confusing a square with a triangle. Furthermore, these errors tended to disappear as the children got older. The older children certainly were better at saying when visual and tactual shapes were equivalent. This experiment or versions of it have now been repeated many times[20, 28, 29] and the original results on the whole have proved extremely reliable.

How do we interpret this result? It seems at first to suggest that the older children were more adept at linking visual with tactual information than younger children. This may indeed have been so. But there is another possibility, the mistakes which the younger children made had nothing to do with cross-modal difficulties. Perhaps these children were simply unable to perceive the shapes tactually (or even visually). The task basically contained two elements. First, the child had to perceive the visual and tactual shapes properly; then he had to link the two types of perception. Errors could be the result either of difficulties in the original tactual (or visual) perception, or of failures in linking these two modalities. The first type of error should be called within-modal, the second cross-modal.

Thus, this experiment and its many replications do not tell us about the development of cross-modal abilities. We cannot tell whether the older children really were better than younger children at making cross-modal connections. There is, however, an excuse for this disappointing start to the literature. Piaget and Inhelder were not specifically concerned with cross-modal organization. They talked rather in terms of finding out about "representation."

But this excuse cannot be made for the next series of experiments which definitely were concerned with cross-modal development. In the end, these studies produced results just as ambiguous. These are the influential experiments of Birch and Lefford.[6,7] They set out to test the very simple hypothesis that the different sensory systems first develop separately in children and only later are brought together in some form of cross-modal organization. Consequently, older children should be much better than younger ones at linking equivalent information which comes to them through different modalities.

To test this prediction, they devised a series of cross-modal tasks in which children had to judge whether a shape presented in one modality was the same as one presented in another. Three types of presentation, each representing a different modality, were involved. These were *visual*, in which the child saw but did not feel the shape; *tactual* in which he felt it without seeing it; and *kinesthetic* in which the child held a stylus in his hand which was then moved for him around the shape. From these three presentations, Birch and Lefford produced three cross-modal tasks, each of which involved comparing a series of pairs and shapes. In one task (visual-tactual) the child saw one shape and actively felt the other with his hands. In another (visual-kinesthetic) he saw one shape and one hand was moved for him around the other shape, a mode of presentation called kinesthetic. In the third (tactual-kinesthetic), he felt one shape actively and had his hand moved around the other one. The term they actually used for the tactual presentation was "haptic."

Birch and Lefford predicted that the older the children were, the better they would be at all three tasks. Indeed these were the results they obtained. The older children were better in these cross-modal tasks, and their superiority was particularly marked in the two tasks which involved the kinesthetic presentations. The experimenters concluded that these results support their hypothesis that cross-modal ability develops at a comparatively late stage in childhood.

This conclusion may be correct, but again it may not. The difficulty which the younger children had, particularly with the discriminations involving kinesthetic presentations, may have been in the original perception and not in connecting perceptions across modalities. The experiment may simply be showing that the older children get better at distinguishing shapes kinesthetically. Therefore, we cannot tell yet whether the Birch and Lefford hypothesis is correct. Furthermore, we are not helped by another set of studies published in the fifties and sixties by Abravanel,[1] Blank and Bridger,[8] Conners et al.,[15] Fisher,[20] and Lovell[29] which also involved only cross-modal tasks and therefore leave us quite unsure whether the younger children's difficulties lay within or across modalities.

How does one avoid this apparent impasse? The answer is very easy and has been available for some time. Simply give the child within- as well as cross-modal tasks. Test whether he can match tactual with tactual shapes and visual with visual, as well as visual with tactual. Only if the child consistently gets a discrimination right in the within-modal tasks, but wrong in the cross-modal ones, can one be sure that his errors in the cross-modal task are genuinely cross-modal. If on the other hand, he errs as much in, say, the tactual-tactual task as in the visual-tactual one; then it is fairly certain that his failures in the cross-modal task are merely failures in tactual perception.[11, 12]

That is not all. If one wishes to make the developmental case that children's ability to make cross-modal connections increases as they grow older, it is not enough to demonstrate that the cross-modal tasks are the harder ones. One must also show that with age greater improvement takes place in the cross-modal tasks than in the within-modal tasks. If, on the contrary, performance improves as much in the within-modal conditions as in the cross-modal tasks, one can conclude nothing about cross-modal development. If seven-year-olds are better than five-year-olds both on a visual-tactual matching task and on a tactual-tactual matching task, and if this age difference is as great in the one task as in the other, one can only suggest that the improvement in the visual-tactual matching task is the result of children becoming more capable at discriminating objects by touch.

Actually three studies on visual and tactual perception were carried out in the sixties which did include these essential controls. All three suggest rather strongly that the Birch and Lefford hypothesis is wrong. The first of these was an experiment by Hermelin and O'Connor,[26] which primarily was designed to compare retarded with normal children. Since it involved one age level only which was around five years, it was not a developmental study. Hermelin and O'Connor gave these children a visual-tactual (V-T) matching task in which the standards were visual and the choices tactual, and a tactual-visual (T-V) task where it was the standard that was tactual. They also gave the children tactual-tactual (T-T) and visual-visual (V-V) tasks. The results showed that the cross-modal tasks were no more difficult than the within-modal ones. This seems to show that any errors that were made on the cross-modal tasks were probably simply errors in the visual or tactaul perception and thus had nothing to do with cross-modal connections.

Another study which included the same four matching tasks (V-T, T-V, V-V, and T-T) was carried out by Rudel and Teuber[38] on children of four and five years. They found that at both age levels the tactual-tactual matching condition was actually worse than the visual-visual matching task. There was no evidence that performance on the cross-modal tasks improved more with age than it did in within-modal tasks.

Much of the same pattern was found in an experiment by Milner and Bryant[31] on children of five, six and seven years. We also showed that the easiest condition was the visual-visual one, then the two cross-modal tasks, and finally worst of all the tactual-tactual task. What does this pattern mean?

One way of looking at it is to note that children always seem to make more errors in the tactual-tactual task than in the visual-visual one. This means that the tactual perceptual input is not as effective as the visual one. In turn this means, to put it crudely, that in the visual-visual task there are two good inputs, in the visual-tactual and tactual-visual tasks there is one good and one bad input, and in the tactual-tactual task two bad inputs. Thus in the last condition there is more chance for error than in the other three tasks. It follows from this analysis that the relative difficulty for all four tasks is decided by the discriminability of the two perceptual inputs. It seems to have nothing to do with failures in cross-modal organization.

These studies provide no support for the Birch and Lefford hypothesis[6,7] and some compelling evidence against it. It is the same with more recent investigations. No subsequent study involving the visual and tactual perception of shape shows any convincing sign of cross-modal development in the form of a difference between cross- and within-modal tasks.[30,37] So the hypothesis, insofar as it applies to the visual, tactual and kinesthetic perception of shapes, is almost certainly wrong. If so far we have made no great theoretical advance, we have at least learned something about the experimental problems in this area. This lesson will be useful when we come to consider the experiments which are more directly concerned with reading. But before we come to these, I should like to turn to another hypothesis about cross-modal development.

Language and Cross-Modal Development

It has sometimes been suggested that humans make cross-modal connections through language. The hypothesis is attractively simple. The child holds and sees a ball, for example, and also learns its name. He attaches this name both to the visual and to the tactual impression of this ball, and thus the name becomes the link between the two impressions. The tactual and visual impressions are treated as equivalent because they have the same name. Language then according to this hypothesis is the *tertium quid* through which the modalities are connected. This hypothesis has been advanced at different times, albeit rather tentatively, by Ettlinger,[18] Hermelin and O'Connor,[26] Garvill and Mollander,[22] and Blank and Bridger.[8]

The hypothesis produces some clear predictions capable of disproof. In the end it turns out that most of them have been disproved.

One obvious prediction is that animals, who have no language, will not be able to match objects (shapes) across modalities. For a long time the literature seemed to show that it is extremely difficult to find any sign of cross-modal organization even in animals as sophisticated as the rhesus monkey.[17,18] We can take as an example an elegant experiment by Ettlinger and Blakemore[19] with monkeys. The experiment was a matching one, but the animals had to be taught to match. A group of animals was given three shapes on every trial. Two of the shapes were visual and different from each other, while the third could only be touched and felt. This tactual stimulus was the standard. On some trials it was the same as one of the two visual shapes, while in others it was the same as the other visual shape. The monkeys had to learn to respond to visual shape A when the tactual standard was also shape A, and to visual shape B when the tactual standard was B. They did learn this, and it is tempting to conclude that this must mean that they knew when the visual and tactual shapes were equivalent.

However, as the experimenters correctly argued, this need not be so. The monkeys may simply have been learning to go to a particular visual shape whenever they felt a particular tactual shape without realizing that the two shapes were equivalent. So Ettlinger and Blakemore devised an interesting control task which they gave to another group of animals. These monkeys also had to learn to go to one visual shape when they felt a particular tactual shape, and to go to the other visual shape when they were given another tactual shape. However, in this task the tactual and visual shapes were completely unrelated. Yet these animals learned the task as quickly and as successfully as those for whom the visual and tactual shapes were the same. The experimenters concluded, and one can only agree, that the monkeys in the first group probably did not realize that the visual and tactual shapes were equivalent.

Yet compelling though this conclusion is, the experiment raises some uneasy questions. The very fact that the control group learned to associate specific tactual objects with specific visual ones means that monkeys can at some level link visual with tactual information. If they can learn to associate tactual with visual perceptions, why do they not possess an effective cross-modal organization?

One possible answer is that they do have this kind of organization, but for some reason they were not able to put it into effect in that experiment. This suggestion is bolstered by the results of a recent and ingenious study by Cowey and Weiskrantz.[16] They left monkeys for short periods in total darkness with pellets lying around in their cage. Some of these pellets were edible and these all came in one shape. The rest were inedible and were all another shape. Later, after they had been taken out of the dark the animals were given one example of each of the two shapes, the edible and the inedible shape, and were allowed to choose only one of these. They selected the shape that had been edible 67 percent of the time in one study and 79 percent in another. Thus they were able to connect the same shape which they originally felt with the shape which they later saw. This obviously is a cross-modal connection.

Thus animals without any language in the end do show some sign of cross-modal links. But the question remains whether the language is essential for such links in humans. It could be that language is not essential. To test this we must look to studies of human babies who have not yet learned to speak.

There is now some evidence that even babies of less than 12 months can match some shapes across vision and touch.[13] It is difficult to get babies to match things, but we noticed that babies are attracted to and do reach for objects which make noises. So we constructed little shapes which made a bleeping sound.

We gave each baby one of these objects to hold without seeing it; at the same time made it make a noise. Then we placed that object together with another one of a different shape on the table in front of the baby for him to see. We argued that if the babies consistently reached for the one which they had held and which had made the noise, they must be connecting visual with tactual information. In fact with some pairs of shapes, though not with others, babies did make this cross-modal match. For example, they could make the match with Pair A, but not with Pair B (Figure 1). Here again is a cross-modal connection without language, and this time it occurs in humans.

So it would appear that cross-modal abilities do not depend on language. It is quite possible, of course, that verbal people do to some extent use words when they make some cross-modal connections. What exactly goes on when a cross-modal connection is made and what is the psychological process underlying cross-modal integration are matters which we still are far from discovering. It is perhaps more realistic to turn from this question to the studies which attempt to relate cross-modal abilities to the way children learn to read.

Figure 1. Shapes used in the infant experiment. (From Bryant, Jones, Claxton, et al., 1972)

Cross-Modal Associations and Reading

Many of the themes and many of the problems which we have noted in the general study of cross-modal development also crop up in experiments on cross-modal influences in reading.

Perhaps the best way to start an account of this work is to describe the curious incident of experiments on tactual and kinesthetic influences in learning to read. The curious thing about these experiments is that they have not really been done in a controlled laboratory setting. This is a gap which always surprises me. On the one hand, we have the intuitions and successful practices which go back to formidable educators as Montessori, Gillingham and others which suggest very strongly that children can be helped learn to remember the visual patterns made by letters if they are experienced tactually and kinesthetically as well as visually. These suggestions have been enthusiastically taken up in many educational programs. On the other hand, experimental psychologists have done virtually nothing to clarify the validity of this practice. Yet it should be possible to design an experiment which tests whether or not children remember the shape and orientation of a letter better when they have experienced it by feeling it.

To my knowledge, the nearest thing to an experimental test of this approach came in an experiment by Hendrikson and Muehl.[25] They examined the confusions children make when they have to remember the difference between the letters "b" and "d." They trained some children to move their arm to the right whenever they were shown b and to the left when they saw d, thus emphasizing the directional differences of the two letters with a related movement. However, the movement trained children were no better at distinguishing the two letters than others whose movements were in no way related to the different directions of b and d. Here then is a failure to provide laboratory support for a multisensory program based on kinesthetics. However, the study involved only two letters, only one type of movement, and thus is limited in its application to the general area under discussion.

What would happen if one worked with other letters and with combinations of letters? What would happen if the children felt the letters as some educators have encouraged? What is the effect of producing several different sensory sources about the same pattern at the same time rather than successively? An experimentally based answer to these questions is not yet available. Further investigation, however, may permit a more definite conclusion.

There is more evidence, however, from studies which have tried to link cross-modal abilities and reading directly. These all concern connections between vision and hearing. They start with the well-known work of Birch and Belmont.[4] They had the idea that since reading involves links between auditory and visual patterns, some of the difficulties which some children have in learning to read might be the result of an inability to make cross-modal associations. This suggestion is an extension from Birch's original ideas about cross-modal development. The hypothesis here is that cross-modal ability develops faster in some children than in others, and that these differences between children may influence the rate at which they learn to read.

Their first experimental test of this hypothesis involved 150 Scottish boys whose reading scores were in the bottom 10 percent of three out of four reading tests administered to them. They were counted as backward readers and were compared to 50 other boys whose reading scores did not fall in the bottom 10 percent of any of these tests. The mean age of both groups was around nine-and-a-half years.

The point of the experiment was to compare these groups in a cross-modal task. The modalities chosen were appropriately, vision and hearing. But how does one test for visual-auditory associations? It is usually possible to say what an object will look like from the way it feels, but one cannot always say what a thing will look like from the sound it makes, or vice versa. One door squeaks and another doesn't, despite the fact that they both look pretty much the same. So it must have been a problem for Birch and Belmont to devise an auditory-visual test which took the same form as their cross-modal tasks involving vision, touch and kinesthesis.

Their solution, one which has been adopted in all the many experiments which were later provoked by Birch and Belmont's research,[4,5] was to use the dimension of length. Sounds last for a certain amount of time, and the intervals between sounds can vary as well. Visual patterns also take up a certain amount of space, and so do the gaps between them. One thus has long and short auditory and visual stimuli. It is possible (one has only to think of the Morse code) to treat the auditory and visual information about length as in some way equivalent. One can treat a long sound as equivalent to a long visual stimulus, and a long gap between sounds as equivalent to a long gap between visual stimuli.

Birch and Belmont's auditory-visual tasks involved a sort of inverted Morse code. In each trial they tapped out a sequence of sounds. Each tap lasted the same amount of time but the intervals between the taps was either a long or a short one. In sequences made out of four taps, the first interval might be a short one and the next two long or all three intervals might be long and so on. As soon as the experimenter finished tapping, he showed the child three visual patterns, each made out of dots arranged in a straight line. The only difference between these patterns was in the length of the gaps between the dots. There were long and short gaps, and thus a pattern with four dots might have three long gaps or one short and two long gaps between the dots and so on. Only one of these three lines was meant to be the equivalent of the preceding auditory sequence. This line was the one whose spatial gaps (reading from left to right) made up the same pattern as the intervals between taps. Thus four dots separated first by a long and then by two short gaps were the equivalent of four taps separated first by a long interval and then by two short ones.

The results of this experiment can be told very simply. The backward readers were worse on this visual-auditory task than the normal readers. We can also say straightaway that this has proved a reliable result in subsequent experiments. Many other studies which use Birch and Belmont's cross-modal task or some variant of it, have also shown either that backward readers have more difficulty with it than normal readers or that the ability to make this sort of connection between visual and auditory patterns is correlated with reading ability.[3,5,14,21,27,32,34-36,40,42,43]

What are we to conclude from this result? Does it, as Birch and Belmont suggest, support their hypothesis that children's difficulties in reading are often the result of a failure to make connections between visual and auditory perception? Such a conclusion would be unjustified. Again there are no within-modal controls so that the backward reader may be backward only in visual or auditory perception. He may just be unable to take in, for example, the sequence of the auditory taps. We do not have to look far for the correct control. Make the children try to match auditory with auditory sequence and visual with visual pattern, as well as auditory with visual. Only if backward readers have particular difficulty with the cross-modal task and not with the within-modal ones, can we be sure that their difficulty cannot be explained away in terms of failures in auditory or visual perception. In a later study, Kahn and Birch[27] did recognize this difficulty and attempted to improve within-modal controls. However, these were not strictly comparable to the cross-modal task. Furthermore, they always followed the cross-modal task, thus being open to practice effects.

Lack of within-modal controls is not the only difficulty. Even if we were to find that the backward readers were only backward in the auditory-visual task and not in the auditory-auditory or visual-visual ones, we still could not be sure that their difficulty was really a cross-modal one. For there is another difference between the presentations in Birch and Belmont's task besides the fact that the first was auditory and the second visual. The other difference is that the first was a temporal sequence, distinguished by the length of the temporal intervals between sounds, while the second was a spatial pattern, in which the length of the gaps between dots varied in space. The task then involves integrating temporal with spatial information; it tests whether children can treat long and short in time as equivalent to long and short in space. It could be that the backward readers were deficient in this type of integration. Again the control is not difficult to find. One needs a temporal-spatial matching task which involves only one modality. This would be difficult to do with sounds since it is difficult to think of an auditory and spatial pattern which children would be able to take in. But it is quite easy to have a temporal as well as a spatial visual pattern. One need only show a single dot or a single light which appears and re-appears after short or long intervals.

The Birch and Belmont experiment was rightly criticized by Sterritt and

Rudnick[42] on two other grounds. First, it was not clear whether the auditory presentation was just auditory, since the children may have seen the experimenter tapping. Secondly, the backward and normal readers were not equated for I.Q. However, since these are difficulties which can and have been put right without restructuring the experiment's design, I shall not concentrate on them.

Now we can see that to demonstrate that the backward readers' difficulty was a cross-modal one, we need an experiment in which backward and normal readers have to deal with three kinds of information: (1) visual and spatial patterns; (2) visual and temporal sequences; and (3) auditory and temporal sequences. These patterns can then be matched with each other in all possible combinations. This would make nine types of matching problems: auditory-temporal sequences matched with visual-spatial patterns, auditory-temporal patterns with auditory-temporal sequences, auditory-temporal with visual-temporal sequences, visual-temporal sequences with visual-spatial patterns, visual-temporal with visual-spatial and so on.

To find that the backward readers are worse than normal readers at matching auditory with visual patterns, whether the visual patterns are temporally or spatially arranged, but no worse with the other combinations, would be to have pretty good evidence that there was something to the hypothesis about cross-modal deficiencies in backwardness in reading.

Now the fact that the Birch and Belmont experiment controlled neither for within-modal effects nor for difficulties in linking temporal with spatial information was noticed by a number of psychologists, who then set about trying to sort out where exactly the backward readers' difficulties lie in this sort of situation. This is the main reason why the Birch and Belmont experiments provoked so many further studies. One such study is by Goodnow[23] who was interested in temporal-spatial integration. Although she relates her results directly to the Birch-Belmont hypothesis, she does not consider the question of reading ability at all. This should remind us that there are two separable questions. One, whether cross-modal abilities develop. The other, whether this development if it does occur affects learning to read. Many studies attempted to plug only one of the two gaps, either just putting in within-modal controls or just checking the question about temporal-spatial integration by including visual-temporal sequences.

For example, Muehl and Kremenak[32] gave children of six and seven years within- as well as cross-modal versions of Birch and Belmont's task by including auditory-auditory and visual-visual matching tasks. They found that the auditory within-modal task led to even more errors than the cross-modal tasks. A more recent study by Vande Voort, Senf and Benton[43] also included these within-modal controls and compared backward with normal readers, the ages of both groups ranging from 9 to 11 years. This experiment also confirmed that the auditory within-modal comparisons were at least as difficult as the cross-modal ones, and it also showed that the backward readers were as much at a disadvantage in the within-modal tasks as in the cross-modal ones. This result, of course goes directly against Birch and Belmont's hypothesis which demands that the backward reader's inferiority should be particularly marked in the cross-modal task.[4,5] However, the implications of both these studies remain ambiguous because one does not know if the relative difficulty of the auditory patterns is due to the fact that they are auditory or due to the fact that they are made out of temporal sequences.

A similar objection, though the other way round, can be made to those studies which concentrate only on the temporal-spatial question. An example is an experiment by Blank and Bridger[9] which compared nine-year-old normal and retarded readers in three tasks. One task was a purely visual version of the Birch and Belmont situation. The children were first shown visually a temporal sequence which consisted of a light flashing on and off, each flash being separated from its predecessor by a long or a short interval. Then they were shown three dot patterns with the dots separated by long or short spatial gaps. Their task was to point out the spatial pattern which was equivalent to the temporal sequence. The backward readers were worse on this task than the others. The second task simply involved matching dot patterns. They were shown a dot pattern and then had to say which of three subsequent patterns was the same as the one they had seen initially. The backward readers made hardly any mistakes and were as good as the normal readers on this task. Finally in the third task, the children were shown visually a temporal sequence, but this time they were asked to describe this sequence. This was a task which also caused the backward readers some difficulty. The experimenters concluded that backward readers have no difficulty with spatial patterns but do have particular difficulty with temporal ones. Their failure then is not in integrating temporal with spatial information but in taking in temporal information.

There are some objections to this conclusion. One is that one cannot say much either way about the difficulty of temporal-spatial integration because there is no adequate temporal-temporal matching task to serve as a control. Asking a child to describe a temporal sequence does not test perception, since his failures may simply be due to a lack of the proper vocabulary. Thus we cannot know whether the backward readers' errors in the temporal-spatial task were failures in integration, or in the perception of temporal sequences, or in verbal expression.

However, the most pressing cause for concern here is the fact that, by confining itself to visual sequences only, the study cannot tell us whether or not the errors in the original Birch and Belmont task were in any way caused by failures in linking visual with auditory errors. Simply to show that backward readers are also worse on a purely visual analogue of the Birch and Belmont task does not rule out the possibility that their inferiority might be greater in tasks which demand auditory-visual integration than in those which do not. Exactly the same criticism can be made about a later and closely similar study by Blank, Weider and Bridger.[10]

Therefore, we must turn to tasks which use visually presented temporal sequences in addition to visually presented spatial patterns and auditorily presented temporal sequences, and which combine them in the nine matching tasks outlined above. I have been able to find few experiments which have compared normal with backward readers with all nine problems.

One is a study by Bryden[14] with children whose ages were nine-and-one-half to ten years. The patterns he used were very like Birch and Belmont's except that he included visual-temporal sequences as well as the usual visual-spatial patterns and auditory-temporal sequences. The visual-temporal sequences were made by a light which flashed on and off after short or long intervals.

He found the backward readers were worse on all his nine tasks. They did make more errors, it is true, than normal readers matching auditory-temporal patterns with visual-spatial ones. However, this difference between the two groups was as great in the auditory-auditory, and in the visual-visual tasks. There was no sign that backward readers were particularly bad at any one or two of the nine tasks. They were bad at all of them.

Two other studies, one by Sterritt et al.,[41] the other by Rudnick et al.,[39] also contained the essential, nine conditions. However, these were between-subject studies with different children doing different tasks. The result is that though they tell us something about the relative difficulty of the nine tasks, they cannot tell us much about the tasks' relationship to reading.

These studies do not take us very much further forward, but they do at least tell us that the backward readers' difficulty spotted by Birch and Belmont probably has nothing to do either with cross-modal organization or with the coordination of information about time and space. Does this mean that the answer to our original question about cross-modal connections and reading is that there is no significant link between the two?

Reading and Different Types of Cross-Modal Connections

One obvious thing to note about the long series of experiments on cross-modal organization and reading is that without exception they have all (for no very explicit reason) stuck to some version of the Morse code type of pattern which emerged in Birch and Belmont's experiment. A study by Gregory and Gregory[24] even compares performance on the inverted Morse code with performance on real Morse code. No doubt everyone kept to these patterns partly because that was how the experimental literature started and partly because there is some justification for saying that a long temporal gap is naturally equivalent to a long spatial gap. A single important exception is to be found in a recent monograph by Bakker.[2] He examined the hypothesis that backward readers have difficulty in remembering temporal sequences by giving them lists of familiar objects together. However, his groups of backward and normal readers were not equal in I.Q., thereby limiting the applicability of the findings.

Is this natural equivalence necessary? I think that we should be clear that there are really two types of cross-modal associations. Those that are natural and universal on the one hand and those which are quite arbitrary and artificial on the other. The cross-modal organization underlying these two types of connections may or may not be the same.

A good example of a natural association is the one which exists between visual and tactual information about an object's shape. In this instance, those features which determine the object's visual shape also determine its tactual shape. If I change one, I must change the other. Moreover, if I correctly associate visual shape A with tactual shape A, it is most unlikely that someone in another part of the world will correctly associate visual shape A with tactual shape B. If we differ, we cannot both be right.

Contrariwise, arbitrary associations are not naturally given and do vary between cultures. Reading is a good example of arbitrary associations. There really is no natural reason why a particular set of written symbols should signify a particular set of sounds. In fact, the same sounds are written in different ways in different countries. Arbitrary associations presumably have to be learned from scratch. There is nothing in one's natural environment which will tell one what letter goes with what sound.

If one considers again the inverted Morse code pattern, one can see that it falls into the natural category. The length of auditory time is linked with length in visual space in one's natural experience. The longer one hears the noise of a marble rolling behind a sofa, the further it has probably gone. Moreover, the experiments themselves assumed this natural correspondence, since none of them made any attempt to teach the child to make this type of connection during the experiment.

Therefore, I should like to suggest that they may have chosen the wrong type of cross-modal association. It would have been better instead to have taken a set of sounds and a set of visual patterns which had nothing intrinsically to do with each other and to have arbitrarily designated which went with which. Then we could have seen how children, backward and normal in reading, manage when they have to learn to make arbitrary connections between sights and sounds. Of course there would have to be within-modal controls such that the children would learn to associate sounds with sounds, and visual patterns with visual patterns, connected in a con-pletely arbitrary manner. If the backward readers were particularly bad in the cross- but not in the within-modal task, one could say that after all there was something in the cross-modal hypothesis about reading difficulties.

I do not wish to suggest strongly that such a result would occur. I only wish to make the point that it is not yet ruled out. It may be that the reason why it has been to hard to find any tangible link between backwardness in reading and cross-modal connections is that we have been looking at the wrong kind of connection. Now that we have, at any rate, learned something about how to do cross-modal experiments, we ought at least to use our skill to turn this one last stone.

To summarize, I have shown, I hope, that the question of cross-modal organization and reading is an interesting one. I have also demonstrated that the laboratory experiments in this area got into a bit of a mess. But I hope that I have also shown that by sorting out this mess we have managed to gain a pretty clear idea of the experiments which ought to be done and of how they ought to be done.

First we need a thorough investigation of the way in which tactual and kinesthetic experiences might help children learn to recognize particular patterns. Secondly, we need experiments on cross- and within-modal learning of arbitrary connections and the relation of this learning to reading. I think that this research cannot fail to produce practical and useful information. I am only sorry that it will have to be reported at a later meeting of the Orton Society and not at this one.

References

1. Abravanel E: The development of intersensory patterning. Monogr Soc Res Child Dev No. 118, 1968
2. Bakker DJ: Temporal Order in Disturbed Reading. Rotterdam, Rotterdam University Press, 1972
3. Beery JW: Matching of auditory and visual stimuli by average and retarded readers. Child Dev 38:827–833, 1967
4. Birch HG, Belmont L: Auditory-visual integration in normal and retarded readers. Am J Orthopsychiatry 34:852–861, 1964
5. Birch HG, Belmont L: Auditory-visual integration, intelligence and reading ability in school children. Percept Motor Skills 20:295–305, 1965
6. Birch HG, Lefford A: Intersensory development in children. Monogr Soc Res Child Dev No. 89, 1963
7. Birch HG, Lefford A: Visual differentiation, intersensory integration and voluntary motor control. Monogr Soc Res Child Dev No. 110, 1967
8. Blank M, Bridger WH: Cross-modal transfer in nursery school children. J Comp Physiol Psychol 58:277–282, 1964
9. Blank M, Bridger WH: Deficiencies in verbal labelling in retarded readers. Am J Orthopsychiatry 36:840–847, 1966
10. Blank M, Weider S, Bridger WH: Verbal deficiencies in abstract thinking in early reading retardation. Am J Orthopsychiatry 38:823–834, 1968
11. Bryant PE: Comments on the design of developmental studies of cross-modal matching and cross-modal transfer. Cortex 4:127–137, 1968
12. Bryant PE: Perception and Understanding in Young Children. London, Methuen, 1974
13. Bryant PE, Jones P, Claxton V, et al: Recognition of shapes across modalities by infants. Nature 240:303–304, 1972
14. Bryden MP: Auditory-visual and sequential-spatial matching in relation to reading ability. Child Dev 43:824–832, 1972
15. Conners CJ, Schuette C, Goldman A: Informational analysis of intersensory communication in children of different social class. Child Dev 38:251–166, 1967
16. Cowey A, Weiskrantz D: Demonstration of cross-modal matching in rhesus monkeys, *Macaca mulatta*. Neuropsychologia (in press)
17. Drewe EA, Ettlinger G, Milner AD, et al: A comparative review of neuropsychological research on man and monkey. Cortex 6:129–163, 1970
18. Ettlinger G: Analysis of cross-modal effects and their relationship to language. *In* Brain Mechanisms Underlying Speech and Language. Edited by CH Millikan, FL Darley. New York, Grune & Stratton, 1967
19. Ettlinger G, Blakemore CB; Cross modal matching in the monkey. Neuropsychologia 5:147–154, 1967
20. Fisher GH: Development features of behaviour and perception. I. Visual and tactile shape perception. Br J Educ Psychol 35:69–78, 1965
21. Ford MP; Auditory-visual and tactual-visual integration in relation to reading ability. Percept Motor Skills 24:831–851, 1967
22. Garvill J, Mollander B: Verbal mediation effects in cross-modal transfer. Br J Psychol 62:449–455, 1971
23. Goodnow JJ: Matching auditory and visual series: modality problem or translation problem? Child Dev 42:1187–1201, 1971
24. Gregory AH, Gregory HM: A new test of auditory-visual integration. Percept Motor Skills 36:1060–1065, 1973
25. Hendrikson LN, Muehl C: The effect of attention and motor training on learning to discriminate 'b' and 'd' in kindergarten children. J Educ Psychol 53:236–242, 1962
26. Hermelin B, O'Connor N: Recognition of shapes by normal and sub-normal children. Br J Psychol 52:251–284, 1961

27. Kahn D, Birch HG: Development of auditory-visual integration and reading achievement. Percept Motor Skills 27:459–468, 1968

28. Laurendeau M, Pinard A: The Development of the Concept of Space in the Child. New York, IUP, 1970

29. Lovell K: A follow-up study of some aspects of the work of Piaget and Inhelder on the child's conception of space. Br J Educ Psychol 29:104–117, 1959

30. Miller S: Visual and haptic cue utilisation by preschool children: the recognition of visual and haptic stimuli presented separately and together. J Exp Child Psychol 12:88–94, 1971

31. Milner AD, Bryant PE: Cross-modal matching by young children. J Comp Physiol Psychol 71:453–458, 1970

32. Muehl S, Kremenak S: Ability to match auditory and visual information within and between modalities and subsequent reading achievement. J Educ Psychol 57:230–238, 1966

33. Piaget J, Inhelder B: The Child's Conception of Space. London, Routledge and Kegan Paul, 1956

34. Reilly DH: Auditory-visual integration, sex and reading achievement. J Educ Psychol 62:482–486, 1971

35. Reilly DH: Auditory-visual integration, school demographic features and reading achievement. Percept Motor Skills 35:495–501, 1972

36. Reilly DH: Note on the relation of auditory-visual integration and intelligence. Percept Motor Skills 37:45–46, 1973

37. Rose S, Blank M, Bridger WH: Intermodal and intramodal retention of visual and tactual information in young children. Dev Psychol 6:482–486, 1972

38. Rudel RG, Teuber H-L: Cross-modal transfer of shape discrimination by children. Neuropsychologia 2:1–8, 1963

39. Rudnick M, Martin V, Sterritt GM: On the relative difficulty of auditory and visual, temporal and spatial, integrative and non-integrative sequential pattern comparisons. Psychonomic Sci 27:207–210, 1972

40. Rudnick M, Sterritt GM, Flax M: Auditory and visual rhythm perception and reading ability. Child Dev 38:381–587, 1967

41. Sterritt GM, Martin V, Rudnick M: Auditory-visual and temporal-spatial integration as determinants of test difficulty. Psychonomic Sci 23:289–291, 1971

42. Sterritt GM, Rudnick M: Auditory and visual perception in relation to reading ability in fourth grade boys. Percept Motor Skills 22:859–864, 1966

43. Vande Voort L, Senf GM, Benton A: Development of auditory-visual integration in normal and retarded readers. Child Dev 43:1260–1272, 1972

PSYCHIATRIC ASPECTS OF LANGUAGE DISABILITY

Leon Eisenberg

Man and his language are simultaneously creature and creator of each other. The capacity for acquiring linguistic competence is a species-specific, genetically determined trait shared by no other living creature but universally persent among human groups, all of whom exhibit complex and fully elaborated languages, however primitive the state of their technology.[12] To recognize that it is genetic is at the same time to herald its singular importance for species evolution; that is, the elaboration of hominoid protolanguages conferred unique adaptive value upon the progressive evolution of brain structures capable of subserving ever more effective linguistic features.[10, 24] The "better" the brain, the more likely the progeny were to survive. The interplay between man and his culture is recapitulated within the development of each individual; genetic competence makes it possible but does not guarantee linguistic performance; for that, interactive language exposure during the early years of life is the force that transduces potential, into actual, brain structure.

I mean the statement—that experience shapes brain structure (within the range of possibilities set by the genome)—quite literally, although I acknowledge that it represents an extrapolation from the experimental laboratory and generalizes from what has been shown to be true only in extreme environments. For example, the kitten, at birth, is equipped with a complex visual system consisting of interconnected pathways from retina through geniculate to tectum and to cortex. This pre-formed mechanism responds differentially to geometric features of stimuli in the visual environment.[39] Yet, occluding one eye for the first six weeks of life, and thus depriving it of visual experience, results in shrinkage of the subtended geniculate neurons and a loss of the capacity of that eye to drive cortical neurons in the normally binocular areas of visual cortex.[40] The phenomenon is age-related; the visual system of the mature cat is untouched by even longer periods of monocular visual deprivation if early experience has been normal. However, the monocular effect is no simple subtraction phenomenon. Strikingly, occluding both eyes leaves each, when they are re-opened, able to drive bionocular cells.[41] Thus, it is the absence of visual exposure in the occluded eye *plus* the presence of visual driving in the open eye which alters a network of interconnections initially prescribed in the genetic code but requiring experience to "solder in" the synapses.

Further, the eye of the monocularly-deprived kitten once opened remains incompetent for visually guided behavior in the binocular (that is, nasal) visual field.[30, 32] Paradoxically, lesions of the visual cortex *restore* visually guided behavior, apparently because the direct and intact pathways from retina to tectum are freed from functional inhibition by abnormal cortico-tectal influences as a result of the ablation.[31] What the experimenter does to the kitten, nature has done to the child. Squint or wall-eye, if uncorrected before age five or six, results in marked and permanent loss of visual acuity in the unused eye. Indeed, uncorrected astigmatism itself leads to permanent impairment of ability of the retina to respond to narrow bands of light in the axis of prior astigmatism, even when the lenticular abnormality is by-passed to produce a precise focus directly on the retina.[14]

This digression into neurophysiology is intended to stress the critical dependence of complex functions on a genetically wired set of interrelationships between brain nuclei, on the one hand, and on the sequential and meaningful reinforcement of those patterns by the normal environment for which the species has been designed, on the other. Nature may build in insurance against minor deviations but finds it too expensive to guarantee maturation against major deviations in the "average expectable environment" for that organism. Conceptual and experimental elegance in the laboratory serves to dissect out the delicate epigenetic processes which in the ordinary course of events evolve so regularly that we may mistake them as entirely predetermined. This model, as ancient as Aristotle,[10] may serve to guide our consideration of the development of language.

However much earlier spoken language may have come into existence, it is at least coterminous with *Homo sapiens sapiens* who has been present on earth for some 50,000 years.[18] With language, to the phyletic memory enshrined in the genetic code, blindly discovered through mutation and ruthlessly selected for survival value,[23] was now added an inter-generational Lamarckian memory transferred from parent to child so that each generation could profit from the lessons painfully learned by its predecessors. The discoveries, chance or deliberate, of the individual organism no longer needed to be lost and rediscovered but could be transmitted from parent to child. The accretion of knowledge through cultural tradition conferred an enormous advantage on this bipedal plantigrade primate (the ape who walks on two flat feet) in his struggle to perpetuate his species in the midst of an inhospitable environment. But it exacted a price in the far longer epoch of immaturity for the young necessary to apprentice them to the tasks of learning.[10]

Written language dates back not more than 5,000 years. Its invention permitted further elaboration of the ability to abstract, the capacity for self-consciousness and the manipulation of symbols no longer constrained by the particularities of the things or actions they represented. The priests and officials who were the sole possessors of written language so thoroughly understood its power that they guarded their treasure against defilement by the vulgar. With revolutionary ideals of the Age of Enlightenment universal literacy was announced as a goal that ultimately became a popular slogan; only in the present century and in "developed" nations has that goal been approached. Yet even today, fully half of the world's peoples remain illiterate. Although reading is no guarantee of the attainment of democratic values (the Germans were highly literate just before the Nazi era), ignorance is clearly its enemy. And the man or woman who cannot read in a literate world is increasingly excluded from full participation in its deliberations and decisions.

But just as written language comes after oral language in human history, so does it in individual development. The child first attempts to master reading at a time when he is already the possessor of basic linguistic competence in his native tongue. If the evidence from feral children is to be given credence, it indicates that there is a sensitive period for language acquisition during the years before adolescence which, if foregone, can never be recaptured.[20] To the contrary, adults can learn to read for the first time at an advanced age even if denied exposure for all the prior years. Yet learning to read, although dependent on understanding language, furthers language competence which, in turn, facilitates reading in a benign and expanding cycle.

If I begin my account with these initial remarks on the development of the species and of the individual in relation to oral and written language, it is to highlight their centrality to man's most unique attributes as well as the complexity of the mechanisms underlying their mastery and their functional consequences for personal as well as national history.[12] Indeed, what is remarkable is the regularity with which language is acquired, given central nervous system integrity and language exposure. It is no less remarkable that competence in reading is the ordinary course of things rather than the exception to be explained. What we take for granted in the school-aged child, simply because linguistic competence is so regularly acquired, is an exquisite performance that has evolved from a complex pattern of central nervous system interactions, social experience, and personal attributes.

The skill we measure by tests of reading performance rests upon a complex series of orderly developmental achievements integrated by one superordinate principle: their *meaning* at each moment in the life of the child. The search for a single determinant of reading failure is a conceptual error, a deduction amply verified by the empirical data which have failed to identify pathognomonic and reproduceable stigmata in retarded readers.[25] Of a group of slow readers in the first grade, some, not readily distinguishable from their peers, will be reading with relative fluency by the third. Those who are persisting failures by the third are at high risk for academic failure. Yet cross-cultural studies of poor readers at successively higher grades fail to identify patterns of reading errors, perceptual inadequacies, analytic or synthetic deficits common to all members of the group. In part, this may be explicable on the basis of delayed but slowly progressive maturation; a subsystem that may well have been an important contributor to the reading failure at an earlier time now tests in the normal range for age because of a ceiling effect. If I point out the obvious, it is to plead against aggregating children over a wide range of ages in studies attempting to test the contribution of one developmental attribute or another to reading difficulty. I go further. Although narrower age groups will reduce this one source of heterogeneity, heterogeneity will remain; it is in the nature of an impaired performance which can be disrupted at many different points in its elaboration.[4]

The concept of "specific dyslexia" may be useful provided that we understand "specific" to mean no more than the one dictionary definition: "constituting or falling into a named category." It is in this sense "primary" or "of unknown cause" in the same way that physicians distinguish between "idiopathic" and "secondary" epilepsy. This consideration led to my "operational definition" of specific reading disability as the failure to learn to read with normal proficiency, despite conventional instruction, a culturally adequate home, proper motivation, intact senses, normal intelligence and freedom from gross neurologic deficit.[9] This is an attempt at further reduction of variability by eliminating sources of failure we can identify with greater or lesser confidence. Admittedly, the terms in the definition are not at all precise. If it minimizes some sources of variability in order to separate out a somewhat "purer" group of poor readers, it does so at a clinical cost; the presence of a disrupted home or borderline intelligence does not exclude the possibility that a given child may *also* be hampered by those yet-to-be-determined factors that contribute to "specific" dyslexia. A classification of the sources of reading retardation[9] does at least identify for the reading clinician points of intervention which should enhance reading performance *if* the child does not have other barriers to progress.

To the best of my knowledge, there is no absolute statement that can be made about any one of the factors that have been implicated in reading difficulty unless we limit our consideration to very extreme instances. For example, although poor readers tend to show poor spatial orientation, girls with Turner's syndrome, a chromosomal disorder associated with the behavior anomaly of poor spatial orientation, fail to display reading problems.[1,22] As another instance, although brain-injured and moderately retarded children are likely to be poor readers, a syndrome of "hyperlexia" has been identified in a few of them. This refers to youngsters with facility in oral reading well above grade as well as an avid preoccupation with reading anything that comes to hand despite, in most instances, little or no comprehension of the material read.[21] Clearly, we do not deal with all-or-none phenomena. Even those studies that detect statistically reliable differences between poor and good readers reveal such variability that some poor readers test in the normal range of the attribute under study and some good readers below the mean of the poor ones.[25] None of the features thus far identified has been demonstrated to be either necessary or sufficient to produce reading retardation—except at the very pathological extreme of the function. Thus, although schools serving urban slums have a disproportionate number of retarded readers, there are some proficient readers in the very same classrooms. Within-group comparisons to identify characteristics associated with success might provide a more useful strategy for designing intervention programs than merely redocumenting the sad tale of failure.

These prefatory remarks, ranging from neuroanatomy to social class, provide an essential context for discussing the role of emotional factors in reading disorders. Reading is an accomplishment of the child as a whole person; that is, as an integrated organism. It is dependent no less on the maturation of his personality than on the integrity of his central nervous system. Let us agree: just as the child with neurodevelopmental handicap may occasionally surprise us with his reading proficiency, so may the child with severe psychiatric disorder. But the obverse does not hold true. *Every poor reader is at risk for psychological disturbance,* almost always as *one* result of, rarely as *the* cause of, and frequently as a *further contribution* to, the poor reading.

Let me repeat: every poor reader has psychological problems, although not all to the same degree or in the same kind. I make this statement despite my earlier caveat against absolutes. The luck of the draw (in terms of temperament, a supportive family or a compassionate teacher) may minimize but will not eliminate emotional or behavioral difficulties; identification with a deviant social group may enable the child to avoid intrapersonal distress by tuning school out altogether. Such a youngster may adapt well to street culture but he does so at the price of exclusion from socially legitimated opportunity pathways. However, the statement that he has psychological problems does not warrant the conclusion that each poor reader requires psychiatric treatment. That recommendation will hold true only for those children in whom the psychiatric symptoms appear primary or have become a major problem in themselves, especially when they constitute impenetrable barriers to remedial reading instruction, an issue to which we will return.

The "inevitability" of psychiatric disturbance in the poor reader stems from the pivotal role of success at school for the self-concept of the child. Schooling is, in the first instance, reading. Not only is this the major demand on the child in the early grades, but it is the fulcrum for the rest of his learning. Reading has a multiplier effect, for good or bad, in every academic content area. In the school environment, reading is being. An inadequate reader is, in his mind's eye, an inadequate (that is, bad or stupid) person—and, all too often, in the eyes of his teachers, his parents and his peers as well. Reading exercises may be, indeed should be, fun but they are also the child's work. To invest the energy necessary for success, one must begin with the belief that success is possible. That initial belief is reinforced by the experience of success when the task demands are graded in relation to the child's range of competencies. The child who arrives at school timid, dependent, afraid to risk a new undertaking because of a private conviction that he is doomed to failure, a conviction that may be a logical derivative of parental attitudes, is likely to fulfill that prophesy, in the absence of the intervention of a gifted teacher. His more fortunate classmate, lucky enough to begin with a healthy respect for himself, loses it fast if he finds himself unable to master reading.

Self-esteem is a product of many forces, parental love being paramount among them in the earliest years, with the regard of teachers and peers increasing in importance as the child grows older. But even in infancy, the second major thrust appears; namely, self-evaluation based upon task accomplishment in response to an intrinsic motivation for mastery or competence.[37,38] Anyone who has looked at Bruner's time-lapse motion pictures of a one-year-old child attempting to feed himself will recognize at once the power of competence motivation. Self-feeding begins as an enormously inefficient process. More times than not, the mouth is closed when the spoon arrives; the mouth opens when the spoon is 30° to the left and overshot. A normal child will insist on feeding himself or herself despite the pangs of hunger rather than be a passive recipient of pablum shoveled down. The same forward thrust is evident throughout the years of childhood. The emotional delight of a child who is exercising control over himself or his environment is self-reinforcing. It is not enough to have the person who matters tell you you can do something; you have to experience success in doing often enough to believe it possible. I do not wish to minimize the importance of encouragement and approval by adults in sustaining a child's performance, but most accounts of the matter underestimate competence motivation as an intrinsic force with strength at least equal to external reinforcement. In consequence, we expect "reassurance" to offset psychic distress that can *only* be overcome by acquiring competence and not by being given credit for "trying hard" or praise for washing blackboards when you can't read. To the degree that a remedial reading teacher is able to assist a child in task mastery, she is an effective therapist for his psychiatric symptoms. Indeed, the simile is more than metaphor. Effective teaching requires engagement. The dyslexic child is frustrated, defeated, sometimes apathetic and sometimes overtly angry. The key to his transmutation into a learner begins with his relationship to his teacher. I venture to suggest that this may explain why it has been so difficult to document the superiority of one teaching "method" over another.[3] If the interpersonal sensitivity of the teacher is a key variable, results will necessarily be confounded. Indeed, when one observes teachers at work, the extent of the artistry in the teaching process becomes at once apparent. Part of this artistry is a familiarity with a wide enough range of methods and a willingness to explore them to determine the best fit between child and method. But part is also the intuition and sensitivity to the child's individual needs that leads to subtle adjustments of pace and presentation and to a changing mix of praise, expectation and demand.

The personality traits of the school-aged child influence whether and how much he or she learns. We expect, and often obtain, superior academic performance from children with high scores on I.Q. tests at school entry. The results are frequently ascribed to "genetic endowment" because of the widespread belief in the constancy of the I.Q. Yet, longitudinal studies demonstrate rather considerable individual variability in I.Q. scores, even when group means display relatively little change over time.[33] A comparison of middle-class children who showed an increase in I.Q. (plus 17 points) during the elementary school years with those who showed a decrease (minus 5 points) revealed that the gainers had evidenced more achievement motivation, greater curiostiy and less passivity than the losers at the time of initial testing.[16] These traits have roots in temperamental differences but they are by no means autonomous; they will be enhanced or diminished by the nature of the child's interactions with parents and teachers. Further, the values of home and school shape the goals to which the youngster directs his energies; that is, toward intellectual accomplishment or competence with tools, domestic tasks, athletic skills, machismo, or the like. Just such influences appear to account for the fall-off in academic performance among young women during the high school years as they respond to socialization pressures against competition with men in favor of the press for "feminine" attractiveness.

Task orientation, a requisite for effective learning, is disrupted in the child whose need for social approval is so great that he constantly looks to the teacher for cues for what to do next rather than attending to the problem and its context. The less the child's need for social approval has been satisfied, as with institutionalized children, the more his concern with the behavior of the adult who presents the test or problem and less with the task demands themselves.[6, 42]

Anxiety is usually taken to be a factor that disrupts learning. When anxiety is severe, that effect is undeniable. But the relationship is far from linear. Some degree of anxiety, as a motivator of performance, appears to be a potentiator rather than an inhibitor of effort and hence outcome. Moreover, anxiety has differential effects on individuals with differing personality organization. For some it is a stressor that disrupts performance and for others a "challenge" that enhances it. The complexity of the interaction between personality traits and learning to read has been documented in a remarkable study by Grimes and Allinsmith.[15] They set out to examine the interactions between anxiety and compulsivity as characteristics of children, on the one hand, and methods of teaching as characteristics of the school system, on the other. Scores for anxiety and compulsivity, traits which proved not to be correlated, were determined for each child. These were, I should add, normal children not singled out because they had a need of psychiatric care. Two contrasting school systems were studied, one using structured teaching by the phonic method and the other relatively unstructured, employing the whole word approach. The outcome measure was reading achievement. The results indicated, first of all, that structured teaching produced the highest achievement among children rated high on compulsivity and anxiety. Secondly, compulsivity had no effect on outcome and high anxiety interfered rather than facilitated achievement in the unstructured teaching situation. Thirdly, personality traits and teaching methods showed complex interactions. High anxiety and high compulsivity led to *over*achievement in a *structured* situation whereas high anxiety and low compulsivity led to *under*achievement in an *unstructured* classroom. I cite this study as an indication that the personality characteristics of the learner as well as the social demands of the learning situation must be examined in relation to one another if we are to make sense of the variability of performance in children of similar ability. It is important to note that these results were obtained in the early elementary grades; findings might differ in upper grades where more in the way of initiative is required of the students; that is, success in reading achievement under too highly structured conditions might conceivably exact too heavy a price in restricting risk-taking and initiative.

All of the above assumes that the student, however he be constituted psychologically (and I have cited only a few key traits rather than provide an exhaustive list), accepts the relevance of the tasks set for him by the school. If his major identification is with a community whose values are orthogonal to academic achievement, then he may perform poorly or not at all despite the necessary cognitive abilities and a strong motivation for mastering what he considers salient to his universe. In this connection, the observations of Labov and Robins[19] are quite significant. In the course of his studies of Black English among youths in Harlem, he came to know a group of youngsters with superior verbal skills despite retarded reading achievement in school. On the hypothesis that their poor school performance was a reflection of their identification with a street culture which rejected school, he studied the scholastic achievement of a group of youngsters who did not belong to street gangs although they lived in the same neighborhoods. He found that the young men in the latter group had much higher academic scores. These observations suggest that culture conflict between the value systems of the gang and of the school accounts for some of the observed differences between linguistic ability and reading skills. It has been known for some time that deliquents are very likely to be poor readers and that a disproportionate number of poor readers exhibit conduct disturbances.[27, 29] As with emotional disturbances, disentangling cause and effect is difficult. Although I would not underestimate the contribution of school failure to a delinquent orientation, poor reading and delinquency more likely reflect antecedent factors that contribute to each. In a recent study, Caplan interviewed a sample of more than 800 male youths living in a high delinquency area of

Chicago.[7] The major finding was the modal profile of a youngster with no belief in his chance for achievement through legitimate social routes. The subjects in his sample who were in trouble with the law contrasted with the others in two respects: they were much more pessimistic about the likelihood of finishing high school and they expected to hold jobs with low status and little prestige when they grew up. Particularly noteworthy was the discovery that pessimistic attitudes toward completion of high school were as prevalent at the age of ten as they were in later years. Thus, pessimism about the future appeared to precede later law-breaking.

This sharp separation between the conventional values of life at school and life on the streets makes it worth inquiring whether the likelihood of academic success might be increased by making the content of the materials intended to arouse interest in reading reflect more realistically the important events of the child's life. Warner[2] among the Maori and Freire[5] among illiterate Brazilians report success in teaching reading with materials produced by the students themselves as well as by the teachers in order to deal with everyday experience and to indicate how social action can change that experience for the better. It would be absurd to think that, merely by trading in Dick and Jane readers for parables of slum life, one would eliminate reading failure; the realities of the slum would remain as the major obstacle; yet more relevant reading matter could be a source of support for the child's learning to read even in the face of external adversity.

Finally, there are psychiatric disorders per se that interfere with reading. The most severe of these is childhood psychosis, a category which includes the syndromes of early infantile autism, disintegrative psychosis, and childhood schizophrenia.[28] In many of these children, the psychotic disorder has many of the features of a developmental aphasia or central language disorder;[26] reading is consequently severely impaired. Such children often test poorly on cognitive or information processing measures so that the reading failure may be attributed to functional mental deficiency. Others nonetheless acquire fluency. Some are facile at oral reading and avid in their pursuit of it despite minimal comprehension and failure to make functional use of the incessant reading, much like "hyperlexics."[21] Still others read and understand but are so impaired in their social relationships that their idiosyncratic replies to questions may lead observers to doubt their understanding.[8] In psychotic children, the major therapeutic challenge is the psychosis; remedial reading instruction may be a useful component of a total rehabilitation program but it will not be sufficient in itself.

A second group of psychiatric disorders associated with retarded reading behavior are the hyperkinetic behavior syndromes,[13] sometimes classified as minimal brain dysfunction.[36] Whatever the diagnostic label, short attention span and distractibility are the major symptoms that interfere with effective learning.[13] Behavioral and pharmacologic measures which have been shown to decrease impulsivity and distractibiltiy are the appropriate means to make learning possible; but an appropriate educational opportunity remains essential to success. Unfortunately, most controlled trials of therapy have been short-term and have focused on correcting the presenting symptoms. Measures of academic achievement, by their very nature, require longer time spans of observation to determine whether substantial progress has been attained. Such follow-up studies as are available on hyperkinetic children, many of them treated inconsistently or not at all, indicate that the overall outcome is far from satisfactory.[34] I have argued elsewhere that we must recognize these disorders as chronic and as requiring close medical and educational supervision over the long run in order that permanent educational handicap, poor self-concept and antisocial adaptation can be averted.[11]

The third of the psychiatric conditions that require to be considered are the neurotic and personality disorders, in some of which reading becomes the arena in which parent-child conflicts are fought out.[35] For parents with a high stake in their child's school success, his almost deliberate sabotage of their inordinate expectations is a dramatic mode of retaliation against their demands. In other instances, we may find a child who fears the anger that he fantasies to be aroused in peers were he to be successful, or one whose narcissism is so inordinate that he avoids the possibility of a less than perfect performance by "deciding" not to try; these children wear a cloak of "protective stupidity;" that is, whatever the obloquy one suffers by being called "stupid" seems less awful than the imagined consequences of trying. Indeed, the suffering associated with failure may meet a need to be punished for having harbored "evil" thoughts and feelings. Even in such instances, symptom choice may not be determined by psychodynamic factors alone but may reflect a "point of least resistance" because of an associated language learning handicap.

However generated, reading problems often interlock with parental psychopathology in such fashion that a metastable equilibrium of family emotional economy is established which resists attempts at therapeutic change.[17] This is not at all unique in child psychiatry; we not infrequently encounter symptoms in a sibling when the designated patient improves or decompensation in a parent whose precarious adjustment is maintained only so long as the child's disorder serves as an emotional "sink" draining off otherwise intolerable feelings. In such situations, only attention to the family as a unit will make it possible to meet the child's needs and at the same time to permit the parents to deal with their own conflicts. Remedial reading instruction will almost certainly be doomed to failure for the teacher struggling to help a child who dares not abandon his position as the scapegoat lest a worse emotional cataclysm engulf him. On the other hand, if the healthy side of family ambivalence can be enlisted in an effort to attain constructive conflict resolution, reading instruction may be associated with much more rapid progress than is customarily seen in specific dyslexia.

More common than the psychiatric disorders which antecede, contribute to, or overshadow the reading problem are those secondary to reading failure which may be so prominent that they require treatment either prior to or concomitant with reading instruction for it to have any chance of success. Almost certainly, when the child's problem is severe and long-standing, the parents will require counseling to deal with their own feelings of guilt and despair. Here the task is not the identification and removal of initiating factors, so often thought to be the principal focus of psychotherapy, but rather support for parents who have to face a challenge above and beyond that of normal parenting. Rarely does the reading teacher have either the time or the training to tackle this aspect of management; it is better done by a social worker or school counselor whose first goal should be to clarify for the parents the worker's role as a "psychological extension agent" rather than a personal therapist.

In clinical practice, many problems simply do not fit into neat conceptual categories. A case example may serve as an illustration.

Some twenty years ago, just after I had completed my formal professional training, Margaret Rawson, past president of the Orton Society, referred a young man of ten to me for evaluation. Hans had been in her care for some months but so preempted the remedial reading hours with his compulsion to act out fantasies of hate and aggression that she found herself unable to get him to focus on the reading tasks. His father, a bright, intense, dedicated scientist, was compulsive and perfectionistic. He had been sorely disappointed by the school failure of the son for whom his primary ambition was a brilliant professional career. Hans' mother was depressed, somewhat disorganized, utterly unable to cope with problems of home, husband and son. The younger sister, Katrina, was her one comfort but Hans' bête noire. Mother was near distraction from the repetitive fights between the children, each of whom became angry whenever mother was forced to take the side of the other. To cap this complicated situation, the local principal refused to acknowledge dyslexia as a legitimate disorder and insisted that Hans must be stupid or crazy, probably both. His resentment was fanned by a town and gown controversy between the long-time farmer and merchant residents of the town and the recently arrived scientists, including Hans' father, who worked at a new research facility that was threatening traditional values. My psychiatric evaluation confirmed the dyslexia, personality disorder, family pathology *and* mismanagement by the school. (Mrs. Rawson knew all that before I offered my opinion but she was generous enough to let a young psychiatrist believe he had come to a profound conclusion. With characteristic sensitivity she would, from time to time, ask ostensibly casual questions about one aspect or another of the case that gently kept me from going astray.)

Over the next two years, Margaret Rawson and I divided the therapeutic chores. For the school problem, two elements proved helpful: first, the principal respected the Johns Hopkins Hospital. Therefore, when a staff member said that Hans was bright, that was hard to dismiss; second, the child of a former member of the school board was diagnosed as dyslexic, whereupon dyslexia began to edge its way into the official lexicon of the county. The struggle was a long one, still not completely won. Our clinical work proceeded in concert, each effort potentiating the other, although even a young psychiatrist recognized that Mrs. Rawson's work was more central than his. To begin with, she had to continue to deal with the boy's fantasy life, but I never undertook to teach him to read. Further, as he put less of his energies into wild aggressive play and more into work, Hans derived such satisfaction from his accomplishments as a reader that the progress in psychotherapy went much more rapidly. Moreover the parents became far more responsive to my counseling sessions as Hans' reading achievement became visible to them. My task was largely finished by the end of the first year but Mrs. Rawson continued to provide reading help until the family left town after the father obtained a new position. I am pleased to be able to report that the outcome has been a generally happy one, with Hans going on to college and currently working as a school teacher, although his parents have, intermittently, had rather considerable problems of their own.

Cases with coexisting specific dyslexia, psychiatric disorder, family pathology and school mismanagement are all too frequent. A combined approach to management is critical for success. At times, one or another focal problem defeats the best efforts at treatment; it may not be possible to bring about significant benefit in other areas if a key aspect cannot be changed.

I conclude with this case to illustrate the ultimate futility of interprofes-

sional wrangling about whether emotional disturbance is primary, and learning disorder secondary, or dyslexia the source of the emotional disturbance.
Schools of exclusive salvationism damn too many souls to perdition. Either/
or formulations not only presume a unitary cause for heterogeneous disorders
but also ignore interactions between cognitive and affective human functions.
Clinical experience teaches one rapidly that effective remediation requires
attention to both in each disabled learner although the weight of emphasis
will vary from case to case. It may be convenient to separate cognitive from
affective functions for purposes of discussion, but convenience must not be
mistaken for reality. Real children think *and* feel. Learning is influenced by
the relationship between teacher and learner; language development promotes
discrimination between emotional states and facilitates empathy. Motivation
is a prepotent variable in the learning process. Linguistic competence stands
at the very center of what is crucially human in each of us. We are as we
speak; we work as we read; we become human as we understand each other
through language.

References

1. Alexander D, Walker HT, Money J: Studies in direction sense. I. Turner's syn-
    drome. Arch Gen Psychiatry 10:337–339, 1964
2. Ashton-Warner S: Teacher. New York, Simon & Schuster, 1963
3. Belmont L, Birch HG: The effect of supplemental intervention on children with low
    reading readiness scores. J Spec Educ 8:81–89, 1974
4. Bortner M, Birch HG: Cognitive capacity and cognitive competence. Am J Ment
    Defic 74:735–744, 1970
5. Brown C: Literacy in 30 hours: Paulo Freire's process in northeast Brazil. Social
    Policy 5:25–32, 1974
6. Butterfield EC, Zigler E: The influence of differing institutional social climates on
    the effectiveness of social reinforcement in the mentally retarded. Am J Ment Defic
    70:48–56, 1965
7. Caplan N: Delinquency and the perceived chances for conventional success. Insti-
    tute for Social Research, Ann Arbor, unpublished manuscript, 1974
8. Eisenberg L: The autistic child in adolescence. Am J Psychiatry 112:607–612,
    1956
9. Eisenberg L: Reading retardation. Pediatrics 37:352–365, 1966
10. Eisenberg L: Norman child development. *In* Comprehensive Textbook of Psychi-
    atry. Edited by AM Freedman, H Kaplan. Baltimore, Williams & Wilkins Company,
    1967, pp 1315–1332
11. Eisenberg L: The clinical use of stimulant drugs in children. Pediatrics 49:709–715,
    1972
12. Eisenberg L: The *human* nature of human nature. Science 176:123–128, 1972
13. Eisenberg L: The overactive child. Hosp Pract 8:151–160, 1974
14. Freeman RD, Mitchell DE, Millodot M: A neural effect of partial visual deprivation
    in humans. Science 175:1384–1386, 1972

15. Grimes JW, Allinsmith W: Compulsivity, anxiety, and school achievement. Merrill-Palmer Q 7:247–271, 1961
16. Kagan J, Sontag LW, Baker CT, et al: Personality and IQ change. J Abnorm Soc Psychol 56:261–266, 1958
17. Kline C, Kline CL: Severe reading disabilities: the family's dilemmas. Bull Orton Soc 23:146–159, 1973
18. Kolata GB: The demise of the Neanderthals: was language a factor? Science 186:618–619, 1974
19. Labov W, Robins C: A note on the relation of reading failure to peer-group status in urban ghettos. The Record-Teachers College 70:395–405, 1969
20. Lenneberg E: Biological Foundations of Language. New York, John Wiley & Sons, 1967
21. Mehegan CC, Dreifuss FE: Hyperlexia: exceptional reading ability in brain-damaged children. Neurology (Minneap) 22:1105–1111, 1972
22. Money J, Alexander D: Turner's syndrome: further demonstration of the presence of specific cognitional deficits. J. Med Genet 3:47–48, 1966
23. Monod J: Chance and Necessity. New York, Alfred A Knopf, 1971
24. Morin E, Piatelli-Palmarini M: L'unite de l'homme. Paris, Editions du Seuil. 1974
25. Naidoo S: Specific Dyslexia. London, Pitman Publishing Corp., 1972
26. Rutter M: The development of infantile autism. Psychol Med 4:147–163, 1974
27. Rutter M: Emotional disorder and educational underachievement. Arch Dis Child 49:249–256, 1974
28. Rutter M, Lebovici S, Eisenberg L, et al: A triaxial classification of mental disorders in childhood. J Child Psychol Psychiatry 10:41–61, 1969
29. Rutter M, Tizard J, Whitmore K: Education, Health and Behaviour. London, Longman, 1970
30. Sherman SM: Visual field defects in monocularly and binocularly deprived cats. Brain Res 49:25–45, 1973
31. Sherman SM: Monocularly deprived cats: improvement of the deprived eye's vision by visual decortication. Science 186:267–269, 1974
32. Sherman SM: Permanence of visual perimetry defects in monocularly and binocularly deprived cats. Brain Res 73:491–501, 1974
33. Sontag LW, Baker CT, Nelson V: Mental growth and personality development. Mongr Soc Res Child Dev 23 ser. 68: No. 2, 1958
34. Weiss G, Minde K, Werry JS, et al: Studies on the hyperactive child. VIII. Five-year follow-up. Arch Gen Psychiatry 24:409–414, 1971
35. Weisskopf EA; Intellectual malfunctioning and personality. J Abnorm Soc Psychol 46:410–423, 1951
36. Wender PH; Minimal Brain Dysfunction in Children. New York, John Wiley & Sons, 1971
37. White RW: Motivation reconsidered: the concept of competence. Psychol Rev 66:297–333, 1959
38. White RW: Competence and the psychosexual stages of development. In Nebraska Symposium on Motivation. Lincoln, University of Nebraska Press, 1960, pp 97–138
39. Wiesel TN, Hubel DH: Effects of visual deprivation on morphology and physiology of cells in the cat's lateral geniculate body. J Neurophysiol 26:978–1002, 1963
40. Wiesel TN, Hubel DH: Single cell responses in striate cortex of kittens deprived of vision in one eye. J Neurophysiol 26:1003–1017, 1963
41. Wiesel TN, Hubel DH: Comparison of the effects of unilateral and bilateral ocular occlusion. J Neurophysiol 28:1029–1040, 1965
42. Zigler E: Motivational determinants in the performance of retarded children. Am J Orthopsychiatry 36:848–856, 1966

DEVELOPMENTAL DYSLEXIA:
EDUCATIONAL TREATMENT AND RESULTS

Margaret Byrd Rawson

In the study, treatment, and prevention of the problems of dyslexia, one of the strengths of the Orton Society, built on the example of Dr. Samuel Torrey Orton's own professional life, has been its promotion of interaction between theoretical and applied sciences, and the mutual respect of scientists, researchers and practitioners in several fields. This includes clinicians, technicians, teachers, parents, students or patients, and public. Each is uniquely important in the work of the others and essential in the whole enterprise. Their common purpose is the advancement of knowledge about the language function and facilitation of its development in human beings. And so, at the close of this volume so characterized by interfaces of several disciplines, it seems appropriate to consider an area of common interest in providing effective educational treatment for those with special learning needs of this kind.

I shall resist the temptation to discuss and speculate about background theory, except as it provides a necessary common base for the meeting of our minds on the subject of education and in the field of dyslexia. My predecessors in this series,[23,31,35] and other conference speakers,[10,15,93] have provided much that is relevant, though pertinence dictates that I repeat a few things that some of them have said.

Perhaps one of the most useful purposes served by collecting data for this paper has been the impetus it has given to bringing to light more material on the subject. In recent months I have searched the literature (see prefatory note, reference list) and corresponded and talked with well over 100 selected sources of information, and I am sure I have missed many more. Included have been medical and nonmedical clinics and agencies, independent schools and camps, public school systems and services, a few colleges, and many, many individuals—professionals, parents and pupils or students. From them has come a helpful cornucopia of riches which have added greatly to the substance of this paper.

It will be of no surprise to you that I found great enthusiasm for the topic we are here considering. Everyone seems hungry to know what everyone else is doing, and with what results. There are many goldmines of unworked data in the files and minds of respondents, and some available statistics, varying from raw data in test figures and profiles to a very few sophisticated studies.* Some of the most enthralling contributions are the personal case histories of frustrated search, discovery, and full or partial success which have changed the lives of children and the people around them.[61,80]

People in the helping professions, because of temperament and the pressures of their kind of work, are not very likely to design, initiate, and carry through high quality statistical studies, while those who are research-minded can usually find less amorphous or complicated, and more tractable, raw material elsewhere than in the domains of specialized educational treatments and their results. But times are changing—witness the number of good, sound studies presented at the World Congress on Dyslexia.

Here, then, are some findings, gleaned from 39 years of study and participant-observation in the field of language education and re-education, and a distillation of the enormous enrichment provided by recent contributions of colleagues summarizing what has happened in this specific area not only since the founding of the Orton Society 25 years ago, but since Dr. Orton's landmark paper of 1925, nearly 50 years ago.[69]

Although Orton did not use it, in the interests of conciseness, I am going to use the term *dyslexia* in this paper with some frequency and without apology.[102] If this produces semantic discomfort in any of you, please translate it into your favorite idiom representing language learning differences which sometimes give trouble. Tell yourself that *dys* means poor or inadequate and *lexia* means management of words, so that *dyslexia* refers to ineptitude with language skills. Perhaps we should have an ideographic expression, with no spoken counterpart, as in Figure 1, to flash on a screen whenever the idea comes up, but for the present paper, the *word* "dyslexia" will have to serve for the whole area of meaning.

For this language learning problem, educational treatment is obviously appropriate. Inevitably, treatment will have results of some kind. Our task

---

*See, for example, references 6, 7, 22, 24, 30, 36, 39, 42, 43, 44, 49, 50, 51, 53, 56, 65, 72, 75, 91, 93, 98, 100, 101.

Figure 1. Ideographic representation of the idea of "dyslexia" in Chinese. Drawn for this paper by Che Kan Leong, who says the best translation is, "Reading difficulties in both read and spoken (languages)."

here is to focus as clearly, sharply, and unwaveringly as possible on two things: first, the *educational treatment* of dyslexia, and second, the *results* of this treatment.

We are talking now specifically of *dyslexia* as just defined and not of other problems of learning, such as those related to intellectual, physical, sensory, environmental or general educational inadequacies, which seem neither specific to language, nor causally primary. We speak of *educational* treatment not of medical, physical, emotional, social or other approaches to alleviation. And we are considering *results* primarily in terms of *achieved competence in language skills.* This competence, in turn, provides one of the gateways to life goals which ought to be open to every citizen of a modern, literate society. This is by no means to gainsay the importance of the aspects of life which we are here leaving out; they have been treated in this conference and elsewhere, as they should have been and should continue to be.*

But language, the matrix of dyslexia, and at once the subject and the medium of this presentation, despite its richness, has severe limitations. By its

*See references 3, 11, 15, 41, 46, 48, 52, 64, 78, 84, and 105.

VERBAL LANGUAGE

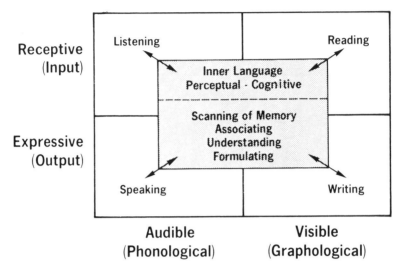

Figure 2. Analysis of verbal language. (After Rawson 1968.)

nature it is time- and space-bound, for it is controlled by the utterance or representation of sounds and longer verbal forms in sequence. These determine the verbal mode of thought, of consciousness and of communication from person to person. Words and phrases can carry both specific and connotative meaning, singly or simultaneously. But no matter how expertly we use them, they cannot represent all of life, or even all of a person's momentary life experience in all its dimensions. Still, within its limitations, verbal language is a useful and versatile tool, and a prime characteristic of man as a species. As we talk, there can and should be parallel awareness that the rest of life is still going on in dynamic interaction with linguistic thought and expression, including all those trains or fragments of thought to which we cannot simultaneously give utterance.[78] Life is whole, though many-faceted.[83] It is to be divided into parts only to make its experience and development manageable within our human capacity to cope with its complexities. One of these complexities is the mastery by each new human being of the skills and nuances of the language of that culture into which he is born or in which he is reared—his mother tongue.

There is order and plan in every child's acquisition of verbal language.[77] The diagram of Figure 2 shows its fractions and their complex interactions. On the left are the audible or phonological components, the basic language of

SENSORY ASSOCIATIONS
IN LANGUAGE LEARNING

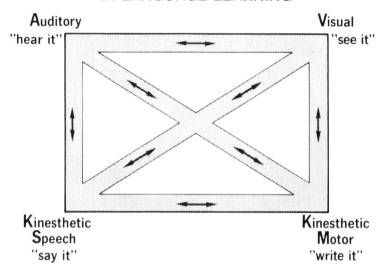

Figure 3. *Sensory associations in language learning. (After A.G. Wolff 1970.)*

listening and speech, common in some tongue to every known culture. Spoken language is first to develop and almost inevitable in each child's life. On the right of the scheme are the visible or graphological components, reading and writing. These are taught and learned later, at what we call "school age," in literate cultures, and often they are mastered with difficulty. Cut the other way, the diagram shows, above, the receptive or input language (listening and reading) and, below, the expressive or output language (speaking and writing). All of these fractions interact continuously, as indicated by the arrows, through the mediation of the perceptual and cognitive processes of inner language, which goes on inside the brain. The diagram in Figure 3 modified from one originated in England by Agnes Wolff, shows the multisensory, intersensory linkages for learning of the language modalities. If we superimpose it upon Figure 2, it is easy to see how well the two models fit each other—language, and its learning.

The rationale which we educators need to keep in mind is this. While symbolic thinking seems to be species-specific to *Homo sapiens,* its development into formulation and expression in a language must be learned from the individual's culture. This learning can be mediated only by the separate and integrated use of the sensory processes through whose gateways alone, as far as we can know consciously, man-on-the-inside is related to the-world-on-the-outside. The modalities particularly involved in language learning, as shown in Fig. 3, are the auditory and kinesthetic-speech and the visual and kinesthetic-motor-tactile senses, which relate, respectively, to the phonological and graphological modes of symbolic forms. The arrows suggest the mutual interaction of these senses as the learner hears while he speaks and looks while he writes, weaving a living tapestry of all the possible permutations. The keener each sense and the better it is both individually controlled and related to the others involved, the more effectively can the person function as *Homo sapiens,* the voluntary language user.

An effective educational approach will take into account the sensory aspects of language learning which all human beings have in common, and the almost infinite variations of individual capacities and their uses in learning. Our aim is to help the person develop each of the aspects of his learning, both separately and with the support and participation of the others.[17, 32,33, 69, 70, 75]   The goal is a harmoniously developing, well-integrated individual; the method of choice is individualized multisensory learning, balancing cognitive direction for understanding on the one hand, with controlled practice for mastery on the other. We include, especially for the dyslexic, emphases on needed special development, judicious management of learning patterns, and use of strengths to support areas of weakness, while the latter are, themselves, being strengthened.[92] Man is a thinker, so in this kind of learning, conscious, rational mind is the master, the coordinator of the learning processes and the ultimate reliance in the face of forgetting or uncertainty. Self-recognized success in the gradual and solid achievement of competence provides improved self-esteem and optimum motivation.[79]

What Kind of Person is the Dyslexic?

There is considerable evidence to support the view that in the general population facility in learning the forms of language is a largely independent trait, compounded of several related aptitudes, in each of which individuals vary normally over a wide range of ability.[27,58,69,70,75,82]

So far, what we have been saying applies to each learner of language, whatever the nature and level of his facility, but what of those for whom natural endowment has not made language learning easy? What distinguishes them, and so provides our specific educational challenge?

Many studies of specific dyslexia give evidence that a large percentage of the individuals we are concerned with is completely representative of the population as a whole with respect to most aptitudes. They can be found in expected proportions: throughout the full range of intelligence; with all kinds of physical, including sensory, make-up; with varying degrees of primary emotional stability; with the usual range of developmental history; and representing divergent socio-economic conditions and varieties of educational opportunity. They differ from their fellows in one respect only: for whatever reasons, they are unable readily to master the skills of their mother-tongue language to a degree consistent with their other aptitudes, their personal and social needs, their other opportunities, and their reasonable expectancies.

Some individuals may be slower or quicker in one or more of the fractions of lanauge learning ability. This appears most often to be a family affair, consonant with normal genetic variation.[69,70]

Orton's observations[69] led him to believe that his patients were not so much deficient or defective, as his predecessors had thought, but rather that they represented "normal neurophysiologic variations" in aspects and patterns of harmonious development. Jean Symmes[100,101] of the National Institutes of Health came to the same conclusions on the basis of a recent well-designed diagnostic study of primary dyslexia. This conviction, which most of us share for most dyslexics,[75,99] has a radical influence on our educational strategies and the optimism of our outlook for the children's future.

There seem also to be a few cases of disabilities deriving from each of several specific, probably non-genetic, causes,[58] such as injuries or special deprivations, perhaps at critical life-stages. The number in each such category may be relatively small, but in the aggregate they do somewhat thicken the low end of the normal, bell-shaped curve which otherwise describes the distribution of persons on a language learning facility scale.[43]

Because this is a complex trait which can, in each person, have variations of much or little in each of its fractions, in kind or rate of development, definitive diagnosis of the individuals and delimitation of the identity of dyslexia itself may both be difficult. From this two things follow.

First, if we find no single diagnostic sign or pattern, but only a variable group of possible indicators, how do we know that dyslexia really exists? This question admits the possibility of denial of unwelcome reality and of responsibility for doing something about it, especially in schools. But if, to quote Abelard,[1] "By doubting we are led to inquire, and by inquiry we perceive truth," then insecurity can result in progress.

Secondly, if we admit, as I believe most of our readers would, that there *is* something there, it becomes important for treatment or education to ask the diagnostic questions. Does this child belong in this category? By what criteria? Is it just one difficulty, and how bad does that one have to be and at what point in his history? Or is it his low position—how low?—on several scales—how many, in what proportion to each other, and when? What combination of negative forces will bring defeat, and what positive ones will help him to cope? Are these factors part of his general nature, of his specific language learning aptitude, or of his life-circumstances, and in what proportions? Since there is a hardly countable variety of combinations of kind and degree, this is hardly a simple problem, nor amenable to simple solutions.[48,52,63,82]

Still, in the process of making knowledge and understanding part of ourselves and so developing clinical judgment, perhaps we can move from the initially chaotic to the complicated to the more systematically complex. Then, perhaps, we can find organizing principles which will simplify the task. To achieve this over-arching structure, resisting the lure of fragmentary aspects and panaceas, is a valid and purposeful use of abstraction.

In our field, we are especially fortunate in those giants of past and present from whose shoulders we can focus on the children's problems and their solution. For one outstanding example, there is Lauretta Bender,[9] who has observed that dyslexic children's learning, and perhaps their general behavior, is commonly characterized by too great or too long continued plasticity, defining that term as, "carrying within itself potentialities which have not yet become fixed." This very plasticity is one of the most valuable ingredients in human adaptability. Brought under control, it emerges as flexibility, a necessary condition of innovation and creativity, and is one of the several positive traits associated with the dyslexic constitution. In the extreme, however, plasticity can make it difficult to keep one's affairs and possessions organized and to learn certain language skills to the point of automatic reliability. Appropriate education needs to be directed to the adequate establishment of control of this plasticity, not into a plaster-of-Paris-like rigidity, but into a voluntarily controlled flexibility more like plasticine.

On another level, we can say that rote memory is the weakest link in the dyslexic individual's chain of mental attributes.[37,85] This is not memory for events, places and facts, or other aspects of living. These may range, as do other people's, from near-perfect to very poor. The dyslexic's particular memory inadequacy seems to be with the sequences of language symbols which in themselves have no specific meaning.[27] He has trouble holding them in mind long enough and securely enough to process them into the language forms which do carry meaning. As one small boy said, "I can think but what's wrong is my words. I forget them and I can't manage them."

The Language to be Learned

This is the kind of person the dyslexic is. Now let us turn our attention to the language he so often finds it difficult to learn, and how best to teach it to him in the light of his special needs.[57, 59, 77]

As we look at the world's language systems we find two basic types—the ideographic[55] and the alphabetic.[28,95] We recognize that each, in modern times, makes use of some features of the other, and also that many languages are written syllabically. The variations are fascinatingly endless, but right now space demands that we oversimplify by looking only at the main character-istics of the *two basic* bridge systems by which ideas can traverse the gap between two human minds.

In ideographic languages, such as Chinese, the plan is shown in Figure 4, with two parallel spans from one mind to another, each span designed for two-way traffic. One route is vocal-auditory, the spoken language. The other carries meaning by a primarily visual-graphic system, whose thousands of ideographs are understood by all persons literate in the language, however mutually unintelligible their spoken dialects.

But it is with the second, or alphabetic-phonetic, languages that most of us Occidentals are familiar. Figure 5 shows this system, in basic contrast. This is a linear route, by which the idea in one mind is first encoded into speech. This, analyzed into phonemic units, is then encoded a second time, into graphemic units of one or more letters of a limited alphabet clustered into words. These can then be decoded back into the speech common to the communicants, who thus read each other's messages. Of primary importance in the graphic symbols is the shape and orientation of letter elements and their sequence in written word units, which correspond in spatial arrangement to the order in time of the component sounds of the spoken words, the ultimate carriers of meaning.

In both ideographic and alphabetic systems, the language processes are common, but the intermodal connections are different. Both make multi-sensory and intersensory demands on learners, although the interrelationships of auditory and visual forms are different, dictating a somewhat, but not entirely, different set of educational strategies and tactics.

IDEOGRAPHIC
LANGUAGE SYSTEMS

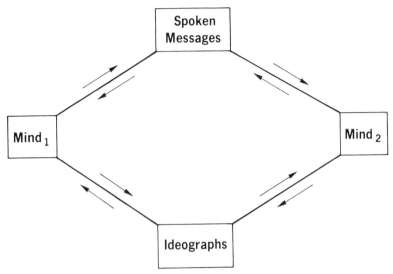

Figure 4. Transmission of thought in ideographic language systems.

The speech code is inherently more complex and difficult, as modern linguistic science is demonstrating,[35, 54, 61] but appears to be a built-in, universal human aptitude. The relatively simpler coding task of the historically much newer graphic mode surprises theoreticians by proving far harder for people generally to learn. Perhaps this is because it requires an additional level of abstraction and greater maturity.

In the alpha-phonetic languages, persons with good memory for visual symbol patterns can learn word forms as if they were ideographs. Perhaps they unconsciously generalize and subliminally realize the built-in letter-sound relationships. One mark of the dyslexic is his difficulty in doing just this.[8, 27]

We see a common core in our dyslexic group of children, and we can identify common principles in the educational treatment approach in use in many settings. Most of us know most about how this applies in English-speaking countries, but, as is often the case, parallel needs, as they have been identified elsewhere, have given rise to comparable theories and treatment procedures. One is struck with the similarities and cross-references in the large and growing professional literature of the field in many languages. Children in

ALPHABETIC
LANGUAGE SYSTEMS

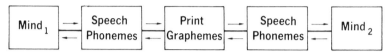

Figure 5. Transmission of thought in alphabetic language systems.

Prague[59] and Amsterdam,[7] in Warsaw[57] and Vienna,[53] in New York,[20] Vancouver,[51] and Melbourne,[95] and in Latin America[98] have a common look about their work, despite the Babel of their vocabularies. These children are all, it seems, responsive to similar teaching approaches. And why not? The language function is common to humanity, and knows no linguistic barriers.

How, Then, Shall We Teach?

In recent years we have come to phrase the old objective as, "Let us teach the language as it is to the person as he is." Whoever and wherever he is, the child will need a regime in which all the best principles of pedagogy are practiced. If he is at the dyslexic end of the scale, he is likely to thrive if he has certain kinds of special care. Light has been shed on this need from many sources over the years, but for now, vastly oversimplifying, we may summarize them as follows.

Language is a continuum which does not begin at school entrance,[3,26,45,66,103,105] nor even in kindergarten, so it will first be necessary to make sure that the child has developed good basic language competence, as most children have by the age of five or six. Many children who are going to develop reading and spelling problems come to school apparently well grounded in spoken language, though many others show inadequacy here. So the spoken language of the beginner or the older dyslexic should be evaluated and, where necessary, given remedial attention, in addition to the general "language arts" enrichment which is the province of the whole of education for all children.

Perhaps we should look at the sensory linkage diagram of Figure 3 again for at this point it provides a good working model for the teacher. Orton's first principle in teaching,[68,69] which has stood the test of time, was to reduce the language to its most basic elements, the sounds and letters—the phonemes, and the graphemes which symbolize them. These are learned well, through all the senses, singly or conjointly, with due regard for the learner's needs and his increasing capacity to handle the multisensory stimuli. He hears and says, sees and writes, in various combinations, with awareness of what he is doing and why. The sounds and letters are not presented haphazardly but in planned sequence, a few at a time, with constant review for thorough, cumulative mastery. As soon as the student has a few symbols to work with, he learns to synthesize by blending them into words, to read simple sentences, to analyze the same dependable words into their components and to write them. Figure 6 is presented only to show at a glance that the most basic principles of English spelling can be outlined on a single page.[77]

Difficult as all this may be at the start, it does seem essential, and I have yet to meet the child of normal intelligence and reasonably intact senses who cannot learn to do it. Automatic retrievability is highly desirable and comes in time, but it is the *direct* goal only with the limited number of elements and a very few phonetically irregular but indispensible sight words.

From the beginning, the student relies primarily on the cognitive approach as he becomes adept at analyzing and synthesizing patterns, a useful skill when one is faced with new or forgotten words or with learning the essentially rational system of English spelling. By this route, as Orton thought,[69, 70] one may establish the effectiveness of the language-dominant cerebral hemisphere of the brain, through strengthening the physiological habit of its use in attending to consistently oriented patterns of language symbols.

In summary, dyslexic students seem to come out best if we make our teaching program structured, systematic, sequential, cumulative, and thorough, responsive to individual needs and, withal, humanely and joyously therapeutic. A clear goal, clinical acumen, and pedagogic skill are all both necessary and attainable.

Instructional Materials

One master-teacher has said, "Give me pencil and paper, or even a stick and a patch of dusty ground, and I can teach any child to read." Of course she can, for the text is in her head; but even without that degree of expertise, the *essential* equipment for teaching is simple and inexpensive—writing materials, preferably including a chalkboard, and some well-chosen books. All the other teaching aids serve, often superbly and invigoratingly, the interest and delight of both child and teacher, but one *can* do without any or all of them.

Major Principles of English Spelling

BASE WORDS

1. Closed monosyllables: *bit* to *splash*
   Pattern v̆ c [vowel + consonant(s)]

2. Polysyllables, closed: *gambit, rabbit, establishment*
   v̆ c' • c v, v̆c' • c̣v

3. Monosyllables with double (or "reinforced") consonants: *bell, batch*
   v̆cc

4. Final-e, long vowel: *safe*
   -v̄cȩ, an instance of -v̄cv

5. Open syllables, stressed, long vowel: *me, pó-ny*
   -v̄ or v̄' • cv

6. Patterns for 2-syllable words
   a. *gambit* (-v̆c' • cv–)
      rabbit (v̆c' • c̣v–)
   b. *pony* (-v̄' • cv–)
   c. *robin* (-v̆c' • v–)
   d. *begin* (-v̄⁺ • cv'–) (an unstressed "long vowel" sounds "half-long")

7. Two-syl., cons + *le* words. See patterns 6a, b, above & Fig. 4

8. Consonant-spelling choices

9. Other spellings for long and variant vowel sounds

DERIVATIVES

10. Plurals

11. Possessives

12. Addition of suffixes
    a. After final consonant (Table 2)
    b. After final ȩ
    c. After final *y*

13. Addition of prefixes; assimilation (Figure 5)

14. Word building: simple compounds, root compounds; affixes; etymology

GENERALIZING SPELLING EXPERIENCE

15. Double consonants, summary (Figure 6)

16. Relation of syllabic stress to vowel quantity and spelling signals; dealing with *schwa*

17. Functions of final *e*

18. Four principles for spelling long vowel sounds

19. Customary usages: *y* and *i* as alternative spellings for vowel and consonant sounds

20. Vocabulary of language terms

Figure 6. Major principles of English spelling. (Reproduced from Rawson 1970.)

The history of any science or art is filled with ideas and observations which seem unrelated until some creative person brings them together in a new arrangement and focus. Then we have a work of art, a theory, or a technical breakthrough. Such advances are likely to lead to further appreciation and knowledge and to manifold and growing applications.

Just as Orton performed such a synthesis as he worked with his associates in the theoretical areas of language and language differences, so he mobilized an equally creative group of other colleagues who began to produce clinical, scholarly and pedagogic procedures and materials.[17,32,33,65,68] Reminiscences of his wife, June Orton, and others from early days in Iowa and New York point out the converging and diverging lines of development. Some of these descend directly from Orton and some through Gillingham. A few others starting independently toward solution of the same problem, joined them later. In time they developed work-plans, manuals and other instructional materials from which we continue to learn and draw practical help. Of the publications particularly relevant to the Ortonian educational approach there come to mind those of June Orton,[67,68] Childs,[18,19] Rome and Osman,[81] the Massachusetts General Hospital Group,[74,97] Cox,[21] Slingerland,[94] Hathaway,[40] Bannatyne,[8] Traub,[104] Pollack,[73] Bowen,[13] Anderson,[2] Eleanor Hall,[38] Spalding,[96] Ansara,[4,5] Smelt,[95] Saunders and associates,[87,88] Durbrow,[29] and perhaps as many more. Many of these provide self-consistent cores around which to build a teaching plan, to be enriched by drawing on the others, which are compatible but not, usually, congruent. This is a process of enriching structure, and is a far cry from the eclecticism which puts bits and pieces together into a crazyquilt of confusion for the learner.

I know of several teachers who have in preparation their own new formulations or variations, being developed as they work with children. This is good, for there is much to be said for being in the learner's shoes oneself, the while one is teaching neophytes. We are here working with an *approach* rather than a *method,* which is, as Bannatyne has pointed out, *structured* but not *programmed,* and is therefore adaptable to individual needs. It makes an invigorating contrast to the experience of the assembly-line worker who must follow the guide in the teacher's edition of a reading series.

One kind of thing we do *not* need for our teaching is a plethora of gadgetry, however attractive it may be to the toy-loving, button-pushing child in each of us. Trampolines and movement programs, visual aids and listening experiences are important in their own right at the appropriate times and places. They belong in the life of *every* child, including the dyslexic one. They can be educative in many ways, but we should not let ourselves be seduced into expecting them to teach reading and writing. To the extent that they are substituted for the direct approach, they may divert time, energy, money and acceptance of responsibility from the proper focus. Eye-hand coordination, visual and auditory discrimination, and self-confidence can be achieved directly during the learning of critically needed language skills.

Educational Patterns in Practice

There is a sequence of growth in any specialized field which I first heard formulated by Roger Saunders:[86] first there is recognition of a condition; then treatment; then research; and, finally, prevention. This cycle we can see repeated in the over-all development of the knowledge and treatment of language difficulties.

A historical sequence typical of what we have often observed is that, after failure and frustration a youngster comes to a clinician who can identify his problem and either start his rehabilitative education or refer him to a competent teacher-therapist. The understanding and cooperation of the child's teacher and school principal are elicited. The child makes progress, so the teacher wants to learn more, in order to help him and other children. The principal, psychologist and others begin observing and testing all through the school. A program is set up for more thorough evaluation in the school, and some special teaching facility is developed—a resource room, class or tutoring program. Records are kept, examined and found impressive. Children in need of help are identified earlier, and eventually they are screened in first grade, kindergarten, and now even in nursery-age speech and language development programs. Appropriate instruction is provided for "at-risk" children and other beginners are shifted to join them if their needs warrant. Perhaps the whole school shifts to a code-emphasis method of teaching reading and spelling,[12, 16] probably with grouping of children for language teaching to accommodate their differing needs and rates of learning.[76] Close scrutiny of each child's growth will still bring to light those in need of special, individual care. So far I have not been aware that the later histories of these remedially or preventively taught children have been followed to see whether they may need "booster shots" at such critical periods as the beginning of algebra, foreign language, or the production of term papers, but this would seem to be a constructive idea. This sequence has been repeated, in whole or in part, many times in the past 49 years.

Although in America two names, Orton[69, 70] and Gillingham,[32] stand out in the history of dyslexia education, and especially at this anniversary conference, this by no means points to a personality cult nor a panacea solution, which would have been the antithesis of their spirit. The roll of scientists, physicians, psychologists, and educators in many lands is long.

Schools with programs for meeting dyslexic children's needs have been of several types. Independent schools came first, perhaps because in the early days children were most often referred from and to them, and because they were freer to innovate. More and more, public schools are finding a solution here to some of their problems.[30, 39, 56, 89, 94] There have been special education schools for severely disabled youngsters which have devised departments and programs for dyslexic children. Day and boarding schools especially designed for dyslexic children are not entirely novel—we know one which is going strong after nearly 40 years, but most of them are of more recent establishment. There have been, and are, several good summer camps and summer school programs especially planned for dyslexic children. Hospital-related clinic schools go back to Dr. Orton's original multidisciplinary group at the Iowa State Psychopathic Hospital in 1925–1927.[65] Then there are nonhospital clinic teaching facilities, of which there is none better than that of Paula Rome and Jean Osman, at the scene of the World Congress in Rochester, Minnesota. On the lists, too, are more individual therapists than one would believe unless one had been searching through history as I have. Some people go back to the 20's and some have only just graduated from college. Teachers' aides, volunteers, or paraprofessionals, and parents,[88] too, are beginning to play roles of increasing importance.

People and facilities in all or most of these categories are to be found in other countries, too. Sometimes their activities are comprehensive and well-organized, as in Czechoslovakia, well-reported in the writings of Matějček.[59] In other countries they are more fragmentary, and in some places they are falling victim to the current back-to-only-the-regular-classroom-for-everybody vogue.

As we think of the thousands of children who have been rescued from educational and life failure, though, we have no justification for smugness or self-congratulations—we need only think of the millions who have not been recognized or reached.

Teacher Education

Teacher education should have a chapter of its own. It has gone through much the same evolutionary pattern as in most other professions, but isn't as far along as in many of them. At first it was Samuel Orton or Anna

Gillingham on one end of Horace Mann's proverbial log and a succession of apprentices on the other. For some of us, who were largely self-taught, finding wisdom wherever we could, even the log was a second-order metaphor. As these arrangements became more formalized, with Gillingham's and other programs giving regular courses and requiring long-time commitment, people began to receive valued but not university-negotiable certificates. College and university credit for work specifically related to dyslexia began in 1959, grew slowly, but is now accelerating. There are graduate courses, perhaps in psychology or learning disability programs but seldom under the aegis of "education." More people are getting relevant master's degrees, and there are even occasional doctorates. Since finding the teachers to whom universities are willing to grant faculty appointments has been a serious bottle-neck in the teaching of teachers, we must applaud the present trend heartily.

Short courses, and various institutes and workshops are popular as introductions to the field, which is all they can possibly be. They have both merits and hazards when presented by responsible organizations, such as some associations for children with learning disabilities, the Orton Society through its conferences and branches, and that unusual publisher-with-a-conscience about how the books he sells may be used, Robert Hall of Educators Publishing Service. Some of the introductions lead on into longer courses, with supervised teaching, with or without university credit. Self-education is still very much worth the effort, too, and, with the growth of the literature, more and more feasible.

Educational Management Programs

Aside from what happens in private practice of clinicians, with what sorts of management practices shall we implement our programs, especially in schools? Some compromises with administrative reality we can make, but there comes a time when one must put one's foot down firmly, saying, "Beyond this point we cannot go. These minimum standards must be met, or our effort, too thinly spread, will be worse than wasted. With only one childhood granted him, no child can afford to have it used up that way!"

However we may place children in *groups* for instruction and for school living, the guiding principle lies in the awareness that people learn as *individuals*.[76] We may favor a small group for the younger child, unless his disability is severe, and individual teaching for the older student; a class for the mildly dyslexic youngster in a preventive program, and clinical tutoring for the one with severe problems or a history of failure and frustration. We may have one plan where we have qualified specialists to do the teaching, and another where the classroom teacher must learn how, if she has time, or an untrained teacher aide or parent is involved.[47,62,82] We could wish for a qualified tutor for every child in trouble, but with too many children and not enough teachers we will do what we can within the limits of professional responsibility and integrity. Respondents the world over and representing several languages and educational systems have reported both the values and the limitations of each of these arrangements. They are all trying to keep the whole child and the total environment in mind as much as possible, and to maintain balance between stability and versatility, scholarly rigor and human warmth, and all the other opposites with which we are all familiar. As an article of faith, and the judgment of observation, we may say that language teaching *is* therapy, but that, on the other hand, unless it is therapeutic in management and in spirit, it will not be effective teaching. The full appreciation of this among dyslexia therapists is a rewarding finding in programs for all ages and in dozens of locations.

Results

But can children who have actually failed, or were predicted to be at serious risk of failure, really learn? A quick tally of the program participants at the World Congress alone brings up names of at least 47 persons, all on the educational firing line, who could give affirmative evidence, and I have heard from many more in that audience and elsewhere, at home and abroad.

Children themselves think educational treatment works. The reported consensus seems to be, "Boy! It's great. I'm beginning to learn how, and I don't think I'm dumb anymore. [and wistfully] . . . I hope it lasts." Or if they have been at it a while, "I know I can do it now, I'll get there! And it's interesting and even *fun*!"

The parent of a child newly diagnosed and embarked on language therapy often says, "He's a different boy, and our family life and reports of his behavior at school are different, too." Then there was the not atypical phone call a year after therapy had ended: "Do you remember telling me that someday I'd say, 'Tommy, get your nose out of that book and go out and play ball'? Well, it has just happened and I thought you ought to know."

From the teacher of a third grade class of 25 came this: "Last year I had half these children in a smaller class for emotionally disturbed youngsters. They had me climbing the walls along with them, but with the approach I'm using now all but one of them have settled down to work happily in activities from which they know they are learning."[89] These reports won't surprise those experienced in this field. There have been schools with preventive and re-education programs dating back to the '30's, and there are more of them all the time, public now, as well as independent. They have raw data and case stories which aggregate in support of the statement of one long-time secondary school headmaster[44] who says, "I have worked with roughly over a thousand boys during almost 40 years since Dr. Orton started us in this field and I know of *no* [his emphasis] boy whose reading skills were not strengthened. Reading speed rises very gradually in most cases, but comprehension reaches a healthy level. Spelling gains have been more modest . . . " We regret the approaching retirement of such a man, except that it will give him time to make a careful study of his records, which he has promised to do.

There is also the reading service director of 30 years experience and unblemished probity who says, "We don't *say* much about the records of success of our full-time 'graduates.' But we do *keep* careful records, for 'by their fruits ye shall know them.' However, since most people find 96 percent school and job success unbelievable, we long ago decided we'd rather just go on teaching than argue with them."

These statements, which sound so like the "testimonials" of which we are properly wary, are the more convincing because they are repeated from so many reliable sources. It is dilemma; we do not like to seem to blow our own horn, but neither should a welcome light be hidden under a bushel. We would all agree, I am sure, that these anecdotal facts need to be supported, as increasingly they are coming to be, by comparative scores and controlled studies, with careful description of populations, settings, and methods. Meanwhile, informally and in brief personal reports, we have begun to amass some numerical and descriptive data. From several teachers and whole schools I have received test data of sufficient detail and objectivity to be encouragingly convincing.[30,45,56,90] There are already a few studies based on larger numbers and statistically reported, analyzed and validated.[42,50,75] Kline[51] and others have presented reports of this kind some of which are printed in the 1975 *Bulletin of the Orton Society.* Although at best their number is not large, not all of those published earlier or elsewhere could be included in the reference list for this paper.

Whatever the specifics of instruction, though, with the kind of regime I have been describing, reports generally seem to tell the same story of normal or accelerated progress where before there had been much less or none, or where slower than average growth was expected from predictive testing. The earlier histories of the children and the status of untreated age-mates have provided comparisons and, in some cases, satisfactorily conventional control groups.

Children who are not too handicapped linguistically and are taught in preventive classes or in regular classes with well-planned phonics programs, may make good progress from the start, and may never be aware of the problems they might have had under less benign circumstances.[30, 94, 96] This emphasizes the point that we are concerned with degrees of normal variation, rather than disease or defect.

Most achievement tests by which progress is measured in schools are geared to the traditional basal reader approach to reading and the accompanying language arts programs where vocabularies are controlled by frequency of everyday usage rather than phonic dependability. So it is often not until the phonemic-graphemic or coding skills are well-established that scores on standard tests will show how much learning has taken place. The Gillingham-Stillman-Childs Phonics Proficiency Scales[34] and the new Dallas Benchmark Scales (in preparation) are useful measures of learning of basic language skills. After children show mastery in these tests, they are generally ready to take off into rapidly accelerated independent learning. Their scores on standard tests may then climb steeply and their progress will be limited only by such factors as intelligence and drive, and minimally, if at all, by dyslexia.

Perhaps we can let a diagram (Figure 7) suggest what might happen to a child in the much-measured elementary and middle school years. If he makes the expected year's growth in each year of his life he will be right with the crowd, as x, in up-hill motion. Of course, he may be ahead, in the y area, or he may be lagging behind, with z. Studies show that with help at an early age he may catch on quickly, because he has few bad habits to unlearn, and a short distance to run, or he may go slowly, because of immaturity or the severity of his handicap. If he is older[7] added understanding and drive may help him to move faster to close the widening gap between his position and his goal, or the burdens of failure and frustration may hold him back at the start of his re-education. Statistical studies in hand from preventive programs, second and third grade classes, older groups and individuals in one-to-one therapy show all of these patterns and some others. Personal experience of teachers, backed up by at least two studies of large numbers,[49, 90] bear witness to the fact that the children most likely to hold their gains are the ones who stay with the programs until they are not just up to grade but well into the y area, and self-propelling. Experience says that the outlook can be good for older students and adults, too.

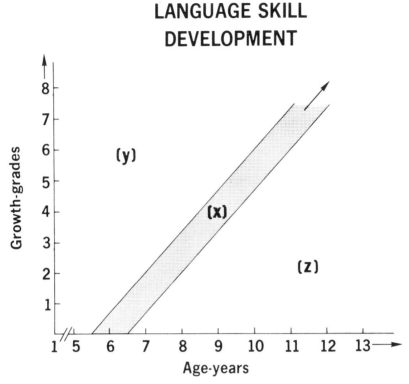

LANGUAGE SKILL DEVELOPMENT

Figure 7. Language and skill development.

Prognosis

These children *can* succeed, if circumstances are even reasonably favorable and if they are given appropriate help over a long enough period. This must be at least a year, and preferably they should have two or three years, because there is much to learn about the language, and often much for the student to unlearn and to catch up on. No dyslexic child, I think we can say, *need fail because of his dyslexia.*[75] With appropriate education, there is a way out. It is often long and slow, seldom spectacular in the beginning except for change of attitudes, but with the kind of education or re-education they need, the process is filled with hope and challenge, interest and deep satisfaction, and progress continues into later schooling and adult life.

This can be shown in the life histories of many individuals known to those among us whose early students are now parents, even grandparents, often of dyslexic children who are now our pupils. There have been a double handful, only, of long-time follow-up studies. These are usually of clinic populations given remedial help of different kinds with fair to good success, the over-all judgment being, "at least they are self-supporting and a few have done well." The individual careers reported in case histories by my old friends and recent respondents, and the results of my own Rose Valley study, seem to warrant much more optimism. There is room for more and better longitudinal studies and the data exist for doctoral students and retiring headmasters.

As a preliminary to his study, one headmaster says, "About 90 percent of our former students and graduates have continued their educational training with success,... I estimate that approximately three-fourths have bachelor's degrees, with several master's and even doctor's degrees ... Perhaps partially because of their earlier disability, students have developed greater than average perseverance and habits of industry to cope with the academic challenge."[44] Perhaps it is that in learning to meet the demands of organized language, well-taught dyslexics themselves become better organized for all of living.

Even with the best of help, our students will always be somewhat dyslexic, I suspect, for this is a matter of constitutional type. They may continue to be unreliable spellers, but the range and quality of their reading is generally in line with their other competencies, if not always so rapid as they would like, and their writing (or typing) can be at least legible. They are likely, on the other hand, to continue to show high aptitude in spatial and visual thinking and creativity. They can make use of other nonverbal, and often verbal, aptitudes of a high order, and other useful qualities such as we have seen in many of them. Hundreds, thousands, of them have learned to cope with language and generally to make it do their will well enough so that they can achieve in school and life in accordance with the full range of their endowment—a truly favorable outlook.

Further study will bring improved understanding and practice, but we need not wait for tomorrow. We have already learned enough to teach almost all children to read well.

Guidelines for the Future

If space permitted, I should set forth at some length our need for carefully designed, statistically validated and widely published research studies, and for making use of the material already gathered. We might talk about the refinement of instructional materials and the improvement of teaching practices, about assimilation of the new into the framework of the old and tried—enriched structure, not superficial eclecticism. There is also much to say about recruiting both older and younger people as teachers, about educating them well, and about preparing for appointment to university faculties persons who could teach teachers increasingly well.

In its recent exploratory report on significant research projects, one of the Orton Society's nine interdisciplinary task forces has this to say:

> The Orton Society is unique as an organization, for it stands at the confluence of many disciplines. Specialized scientific investigators appreciate cross-disciplinary illumination and a closer contact with educational and practical reality. Educational practitioners find their understanding broadened and deepened from participating in the learning about controlled scientific investigation which satisfies the highest standards of excellence.[71]

In the field of public education, which is a major concern of the Orton Society and the professions it represents, there is challenging work ahead for everyone—for professional workers involved directly with dyslexic persons and for members of other professions, including knowledgeable and forceful parents. We who are conversant with the field would do well to remember that it may be hard for others to hear and accept an approach so different from the ones to which they have long been attuned. Rather than being impatient with them, we should simply say and do what we can as forcefully and effectively as we know how, with determination but with restraint and understanding in the manner of our presentation. Then, perhaps, when they hear the *next* paper, or *their* child turns out to be dyslexic, they will be *able* to hear, having absorbed more than was apparent to them or to us when we talked with them. If people seem unreceptive and tempt us to say with Uncle Remus, "A one-eyed mule can't be managed from his blind side," we should realize that the other chaps have quite probably identified *us* with the intractable Mr. Long Ears.

There is exciting new knowledge about the language function and phenomena to strengthen and enlarge our concepts. In our field we who have focused on specific developmental dyslexia *do* have something very good to offer. Children, older students and adults continue to be rescued from the personal and social devastations of failure, and restored to academic, social and economic effectiveness, to self-confidence and human dignity. Increasingly, appropriate early language intervention and teaching are preventing trouble for many language-different children. Programs are flourishing in many settings, and in many lands. The world seems increasingly ready to hear what we have long been saying and to see what we are doing. We need not be too modest about promoting our ideas and programs—*except in the manner of our doing so.*

The field of language and language education is as interesting and rewarding as any there is. May it keep growing, and may our next quarter and half century of helping it do so be as exhilarating as have been the first 25 years of the Orton Society's life and the whole period since Dr. Orton's pioneering presentation of 1925.

References

NOTE: The author's 1974 inquiries brought a wealth of diverse and appreciated information which made this summary report possible. References given here include primarily works already published or nearing publication, and therefore likely to be available. Each work is keyed to its major contribution to the text, viz. G(eneral), N(ature of dyslexia), E(ducational procedures and materials), and R(esults of educational treatment).

Other specific acknowledgement, as well as supporting statistical data, here regretfully omitted for reasons of space, must await publication of the fuller study now in preparation. Correspondence with persons having further relevant data would be most welcome. Address the author at: Foxes Spy, Route 12, Frederick, Maryland 21701.

1. Abelard P: Cited by Bronowski J.[14] G
2. Anderson CW, Main HG: Multi-Sensory: A Workbook of Resource Words. Minneapolis, TS Denison & Co., 1973. E
3. Ansara A: Maturational readiness for school tasks. Bull Orton Soc 19:51–59, 1969. E
4. Ansara A: Language therapy to salvage the college potential of dyslexic adolescents. Bull Orton Soc 22:123–139, 1972. E
5. Ansara A: The language therapist as a basic mathematics tutor for adolescents. Bull Orton Soc 23:119–139, 1973. E
6. Atzesberger M: Excerpts from a study for Rheinland-Pfalz Education Office, West Germany (Courtesy E Klasen, Munich). 1974. R
7. Bakker DJ, Satz P: Specific Reading Disability: Advances in Theory and Method. Rotterdam, Netherlands, Rotterdam University Press, 1970. N
8. Bannatyne A: Reading: An Auditory Vocal Process. San Rafael, California, Academic Therapy Press, 1973. N
9. Bender L: Problems in conceptualization and communication in children with developmental alexia. *In* Psychopathology of Communication. Edited by Hoch, Zubin. New York, Grune & Stratton, 1958. N
10. Bender L: A fifty-year review of dyslexia. Bull Orton Soc 25:5–23, 1975. N
11. Blom G, Jones AW: Bases of classification of reading disorders. *In* Reading Forum (Monograph 11). Edited by E Calkins. Bethesda, NINDS, NIH, 1970. N
12. Bloomfield L, Barnhart CL: Let's Read: A Linguistic Approach. Detroit, Wayne State U Press, 1961. E
13. Bowen CC: Angling for Words. San Rafael, California, Academic Therapy Press, 1972. E
14. Bronowski J: Science and Human Values. Revised edition. New York, Harper & Row, 1965. G
15. Brutten M, Richardson SO, Mangel C: Something's Wrong With My Child. New York, Harcourt Brace Jovanovich, 1973. N

16. Chall J: Learning to Read: The Great Debate. New York, McGraw-Hill Book Company, 1967. F
17. Childs SB [Editor] : Education and Specific Language Disability: The Papers of Anna Gillingham, M.A., 1919–1963. Towson, Maryland, Orton Society, 1968. N,E
18. Childs SB, Childs RdeS: Sound Phonics. Cambridge, Massachusetts, Educators Publishing Service, 1973. E
19. Childs SB, Childs RdeS: The Childs Spelling System: The Rules (revised). Cambridge, Massachusetts, Educators Publishing Service, 1973. E
20. Clarke L: Can't Read, Can't Write, Can't Talk Too Good Either: How to Recognize and Overcome Dyslexia in Your Child. New York, Walker & Co., 1973. N
21. Cox AR: Structures and Techniques: Remedial Language Training for Use With Alphabetic Phonics. Cambridge, Massachusetts, Educators Publishing Service, 1974. E
22. Critchley M: The Dyslexic Child. Springfield, Illinois, Charles C Thomas, 1970. N
23. Critchley M: Developmental dyslexia: its history, nature and prospects (this volume).N
24. Cronin EM: Raskob Letter Box and Teacher's Manual. Oakland, College of the Holy Names [undated] . E
25. Danenhower HS: Teaching adults with specific language disability. Bull Orton Soc 22:140–152, 1972.E
26. de Hirsch K: Preschool intervention. In Reading Forum (Monograph 11). Edited by E Calkins. Bethesda, NINDS, NIH, 1970. N,E
27. Doehring D: Patterns of Impairment in Specific Reading Disability: A Neuropsychological Investigation (Reprinted 1973). Montreal, McGill Press, 1968. N
28. Downing J: Comparative Reading: Cross-National Studies of Behavior and Process in Reading and Writing. New York, Macmillan Company, 1973. G
29. Durbrow HC: Learning to Write. Cambridge, Massachusetts, Educators Publishing Service, 1968, 1973. E
30. East RC: Excerpts from: A study of the effectiveness of specific language disability techniques on reading ability of potentially retarded readers. Bull Orton Soc 19:95–99, 1969. R
31. Eisenberg L: Emotional aspects of language disability. (this volume) N
32. Gillingham A: Collected papers, 1968. See Childs SB.[17] N,E
33. Gillingham A, Stillman B: Remedial Training for Children With Specific Disability in Reading, Spelling and Penmanship. Cambridge, Massachusetts, Educators Publishing Service, 1956, 1960. E
34. Gillingham A, Stillman B, Childs SB: Phonics Proficiency Scales. Cambridge, Massachusetts, Educators Publishing Service, 1966, 1970, 1971.
35. Gough PB: One second of reading. In Language by Ear and by Eye. Edited by JF Kavanagh, IG Mattingly. Cambridge, Massachusetts, MIT Press, 1972. G
36. Hagin RA: Models of intervention with learning disabilities: ephemeral and otherwise. School Psychol Monogr 1:1–24, 1973. E
37. Halacy DS Jr: Man and Memory. New York, Harper & Row, 1970. G
38. Hall ET: Learning the English Language: Skillbooks I and II & Teacher's Manuals. Cambridge, Massachusetts, Educators Publishing Service, 1974. E
39. Hall RG: A Report on the Achievement of Specific Language Disability Children Taught by the Slingerland Multi-sensory Approach to Language Arts. Cambridge, Massachusetts, Educators Publishing Service, 1974. R
40. Hathaway ET: The Teaching Box. Cambridge, Massachusetts, Educators Publishing Service, 1973. E
41. Hayakawa SI, Hamilian L, Wagner G: Language in Thought and Action. New York, Harcourt Brace & Jovanovich, 1964. G
42. Herjanic BM, Penick EC: Adult outcomes of disabled readers. J Spec Educ 6(4): 397–410, 1972. R
43. Hermann K: Reading Disability. Springfield, Illinois, Charles C Thomas, Publisher, 1959. N,R

44. Howard N: Personal communication. R
45. Jansky JJ, de Hirsch K: Preventing Reading Failure. New York, Harper & Row, 1972. N,E,R
46. Johnson DJ, Myklebust HR: Learning Disabilities: Educational Principles and Practices. New York, Grune & Stratton, 1967. N,E
47. Jordan DR: Dyslexia in the Classroom. Columbus, Charles E Merrill Publishing Co., 1972. E
48. Kirk SA, Kirk WD: Psycholinguistic Learning Disabilities: Diagnosis and Remediation. Urbana, U of Illinois Press, 1971. N,E
49. Klasen E: The Syndrome of Specific Dyslexia. Baltimore, University Park Press, 1972. N,R
50. Kline CL, Kline CL, Ashbrenner M et al.: The treatment of dyslexia in a community mental health center. J Learning Disabilities 1(8): 456–466, 1968. N,R
51. Kline CL, Kline CL: Follow-up study of 216 dyslexic children from a group of 750 children evaluated in the past four years. Bull Orton Soc 25:127–144, 1975. R
52. Kolson C, Kaluger G: Clinical Aspects of Remedial Reading. Springfield, Illinois, Charles C Thomas, 1970. N,E
53. Kowarik O: Excerpts from a study of educational treatment of 356 reading disabled children in Vienna, Austria, with follow-up, 1962–1972. Personal communication, E Klasen, Munich, Germany. E,R
54. Lee LL: Developmental Sentence Analysis: A Gramatical Assessment Procedure for Speech and Language Clinicians. Evanston, Illinois, Northwestern U Press, 1974. E
55. Leong CK: An oblique glance at reading disability. Bull Orton Soc 22:69–79, 1972. N
56. Ley D, Metteer R: The mainstream approach for the SLD child: a public school model. Bull Orton Soc 24:130–134, 1974. E
57. Markiewicz J, Zakrezewska B: Dual remedial training of dyslexic children in Poland. Bull Orton Soc 23:39–51, 1973. E
58. Masland RL: Etiological variants in dyslexia. Personal communication. N
59. Matějček Z: Dyslexia: diagnosis and treatment. Bull Orton Soc 21:53–63, 1971. N,E
60. Mattingly IG: Reading, the linguistic process, and linguistic awareness. In Language by Ear and by Eye. Edited by JF Kavanagh, IG Mattingly. Cambridge, Massachusetts, MIT Press, 1972. G
61. McClelland J: Shadow and substance of specific language disability: a longitudinal study. Bull Orton Soc 23:160–181, 1973. N,E,R
62. Miles TR: On Helping the Dyslexic Child. New York, Barnes & Noble, 1970. N,E
63. Money J [Editor] : Reading Disability: Progress and Research Needs in Dyslexia. Baltimore, The Johns Hopkins Press, 1962. N,E,R
64. Money J [Editor] : The Disabled Reader: Education of the Dyslexic Child. Baltimore, The Johns Hopkins Press, 1966. N,E
65. Monroe M: Children Who Cannot Read. Chicago, U of Chicago Press, 1932. N,R
66. Oliphant G: Auditory perception and reading disability. Bull Orton Soc 22:27–40, 1972. N
67. Orton JL: A Guide to Teaching Phonics. Cambridge, Massachusetts, Educators Publishing Service, 1964, 1973. E
68. Orton JL: The Orton-Gillingham approach. In The Disabled Reader: Education of the Dyslexic Child. Edited by J Money. Baltimore, The Johns Hopkins Press, 1966, pp. 119–145. (Also Orton Soc Reprint 11.) E
69. Orton JL [Editor] : "Word-Blindness" in School Children and Other Papers on Strephosymbolia (Specific Language Disability–Dyslexia), 1925–1946, by Samuel Torrey Orton, M.D. Towson, Maryland, The Orton Society, 1966. N,E
70. Orton ST: Reading, Writing, and Speech Problems in Children. New York, WW Norton & Company, 1937. N,E,R
71. Orton Society: Draft of an initial report on Task Force No. 3: Outlines for significant research projects. Unpublished data. N,E,R

72. Owen FW: Palo Alto (CA) Unified School District: Educationally Handicapped Program Progress Report. Mimeographed, 1973. E,R
73. Pollack C, Lane P: The Hip Readers. Brooklyn, Book-Lab., 1970. E
74. Rak ET: Spellbound. Cambridge, Massachusetts, Educators Publishing Service, 1972. E
75. Rawson MB: Developmental Language Disability: Adult Accomplishments of Dyslexic Boys. Baltimore, The Johns Hopkins Press, 1968. N,R
76. Rawson MB: Teaching children with language disabilities in small groups. In Reading Forum (Monograph 11). Edited by E Calkins. Bethesda, NINDS, NIH, 1970. (Also in J Learning Disabilities 4(1): 17–25.) 1971. E
77. Rawson MB: The structure of English: the language to be learned. Bull Orton Soc 20:103–123, 1970. E
78. Rawson MB: Perspectives of specific language disability. I. The past—what has been learned. Bull Orton Soc 21:22–34, 1971. N
79. Rawson MB: The self-concept and the cycle of growth. Bull Orton Soc 24:63–76, 1974. E
80. Robinson MH: "Kenneth Johnson": a progress report on a search for literacy. Bull Orton Soc 19:134–140, 1969. E,R
81. Rome PD, Osman JS: Language Tool Kit. Cambridge, Massachusetts, Educators Publishing Service, 1972. E
82. Roswell F, Natchez G: Reading Disability: Diagnosis and Treatment. New York, Basic Books, 1971. N,E
83. Rotzel G: The School in Rose Valley: A Parent Venture in Education. Baltimore, The Johns Hopkins Press, 1971. (Also, Ballentine PB) G,N,E
84. Ruchlis H: Guidelines to Education of Nonreaders. Brooklyn, Book-Lab., 1973. E
85. Saunders RE: Dyslexia: its phenomenology. In Reading Disability: Progress and Research Needs in Dyslexia. Edited by John Money. Baltimore, The Johns Hopkins Press, 1962. (Also reprinted, Bull Orton Soc 13:75–82.) N
86. Saunders RE: Perspectives of language disability. II. The present-where do we stand? Bull Orton Soc 21:35–44, 1971. N,E
87. Saunders RE, Gialas A, Hofler DB: Lincs to Writing, Reading and Spelling. Cambridge, Massachusetts, Educators Publishing Service, 1969, 1973. E
88. Saunders RE, Malin DH: Parents as tutorial participants: an experiment. Bull Orton Soc 20:99–101, 1970. E
89. Saunders RE, Malin DH: Dyslexia, Prevention and Remediation: A Classroom Approach. Film. Contact authors, or Orton Society, 1971.
90. Schiffman G: Dyslexia as an educational phenomenon: its recognition and treatment. In Reading Disability: Progress and Research Needs in Dyslexia. Edited by John Money. Baltimore, The Johns Hopkins Press, 1972. N,E,R
91. Silver AA, Hagin RA: Specific reading disability: follow-up studies. Am J Orthopsychiatry 34:95–102, 1964. (Also reprinted, Bull Orton Soc 14:8–15.) R
92. Silver AA, Hagin RA: Profile of a first grade: a basis for preventive psychiatry. J Am Acad Child Psychiatry 11:645–674, 1972. N,E,R
93. Silver AA, Hagin RA: Fascinating journey: paths to the prediction and prevention of reading disability. Bull Orton Soc 25:24–36. N,E
94. Slingerland BH: A Multisensory Approach to Language Arts for Specific Language Disability Children. Cambridge, Massachusetts, Educators Publishing Service, 1971. E
95. Smelt ED: How to Speak, Spell and Read: A New Way to Learn English. South Melbourne, Australia, Melbourne YMCA [1 City Rd. 3205], 1972. E
96. Spalding RB, Spalding WF: The Writing Road to Reading. New York, William Morrow & Company, 1972. E
97. Steere A, Peck CZ, Green L: Solving Language Difficulties: Remedial Routines. Cambridge, Massachusetts, Educators Publishing Service, 1971. E
98. Strong LR: Language disability in the Hispano-American child. Bull Orton Soc 23:30–38, 1973. N,E

99. Stuart MF: Neurophysiological Insights Into Teaching. Palo Alto, Pacific Books, 1963. N,E
100. Symmes JS: Deficit models, spatial visualization, and reading disability. Bull Orton Soc 22:54–68, 1972. N
101. Symmes JS, Rapoport JL: Unexpected reading failure. Am J Orthopsychiatry 42(1): 82–91, 1972. N
102. Thompson LJ: Reading Disability: Developmental Dyslexia. Springfield, Illinois, Charles C Thomas, 1966
103. Tower DM: A kindergarten screening index to predict reading failure. Bull Orton Soc 23:90–105, 1973. E,R
104. Traub N: Recipe for Reading. Cambridge, Massachusetts. Educators Publishing Service, 1973. E
105. White SH: Some general outlines of the matrix of developmental changes between five and seven years. Bull Orton Soc 20:41–57, 1970. G
106. Wolff AG: The Gillingham-Stillman programme. In Assessment and Teaching of Dyslexic Children. Edited by AW Franklin, S Naidoo. London, Invalid Children's Aid Society, 1970 [contact British Dyslexia Association, 18 The Circus, Bath, England]

INDEX

5, 176, 177; punctuate elements in, 136, 137; and reading, 188; sensation divorced from, 175; structural invarient in, 182; surfaces and light in, 166–167; theories of, 131; transformational invarient in, 182, 183
Visual-phonetic analysis and synthesis, 61
Visual proprioception, 176, 177
Visual spatial tasks, 51
Visual storage, 150
Visual symbolic behavior, 5
Visual symbols, 28
Visual-tactual tasks, 199
Visual-visual tasks, 199, 200
Vocabulary, estimated size of, 23
Vocabulary expansion and decoding, 89
Vowel stress, dependent on syntactic category, 25

Wang, M. D., 109
Ward, A., 47
Warrington, E. K., 155
Webster, J. C., 104
Weider, S., 209
Weiskrants, D., 202
Weisstein, N., 158, 159
Wernicke, C., 44
West, R. A., 121
Weyl, H., 184
White, B. W., 173
White, S. H., 69, 70, 71
Wickelgren, W. A., 111
Wilbanks, W. A., 118
Winograd, T., 148

Within-modal tasks, 199
Wittrock, M. C., 89
Woodhead, M. M., 104
Woods, B. T., 51
Word, recognition, 28, 29; similarity ratings, 19
Word-blindness, 9, 10
Word-deafness, 45
Word familiarity, 88
Word form aspects, 25
Word form and meaning, 23
Word grouping and sentence meaning, 3, 31–32
Word meaning, arbitrary, 30, as mental events, 16, as neural events, 17, in semantic components, 18; and sentence meaning, 31–32; and syntactic properties, 21–22
Word order and sentence meaning, 31–32
Word recognition, 30
Word understanding, 22
Words, as connectors of language forms with meaning, 16; crucial properties of, 19; meaning of, 16, 17; memory of, 30–31; related, 17, 18; *See also* Lexicon
World Congress on Dyslexia, 1, 232, 246, 248
World Federation of Neurology, 12
Writing, importance of symbol-order in, 56
Writing systems, alphabetic, 2, 27; as connectors of phonological representations with verbal symbols, 26